A PORTRAIT OF THE PERSON

A Portrait of the Person

A Personality Theory for the Clinician

ZOLTAN GROSS, PH.D.

Global Village Press

SANTA MONICA

1992

To my remarkable, beautiful mother

First Edition

Published by
Global Village Press
2210 Wilshire Boulevard, No. 262
Santa Monica, California 90403-5784

Book design & typography by Jim Cook

Library of Congress No. 92-072781

A Portrait of the Person

CHAPTER IX

THE PERSON AS A WHOLE / 194

CHAPTER X

THE TRIPARTITE PERSON / 223

Table of Illustrations

Preface

Now that I have finished writing this book, I can write its beginning. I could not make an introductory statement about my theory until I had grasped its holistic structure. As it took shape, images of Escher's drawings and mobius strips repeatedly came to mind. These are stilled images of movement, which helped me realize I was writing about psychological process rather than entities, structures or states. Through the development of this *Portrait of a Person,* I learned to see psychological phenomena as ongoing flows of process without beginnings or endings. Psychological theory has always been encased in thinking that has been trained on the motionlessness of objects. My portrait of the person is a description of the movement of personality, as I have come to understand that individuals, persons, are continuous flows of information processing.

This book is not the start of a revolutionary new idea; it is a continuation of lines of thinking about personality that began with the diminution of the influence of logical positivism on psychological theorizing. And *Portrait of a Person* certainly is not the end of anything. The Portrait that I have drawn is only a sketch, crudely describing relationships between different kinds of regulatory processes which comprise the person. The mind, consciousness, self, emotionality and personal reality are only roughly outlined. Despite the incompleteness of my description of the person, I believe I have meaningfully described the relatedness of these psychological systems to one another, and I hope my description of the relatedness between personality processes can be a turning point in the way that we think about personality.

I wrote this book because I wanted to be able to theoretically describe my psychotherapeutic work. I have always known that there was a method to my madness, but I had great difficulty in articulating that method with any clarity. This was due, largely, to the static orientation of my thinking about personality. The paradigmatic shift of the theory enabled me to describe process—the essence of psychotherapy.

Writing this book has been as much an exercise in unlearning as it has been one of learning and discovery. I began thinking about this book within a logical positivist orientation, which had been the foundation of my training as a psychologist. This orientation was buttressed by an areligious bias that is a part of my personality. I thought that feelings and emotions were synonymous terms. I also thought that self and ego referred to essentially the same personality process. Most of what I knew about personality has changed. I am now surprised to find myself understanding ancient mystical ways of knowing about personality process. My theory of personality is clothed in the language of information processing and neuropsychology; but philosophically, it is related to Taoist, Zen, Kabbalistic, and Sufi traditions of knowing about personal process.

As I was learning how to think differently about personality process, I also had to learn how to write communicatively. In the beginning, I clothed the embarrassment of my ignorance in the obscurity of German sentence structures. I am touched by the remembrance of the patience of good friends who read early drafts of chapters or sections of this book. Most of them loved me enough to tell me what a dreadful writer I was.

Dr. Harvey Ross sustained me in the early years of my confusion. Without his support and warm intolerance, I doubt I would have been able to complete this task. Dr. Joseph Rabin, another staunch friend, showed me how my uneasiness about challenging old, established ways of thinking about personality was reflected in the awkward and defensive sentences I was writing. He also quarreled with me about my desire to introduce neurological concepts into the theory. I was both delighted and reassured when I won his reluctant admission that the idea of a neurological ego facilitated the description of the theory. Dr. Daniel Levenson, with a kind gentleness, reminded me of the fact that I was a psychotherapist and not a German philosopher. Otto Schweid had a sense of the structure of the theory and encouraged me to pursue it. Dr. Charles Ansell, from his psychoanalytic perspective, struggled with me, respected me and helped me to think through essential parts of my earlier confusions. Dr. Howard Freeman's encouragement, support, and friendship also diluted the loneliness of my adventures.

On the editorial side of writing this book I am indebted to many friends. Dr. Susan Harris, Mary Jadiker, Dorothy Sauser, and Felice Bankier all spent hours teaching me to be grammatically correct and to state my ideas coherently. Rhoda Blecher taught me to simplify my writing. Her input enabled me to see the elegance of a clean, sparse sentence. Molly Maguire Silverman helped me to find the narrative line of the book. She also opened a door that enabled me to admit, albeit reluctantly, that I had a meaningful relationship to spirituality. I also want to thank Ira Gerber, who helped me master the word processing computer without which I would never have been able to write this book. And last but not least, I want to thank Pat for her love and support during the last years of this writing.

A Portrait of the Person

CHAPTER I

Ulysses and Me

Throughout my career as a psychotherapist, I have always felt that my clinical adventures were similar to those that enthralled Ulysses on his odyssey. My adventures have been as dramatic as his, and I blundered my way into almost as many mysteries as he did. However, there was a difference between our odysseys.

He knew what his destination would look like; he was going home. By contrast, I thought that my destination was a "cure," but since I had never participated in one, I was not sure what it looked like. Furthermore, shortly after I started my adventures, the path that I had been instructed to take to arrive at a cure disappeared. Then, for a long time after the disappearance of the path, I searched a variety of other treatment paths, until I realized the search was futile. Cure doesn't exist in psychotherapy. I had taken a nonexistent route to an absurd destination. At this stage of my career as a psychotherapist, I was unaware that I had embarked on a magical, paradoxical journey marked by strange words and tangled ideas.

My odyssey began when I was a graduate student, serving as a clinical assistant at UCLA. The excitement that I experienced during my first few encounters with "patients" was awesome. My heart pounded, and I had to clutch the seat of my chair to keep myself from visibly trembling. These first engagements left no doubt in my mind that I had found the passion of my life. I was hooked. I was going to be a psychotherapist.

My initial psychotherapeutic orientation was psychoanalytic. All of my teachers, who were psychologists or psychiatrists at the universities where I studied, were either psychoanalysts or were psychoanalytically oriented. Another important reason for this theoretical choice was my acceptance of the commonly held belief that psychoanalysis possessed the most comprehensive theory of personality. I must admit this theory was never very appealing to me, but the practice was breathtaking.

Despite the current debate about the value of psychoanalytic theory, it is the birthplace of intensive psychotherapy—i.e., psychotherapy which is oriented to helping people to change basic personality patterns. Although I no longer work psychoanalytically, I am in its debt, as are all intensive psychotherapists.

At first, my preoccupation with learning how to listen to, and be with, my clients consumed me. I was not much concerned about the nature of understanding, consciousness, or cure. I unthinkingly accepted the explanations of my supervisors and the therapeutic literature. I was so busy familiarizing myself with the equipment on my psychotherapeutic ship that I was not aware of my inability to steer it. I simply loved it. I was good at listening and interpreting, even though I was never completely confident that I was actually helping my clients. Nonetheless, being a psychotherapist was and still is an exciting and poetic experience.

During my student days, I learned to help patients follow the primary rule—that is, to free associate. (At this time, I referred to the people with whom I worked as "patients.")* I listened to their associations and tried to decipher their unconscious content. While I listened, patterns of meaning, like walking ghosts of the past, would emerge from these free associations. At times, I could look through my client's eyes into the world of his or her bewildering childhood. From there, I parsimoniously made interpretations designed to help provide insight into the nature of their problems. These insights were designed to bring into consciousness repressed memories of their conflicted childhood relationships.

Forty years later, psychoanalysis still embodies the belief that bringing emotional conflicts of a person's past into awareness is therapeutically beneficial. The International Psychoanalytic Association's (1990) definition of psychoanalysis states, in part, that:

> Psychoanalysis is viewed as an intensive treatment requiring at least four or five meetings a week, with each session lasting 45 to 50 minutes, in order that the analysand can develop a transference neurosis and in order that resistances and defenses can be interpreted and worked through, enabling the analysand to make conscious what had been unconscious, as follows: The

---

*The word *patient* is commonly used in the psychoanalytic literature to designate the analysand. When discussing psychoanalysis I will use *patient*. When describing my work with people, I will use the slightly less repugnant term *client*.

patient becomes aware of the underlying sources of his or her difficulties, intellectually and emotionally, by reexperiencing them with the analyst.

In this pithy definition of *psychoanalysis* are issues that are central to everything that follows. *Consciousness* is the awareness of the past history of the individual, emotionality and interpersonal relationships, including the therapeutic relationship. *Transference* is a term describing the patient's projection of unresolved childhood conflicts onto the "blank screen" that the psychoanalyst presents. *Blank screen* is the phrase describing the impersonal and anonymous role that the analyst adopts to facilitate the patient's projection. This refers to the "transference neurosis" mentioned in the above quote.

Transference also applies to patterns of behavior and experiences that had their origins in the patient's early childhood. The reexperiencing of "sources of difficulties" means recalling past interpersonal relationships and the feelings associated with them and bringing these issues into the forefront of consciousness. Consciousness is a central psychological term to which I will be devoting a considerable amount of time.

In the beginning of my career, I must admit that it was not clear to me why bringing forth unconscious childhood memories was supposed to have curative powers. Although it seemed logical—because consciousness and understanding are frequently regarded as almost synonymous terms—in fact, it was one of the many seemingly reasonable and commonly accepted explanations that I found to be simplistically misleading. I believed that somehow, if one was able to become aware of repressed drives or memories, a person would be liberated from the tyranny of the unresolved conflicts that supposedly created the particular neurosis. However, my work with Karen, a client of mine in the early years of my career, made me realize that the psychotherapeutic vessel I was using to take me to my uncertain destination was actually rudderless.

The theoretical route, which I took in order to find a rationale for psychotherapy that I could use, was formed by the interaction of my clinical practice and my explorations into the theoretical literature. The dichotomy of clinical practice and theoretical exploration is a recurrent issue in this book. In order to describe the theory, I found myself thinking about personality process in ways that differed from standard, commonsense assumptions. My departure from common sense enabled me to think about personality process in a new way. Defining the primary concepts of personality will occupy much of my discussion throughout this book.

An Uncommonsense Way of Thinking about Psychology

As I tried to theoretically describe the dynamics of the two-person psychotherapeutic relationship, I realized that I had no firm conceptual footing that would enable me to continue my journey. None of the basic terms of the theory had clear-cut definitions. *Emotion, person, feelings, consciousness, mind*—all of these and others were vaguely and variously defined.

As I thought about it, I came to understand that psychological phenomena are labeled in essentially the same way as physical objects are labeled. That is, we attach words to feelings in the same way that we label physical things, like tables and stones. In other words, the phenomenal appearance of psychological process is labeled in the same cognitive way that objects are. This is a commonsense way of thinking about things. Fletcher (1984) defines common sense as (1) a common set of assumptions, (2) a set of cultural maxims and shared beliefs, and (3) a shared way of thinking about the social and physical world. Each of these definitions is firmly embedded in cognitive constructions based on the experience of sensory information.

Physical objects and feelings are two very different kinds of phenomena. Physical objects reside in the outside world regardless of what happens to us emotionally, whereas feelings move about within us, taking on different meanings and experiential qualities as our relationships with others change. This way of labeling psychological process creates a subtly erroneous way of thinking about it.

As I delved more into the complex ways in which we classify information, I came up with a unique system of definitions. While learning this new way of thinking about and defining psychological process, I found that I had departed from the commonsense way of thinking that is the foundation of conventional psychological theorizing. With that realization, I also abandoned common sense as a therapeutic tool.

In some respects, my way of thinking about personality is comparable to the evolution of abstract art forms—the work of Jackson Pollack is an example—from the "realism" of, say, Rembrandt. My ideas regarding personality also can be understood through the idea of music, where, liberated from the confines of tonality and melody, the music of Mozart became the atonal nonmelodic music of Stravinsky. The thinking that I will be presenting here has some of the same abstract qualities, and certainly the unfamiliarity, of these newer art forms.

The abstract quality of this theory arises, in part, from the understanding that there is no "little person in the head." Acknowledging such a model enables the theorist to explain personality process in conventional ways, using assumptions that are axiomatically accepted. The most classic example of anthropomorphizing psychological process is the way in which Freud describes operations of the Ego, Id, and the Superego. The Ego is the rational organizer of reality and moderator of the relationship between a relentlessly pleasure-oriented Id and the moral, culturally conditioned, Superego. Each of these is described in the familiar commonsense way that we explain the motivations of people. It is for this reason that Freudian theory is easily comprehensible. Unfortunately, this kind of comprehension masks the inherent confusion of psychoanalytic theory.

My theory can be classified as a postmodern theory of personality. William Bevan's (1991) description of a characteristic of postmodern psychology is relevant to the theory contained in this book. In his description, he says:

> When I suggest that we should look to new models, I am not prepared to say precisely what those models should be. However, I believe that it is essential that they should recognize both the great complexity and dynamic quality of the phenomena with which psychologists deal. They should also be representative; that is, they should allow for successful generalization or translation into settings in which the hands-on, live phenomena that are of principal interest to us occur.
>
> In making these comments on models and methods, I would like to call special attention to *Complex Systems Theory* or, as it is alternatively called, nonlinear dynamics . . . the stability of the patterns that characterize such processes is seen to be a consequence of their nonlinearity. This implies, in turn, that the linear analyses that have been used for so long are simply inappropriate. (p. 479)

My theory is a nonlinear explanation of psychological process that describes the dynamics of moving patterns or systems.

Conventional theories of personality describe states and traits and line them up with static classifications of feelings, drives, and needs to create a motionless picture of the person. My theory is a description of movement. I will be describing cognitive personal transformations as regulatory operations preserving and stabilizing the existence of the individual. Michael's (1991) discussion of "postmodern reflections on social psychology" also describes the characteristics of this theory. Dennett (1991) also makes a similar distinction between thinking within the framework of Cartesian duality—that is, accepting the duality of the mind and body versus a "multiple draft model" of consciousness. The Cartesian Theater finds that psychological activity as starting from a motionless point of observation, whereas the multiple draft model of thinking describes the fluid movement of information processing in the brain.

As I moved into a nonlinear mode of thinking about psychological process, I was confronted with the need to clarify the definitions of the processes I was describing. The adventures I experienced in my search for a definition of the person may not have been as turbulent as my clinical ones, but they were equally chastening.

When I first started to examine seriously the theoretical foundations of my work, I felt incredibly stupid. I was unable to define the central psychological processes that are required to describe the personality operations I observed in my practice. I was chagrined by this. I felt that I could not define them with the clarity that would enable me to continue my theoretical pursuit, and without a system of clear definitions, I was unable to describe personality process.

As I looked more closely at personality, I realized that the road to a theory of personality was pitted with conceptual potholes. I found that most psychological phenomena are conceptually isolated from one another (cf. Staats, 1991). When I thought about it, I realized that the relationship between consciousness and cognition, or consciousness and perception, or feelings and self, is never clearly delineated. I had ignored the theoretical lacunae that exist between these phenomena. As long as they existed, an integrated theory of personality could not be constructed. In each of the theoretical chapters of the book, I will describe some of the epistemological and definitional issues that exist in the definitions of personality process that I present.

Having introduced the conceptual and clinical orientation of this theory, I will describe the overall structure of this text.

An Overview of the Journey's Path

I will use the idea of a journey throughout the description of the theory. This metaphor of the journey serves as a vehicle carrying the conceptual relationships existing in the theory. The ideas and hypotheses of the theory will follow each other in an orderly manner. This journey has two parts. Since the theory grew primarily out of my practice, the first part of the book describes the clinical adventures from which the theory of the dyad emerged. The second part of the book is theoretical. Chapters II, III, and IV are primarily clinical discussions raising questions addressed in the second, theoretical part of the book, chapters V through X. I will use my experiences with clients to illustrate and exemplify the more abstract aspects of the theory; and clinical description to illustrate how my theory relates to clinical practice.

In the first part of this book, I will describe how I overcame obstacles of ignorance with clients who were my comrades on this journey. The basic questions that my theory of personality addresses will emerge from stories of my psychotherapeutic adventures. Delving into relationships (chapter II) raised questions about the structure of the psychotherapeutic relationship, which were largely answered by the theory of the interpersonal dyad. The theory of the dyad in chapter III forced me to recognize the importance of emotional contact, not only in the psychotherapeutic relationship, but in all two-person engagements. When I arrived at my understanding of the dyad, I was ecstatic because I thought I had arrived at the end of my journey. In chapter IV, I describe how the theory changed the nature of my practice and made me confront questions that I was loath to pursue.

Early in the writing of this book, I discovered that I had an ever-present and demanding companion on my journey. He was what I call my "ghost." At first, he annoyed me, and I tried to resist him. At times I wanted to stop my exploration, but he would have none of it. Despite my resistance, he pushed me to scrutinize what was going on between my clients and myself. Eventually, I found that if I stopped resisting him, he would reward me with combinations of ideas that have emerged as this theory of personality. I find that he is most generous with me in the early morning hours. When he is active, he impatiently awakens me between four and five o'clock in the morning. He is a part of me, but he is not the "me" or "I" who is the constant companion of my waking hours. As we move further into the theory, I will introduce him to you and describe the difference between "him" and "me." When I discovered what he was, I became much more secure in my knowledge about the work of psychotherapy.

Despite the resistance that my *self* encountered in going beyond the theory of the dyad, my ghost pressed me to continue the journey, into the second part of this text. The clinical material in the second and fourth chapters led me to the conclusion that deeply emotional interpersonal contact between therapist and client is an essential characteristic of intensive psychotherapy.

In chapter V, I will describe how my understanding of this contact led me to an understanding of *affect hunger,* which is the unending need of our nervous system for stimulation and validation. As part of that understanding, I saw that the *neurological* effects of being alone were related to the experience of loneliness and the pain of aloneness. This realization helped me to see the ego as a neurological system rather than as the psychological system it is usually thought to be.

This neurological system is called by several different names. The names depend upon the theoretical perspective from which it is viewed. Ordinarily, it is called the *core brain.* McLean (1973) calls it the *paleo-mammalian brain.* Weil (1974) describes it as the *hypothalamic-limbic system.* I will refer to it as the *neurological ego.*

With my attention turned to the brain, I realized that its left and right hemispheres organize information into linear and nonlinear formats, and the back and front parts of the brain are specialized to format sensory and nonsensory information. This realization enabled me to understand the mind in a new way. In chapter VI, I will describe my understanding of the mind. This understanding is based on the premise that the brain automatically formats and classifies information in a doubly dichotomous way. It organizes information into linear and nonlinear formats and within sensory and nonsensory formats. This set of ideas raised a curious question. Does the brain organize information, or does the mind do it? If there is a difference between the mind and the brain, what is it? This question led to the definition of consciousness as a *display* function of the mind. Essentially, the definition states that the mind displays information in awareness when it cannot automatically process it.

Then I was confronted with the terminological confusion that exists in psychological theory. It was during my exploration of the mind that I came to the uncommonsense way of thinking about personality that I described above. This understanding enabled me to see that the mind is an emergent product of a regulatory system, which helps stabilize a volatile, iridescent, neurological ego.

Practically everything I thought about in the writing of this theory took me back to the brain. I like to think that this part of the path arose solely from the logic of the theory, but I also think that my ghost led me there. It was he who turned me on to my doctoral dissertation, which studied the effects of the lobotomy operation on learning. Ideas about the biological dynamics of the brain enabled me to have a better understanding of the nature of the individuals I saw in my consultation room.

However, before I could pursue my description and definition of the person, I was confronted with the mind-body problem. Ideas about the formatting systems of the mind and consciousness enabled me to explain why the mind and the body are experienced differently and how they are psychologically related. In chapter VII, I will describe the *emergence* of neurological process into psychological experience. Thinking about the brain and its emergent psychological process enabled me to untangle myself from the terminological confusion created by common-sense classifications.

Instead of simply assuming that our personality operates in synchronicity with our neurological processes, without considering how they are related, I will describe a number of nonmental or nonpersonal processes that interact and emerge into awareness as the psychology that we know, love, and are mystified by.

The biological processes upon which our lives are dependent are not usually accessible to the sensory systems that orient us to the external environment. Nonetheless, we do have nonsensory experiences of our biological process. We experience a wide variety of bodily processes during illness and when we are under emotional stress. We also have experiences of "I" or "me," knowing, and dreaming. These are experiential displays of internal nonsensory process. From these considerations I was then able to construct an introduction to theories of emotionality and personality.

As a result, it was not difficult for me to see that the person was a complex system of cognitive classifications concerning the neurological ego. With this understanding, I was able to arrive at a way of defining the person from which my theory of personality was formed. The classifications of the neurological ego emerge in consciousness as self phenomena, emotionality and personal reality. Personal reality is a term that describes the ways in which we think and know about our relationships with the world around us. It is our morality, social conventions, values, cosmology, *weltanshauung,* even our religions.

The holistic relationship that exists between these systems of classification is described in chapter VIII. In chapters IX and X, I will describe the cognitive classifications of the neurological ego (self phenomena), its relationship to the external environment (personal reality), and its disturbance (emotionality). These classifications are holistically displayed in awareness as our person. The person is the primary psychological system that stabilizes the core brain—the neurological ego.

Reprise

My portrait of the person is both familiar and unusual. It is a sketch of a twentieth-century creature deeply embedded in an active social milieu. The person* that I know is richly and intimately related to his/her social environment, and is responsible for individual behavior and experience. At the same time, the person exists within this environment autonomously, maintaining the integrity of his/her biological systems. The person of this theory is a three-legged creature with its feet firmly planted in its social, psychological, and neurological environments.

This new look at the person reminds me of photographs that I have seen of the earth taken from the moon. In these pictures, one image encompasses and transcends all the previously known parts of the earth and allows them to be seen in a new perspective. Similarly, this developing theory permitted me to create a new picture of personality.

Like the view from the moon, this description of the theory of personality does not contain much detail. Concepts such as consciousness, the person, emotionality, feelings, self, reality, and ego will be viewed from a long distance. Therefore, only their gross relationships to one another will be outlined.

Likewise, a detailed and scholarly map of these areas will not be found here. Lengthy discussions of such densely theoretical issues such as dichotomous information processing and mind-brain models, which

---

*Because my theory is paradigmatically different from commonsense-based theories, I have outlined the major hypotheses of the theory in Appendix A. The paradigmatic shift of this theory has also changed the meaning of most of the labels of psychological phenomena that will be discussed. For this reason, I have prepared a glossary of the major terms of the theory, to be found in Appendix B.

lie in the background of this theory, would obscure and complicate the sketch of the person that I wish to draw. This book is an *introduction* to a clinical theory of personality.

This theory has liberated me to use my person therapeutically. It has helped me to escape the confines of both the blank screen and common sense. The theory of the dyad provided me with a broader view of what was happening in the moment-to-moment interactions between my client and myself because I had more than the binoculars of transference with which to view the process of our work. Instead of being a detached observer looking through a blank screen, I became an active participant in the Theater of the Absurd. This was a rewarding and trying transformation for both my clients and me.

I will continue my odyssey as a therapist in the next chapter, where I enter more deeply into the magic of the therapeutic relationship. In it I challenge old beliefs and use Hellmuth Kaiser's (cf. Fierman, 1965) insight to enable me to find another way of engaging my clients. A new understanding of the nature of the therapeutic dyad grew out of my work with Hellmuth. He helped me find a rudder with which to steer my therapeutic vessel.

Chapter II

The Beginnings of a Psychotherapy of Engagement

One of my major motivations for creating this theory of personality began in the first year of my practice, when an extremely depressed young woman named Karen* was referred to me. I was totally unprepared for the love, excitement, confusion, and despair that were to accompany my work with her.

Karen's Love

The initial stages of our work were wonderful. Her depression lifted within the first three months of treatment, and we were both enormously relieved. With the improvement of her mood, hope blossomed, and my insecurities with respect to my competence as a budding therapist were temporarily assuaged. Karen was able to resume caring for her three-year-old daughter, do her household chores, resist but not conquer her continuing agoraphobia, and return to work in her husband's business as a part-time bookkeeper.

In spite of her progress, troublesome emotional difficulties persisted in her marriage. Beneath the peaceful, affectionate surface of the marriage, Karen and her husband were alienated from each other emotionally as well as being sexually incompatible. I knew that their sexual difficulty was symptomatic, not causative, but I did not understand the reasons for their alienation. Karen described her husband Joseph as a kind and dear man who was very patient with her shortcomings. Unfortunately, his sweetness did not help her to respond to him emotionally or sexually.

Violating the then-current conventional psychoanalytic wisdom

*To preserve confidentiality, all of the client names are pseudonyms and occupational references are fictitious.

against treating a husband and wife together, I asked them to see me as a couple. During that interview, I perceived her husband as a warm and loving man. Overtly, he was extraordinarily patient, and accepting of Karen's sexual avoidance of him. However, as I watched him, I saw his deep-seated anger and recognized his inability to express or openly experience it. When I first asked him why he was not angry with her for sexually rejecting him, he denied feeling anger. Later in the interview, he reluctantly admitted to some impatience with his wife's emotional difficulties and withdrawal from him, but he was hopeful. I suggested that the difficulties they were having arose from their inability to confront the anger that lay beneath the surface of their relationship. This suggestion made no sense to him, though. He believed that love and patience would eventually win her over.

It was not until many years later, working with other clients, that I came to understand that being loved produces pain and alienation in many people who have experienced emotional or physical abuse in very early childhood. I now suspect that this could very well have been true for Karen. When I worked with her, I believed that affection was a universally positive emotion, which always enriched the lives of the loving pair. I did not see that the pain of loving made it difficult for Karen to accept Joseph's unconditional positive regard for her. His reaction to her rejection was covert hostility, which, in turn, triggered anxiety and depression in her.

After the unproductive joint session, I resumed individual treatment with Karen. Her depression continued to lessen, but agoraphobia kept her housebound much of the time. Also, her relationship with her husband remained cool and frustrating. I believed that the solution to her persistent difficulties lay in bringing into consciousness her conflicted childhood relationships. She followed my instructions with a diligence that warmed my heart.

As a matter of fact, I became so enamored of her that I spent hours with my own analyst and supervisor trying to fathom my countertransference toward her. I realize now that my sexual feelings for her did not arise from countertransference; in fact, these feelings became an important clue to the development of my theory of personality. Nonetheless, I was plagued by guilt and anxiety.

The intense sexual attraction between us was mutually and vividly felt, but only obliquely acknowledged. I tried to rescue myself from my confusion and embarrassment by dutifully interpreting her expressions of love as a transference reaction from her lost mother and father or whatever seemed suitable at the moment. I did not know what these feelings meant or what function they had in my relationship with Karen. However, I hoped that if I had a good transference explanation for them, we could continue with our work without anxiety. This was an unfulfilled hope.

My sexual feelings caused me to think about referring her to another therapist. But how could I do this? She was devoted to the therapeutic task, and she was making good progress. She could only interpret such a referral as rejection. Furthermore, I did not have the courage to be honest and tell her that I was unable to work with her because of my sexual attraction. And last, my difficulty did not *seem* to be interfering with our work.

Following my sessions with Karen, feeling like Ulysses tied to the mast when he sailed past the Island of the Sirens, I ran for advice and solace to my supervisor, asking him to bind me more securely to the mast of my therapeutic ship. But, despite my anguished confusion, I stayed within the bounds of my therapeutic task. I cared for Karen so much that I could do nothing to hurt her or jeopardize her therapy. And my lust was no match for my love of the work with her. Leaving my task as her therapist would have destroyed her heroic efforts.

Nonetheless, I remained in the dark about the source of the sexuality that was so confusing to both of us. This sexuality also raised a question in my mind about the paradoxical situation in which we were entangled. Why was the loving that she experienced with her husband difficult, and what was there in our relationship that made it so enticing? Nothing in my personal explorations with my supervisor or my analyst illuminated the basis of what I thought was my countertransference.

Since then, I have come to see the luxury of the psychotherapeutic relationship that can kindle a loving relationship. Where else can a person, seeking emotional help, find someone to empathically listen without wanting something in return? And where else is there a listener so dedicated to using this information solely for the individual's own benefit?

The excitement and creativity of participating in the growth of another individual are so rewarding that the therapist is able to engage and relate to her or his client with a high degree of selflessness. Under these conditions, the therapist is able to serve the client without requiring personal validation. Indeed, this is a rare relationship for both client and therapist.

In therapy, the client can be totally free to express anything to the therapist, who is devoted to the client's growth. I realize that I am stating an ideal here, since no therapist is able to be totally without self-interest in the treatment relationship. However, I do know many therapists who are not only sufficiently skilled, but whose love of the psychotherapeutic art enables them to work in this way most of the time.

In a loving environment, infants receive this type of attention. That is, they are cared for and attended to, with nothing being required of them. Is it surprising that a kind of love emerges from a client/therapist relationship? I have come to realize that this was one of the major reasons behind Karen's love for me. Our feelings were not products of the past. They were reactions to the warmth and nurturing of the present. I did listen and care, and I required nothing of her. *She* was enough.

Karen recovered memories of her childhood that were psychotherapeutically dramatic, to say the least. She was orphaned at the age of three and, initially, could recall nothing about her parents. Shortly after her parents' death, a childless couple from a small community in the Midwest became her foster parents. As she recalled her relationship with them, Karen came to believe that her foster mother had forced her husband to accept Karen as a foster child in order to tighten the bonds of a stable but loveless marriage. Karen was well treated, but not thought of as a daughter. She was not legally adopted into the family, although she lived with her foster parents from the age of three until she married at the age of twenty-two. She did not feel cherished by either of her foster parents.

In the middle of our work, Karen told me that she had had a violent and upsetting dream that she could only vaguely remember. In the following weeks she remembered that her natural mother and father were in the dreams. As she continued to describe them, it struck me that her accounts sounded more like memories than dreams.

Karen's dreamlike memories of her natural parents were terrifying. In them, she experienced panic reactions that shook her awake. These memories alluded to an obscure violence to which she reacted with terror. Then she remembered an uncle, her father's brother. She recalled her mother leaving home for a long time with her uncle. After her mother returned, she saw her uncle murder her mother and father and then kill himself with a shotgun.

Initially, we questioned the reality of these memories. Were they metaphoric fantasies carrying other messages? Or did these horrible events actually occur? While we were raising these questions, Karen remembered that she had an older brother and sister. When her foster parents took her from the orphanage where she and her siblings were sent after the murders, she lost contact with them.

To settle the question of whether the memories were real, and also to try to locate her siblings, Karen returned to her hometown and visited the morgue of the town's only newspaper. There she found an old edition of the paper that had a front-page story about the murders and suicide, which she copied and brought to our next session. The news articles turned out to be quite consistent with the notes that I took on Karen's recollections.

The repressed memories of her childhood had been restored to her consciousness. Bringing this long-forgotten memory into awareness raised intriguing questions about the nature of "cure." I felt fortunate to be able to see a cure so early in my career. Karen's "repressed" memories had been restored to consciousness, and I believed that Karen would shortly be cured. I was eager to see how consciousness functioned as a curative process. Both Karen and I were ecstatic about her discoveries, one of which enabled her to find a brother and sister in a city south of Los Angeles. She was delighted to be able to reunite with them.

However, our joy was short-lived. Her relationship with her husband, daughter, and me deteriorated. She began drinking heavily and engaged in a variety of sexual escapades with men who had no names. Our work became unproductive; her associations were barren. The emotional relationship between us cooled, and therapy became more and more fruitless. For about a year after the recovery of her memories of the murders, Karen and I continued our efforts. During that time, she remembered her natural mother's abusiveness. For example, the scar on her arm had been caused by boiling water that her mother had poured on her when she was caught playing sexually with her older brother. However, the recovery of these memories was without therapeutic effect. They were not helpful in ameliorating her anxiety or in providing her with the ability to relate to her marriage in a less conflicted way.

Karen, in consultation with her husband and others, decided to terminate therapy. While I did not think that the alternative therapeutic program she was contemplating would be helpful, I had nothing more to offer her.

About four years after Karen terminated her treatment with me, she called and asked for an appointment. When I saw her on the following day, an aching lump formed in my throat. She had gained about thirty pounds and looked unhappy and disheveled. After we seated ourselves in my office, she told me that she had pursued a course of LSD therapy, encounter groups, and individual psychotherapy with other therapists, all to no avail. She felt hopeless about her condition. I asked if she had called to see me because she had thought about returning to therapy. She sadly smiled and politely said, "No." I then asked why she had come to see me again. She said she still cared for me and missed our time together. At the end of the interview, I walked her out to her car.

Saying good-bye was awkward. I hated the incompleteness of our contact and my inability to help her. I also wanted to ask her a question that had plagued me for years. After a moment of agonizing silence, I asked her what the recovery of the memories of her parents' murders meant to her. She looked puzzled and said, "You wanted me to remember. I did it for you." I was stunned by this revelation. She drove away, and about five years later the physician who had originally referred her to me told me that she had committed suicide.

Karen is never far from my mind. We had a kind of love I did not then understand. My work with her made me aware of how little I knew about psychotherapy and how much of its theory I had accepted on faith. After she left me standing in the parking lot, I felt a compelling desire to develop a more meaningful understanding about the nature of sex, love, and consciousness in the psychotherapeutic relationship.

Bringing the memories of her parents' murders back into consciousness did not have much therapeutic value for Karen. Whatever positive results were achieved in therapy came from the contact and caring that she experienced in our relationship. Had I known more about the love that is inherent in this type of interaction, I would have understood more about the sexuality that confused Karen and myself, and I could have used it therapeutically. Intensive psychotherapy that is oriented toward facilitating personality change creates an intense emotional relationship between the client and therapist.

The Interpersonal Relationship

The debate regarding the nature of the interpersonal relationship within psychoanalytic psychotherapy has a long and conflicted history. Famous psychoanalysts such as Sandor Ferenczi (one of Freud's heirs apparent), Karl Abraham, and Harry Stack Sullivan, among many others, recognized the importance of the therapeutic relationship. However, the major trend of psychoanalysis until fairly recently has been the use of the couch and the "blank screen" model of psychotherapeutic relationship. Carl Jung (1962) described his understanding of the relationship in psychotherapy as an engagement between two people in the following terms:

> The crucial point is that I confront the patient as one human being to another. Analysis is a dialogue demanding two partners. Analyst and patient sit facing one another, eye to eye, . . . (p. 131).

> . . . the doctor cannot cure without committing himself. When important matters are at stake, it makes all the difference whether the doctor sees himself as part of the drama, or cloaks himself in his authority. In the great crises of life, in the supreme moments when to be or not to be is the question, little tricks of suggestion do not help. The doctor's whole being is challenged (p. 133).

The psychoanalytic tradition of couch and blank screen pulls both analyst and patient in two opposite directions at the same time. While the blank screen presumably offers the patient an opportunity to project onto the analyst unconscious information that can be interpreted, it also prevents them from using the information about what is happening in the immediate relationship. As we shall see in the next chapter, the blank screen prevents valuable information about the relationship from being shared and used. Unfortunately, the recognition by the early analysts of the importance of the therapeutic relationship was not coupled with a theory about its nature.

I, too, came to see the significance of the personal engagement in psychotherapy. It was evident that my person was a significant part of the engagement and the work. No matter how hard I tried to convince myself, I was not a blank screen. The fact that my clients teased me about being the "great stone face" was clear evidence that they had an emotional relationship with me as a person. If this is so, how could I describe the ongoing interpersonal dynamics of the therapeutic relationship? And what guidelines does the therapist use to optimize the therapeutic impact of this engagement? I realized that trying to be a blank screen was contradictory and was handicapping my efforts to be effective. I was trying to be something that I could not be. And in this attempt I could not focus on the interpersonal process as it occurred between me and my client. I could not be both a blank screen and a person at the same time.

After Karen, I felt entangled in an overgrown forest of ideas about what my relationship to the client "should" be. Both theoretical confusions and my need to earn a living confounded my thinking. If I left the analytic fold, where could I go? I was afraid that I would be regarded with suspicion by my colleagues if I stopped doing analytically oriented psychotherapy. Even if I were brave and abandoned psychoanalysis, I had no alternative model to follow that made any sense to me. On the other hand, some of my own analytic work had been meaningful and productive. Analysis was not totally ineffective. My personal analysis had been helpful and enriching, but for reasons that I could not articulate. My ambivalence grew as I faced the constraints of being a blank screen coupled with the meager improvements my clients were making.

The blank-screen role of the therapist, from which ideas of transference and countertransference arose, is fading. In the past, it was believed that if the therapist took on this role, then the patient could project or transfer conflicts of the past onto the therapist's screen. However, this concept had not helped me with Karen. The primary focus of my attention on the dynamics of family interactions during childhood blinded me to the importance of the immediate emotional dynamics of our relationship. It was becoming increasingly apparent that the depth of our relationship was more meaningful than would have occurred as a "transferred" result of the unresolved conflicts of the past. My inability to see the dynamics of our immediate relationship and my confusion about its sexuality caused me to miss a golden therapeutic opportunity.

From the very beginning, sex has been the poltergeist of psychotherapy. It appeared in the first psychoanalytic relationship, where Dr. Joseph Breuer and Anna O. were the first psychoanalytic therapy pair.

The sexuality of that relationship was so distressing that it drove him away from pursuing psychotherapy as a curative enterprise (Breuer and Freud, 1893/1955). I now believe that my inept handling of the sexuality in my relationship with Karen reduced the effectiveness of my work with her.

If I had not loved the work of psychotherapy so much, I, too, would probably have abandoned it. However, the meaningfulness of my relationship with Karen captured my attention, and I intuitively knew that whatever good came from therapy had its origins *in the relationship.* I was also aware of the *power of early childhood relationships* in the formation of the adult person.

These two realizations, combined with empathic common sense, formed the intellectual and emotional foundation of my therapeutic work. These ideas were the buoys that kept me afloat as a therapist, and they are the central insights that brought me to this theory of personality.

Powerful emotions commonly emerge during the work of therapy. *Productive work leads to love and respect. These are extraordinarily difficult feelings for some people to experience.* They disrupt or interrupt habituated patterns of experiencing and feeling. When this happens, a person will attempt to transform the unfamiliar or disruptive feelings into those with which she/he has more skill. As I learned more about the therapeutic relationship, I found that the ideas of both emotional skill and transformation aided me in my understanding of the therapeutic process.

The acceptance or denial of sexuality is frequently experienced when emotional intensity occurs in an intimate situation. Hostages and their captors, parents and children, and patients and therapists are examples of relationships ripe for this kind of emotional transformation. The sexual experience, then, becomes the explanatory "container" within which the emotionality of the couple is held. In the following chapters, I will describe how the explanation, i.e., sexual experience, "contains" understanding that relieves anxiety. Sexual feelings are highly overlearned—that is, many individuals are very skilled in the experience of sexuality. When confronted with an unfamiliar or unusual situation, sexuality in one form or other can be used to transform an unfamiliar emotional situation into one that is readily understood.

The therapeutic relationship is a recent human invention, and it is one that is poorly understood by both therapist and client. It stands outside the familiar conventions of family and friendship; yet the loving experience that is part of it is intimately related to both. When a loving experience emerges in the therapeutic relationship, the client and therapist frequently have difficulty knowing how to use or explain these feelings. Unfortunately, the closest approximation to this loving experience is infatuation, with its attendant sexuality. If the therapeutic relationship becomes fixated on its sexuality, in either its denial or indulgence, the work is either impaired or it stops. I believe that this is what happened to Karen and me. The loving that emerged from the productivity of the initial phase of our work became frozen in the 'container' of sexual denial. As a result, a free flow of communication between us became impossible.

An open recognition that our feelings were an expression of the productivity of our work and the fondness and respect that we had for one another would have allowed us to explore much more important therapeutic issues—the pain of loving and its accompanying sexual confusions. The acknowledgment that sexual indulgence could have put an end to our work might have freed us to continue that work. Instead, Karen's love for me created an unfortunate desire in her to please me. She knew that I was interested in her recalling as much as possible about her early childhood, so she became devoted to this task. Unfortunately, it was not a therapeutic devotion.

Our work was transformed into an unproductive dredging-up of past memories, a subject that she knew would fascinate me. Because of my ignorance and anxiety about *my* sexual reaction to Karen, I was more than willing to be distracted from it by the apparent meaningfulness and drama of the material she was presenting.

Structurally, my relationship with her was similar to the relationship that Joseph Breuer had with Anna O, where the therapeutic pair enabled the patient to (1) achieve a measure of symptom relief, (2) experience a loving relationship that had sexual components and (3) feel confusion about loving and sexuality. It also failed Joseph Breuer.

Dr. Breuer was a highly regarded Viennese neurologist who was also Sigmund Freud's friend and mentor. It was he who turned Freud onto the "talking cure." In the course of his practice, Freud was asked to treat Anna, an extremely distraught young woman whose father, to whom she was devoted, was dying. In the midst of this stressful situation, she would exhibit bizarre behavior. There were times when she refused to speak German and would converse only in English or French. At other times, she would have temper tantrums, or would refuse to eat.

Breuer was called in to treat her as a neurologist, as psychotherapy did not exist. They immediately hit it off, and Breuer spent hours talking with her. She was an enchanting and brilliant woman; in fact, it was she who coined the phrase, the "talking cure."

At times, Anna would be unmanageable until Breuer came into her home. His presence had a calming effect and enabled her to relate more rationally to her family and to her father's condition. On occasion, Anna would regress into infantile behavior; Breuer would literally feed her. All of this was emotionally sustaining, but it was not a cure. Breuer spent so much time with Anna that his wife eventually complained and threatened to leave him. Anna, too, became confrontational and expressed her love and sexual feelings for him. He panicked and abruptly referred her to another physician. Fleeing Vienna, he took an extended vacation with his wife, during which time she became pregnant. Anna also developed symptoms of pregnancy, but these were pseudopsyecis (false pregnancy). The physician to whom she was referred did not help her, and subsequently she was admitted to a psychiatric sanitarium in Switzerland.

Despite his failure, Breuer's work with Anna O. left a deep impression on him. In confidence, he told Freud about Anna and the talking cure. Freud saw in it the potential for the relief of pain and the accumulation of knowledge. It was he who persuaded Breuer to write about Anna O. and include it as a case study in their book *Studies in Hysteria*. Freud believed that the improvement Anna experienced came about because she was able to bring into consciousness her repressed feelings.

Freud's hypothesis of consciousness as a cure had its beginnings in this case. This brings to mind Rollo May's (1963) observation that "Freud had a genius for asking all of the right questions, to which, unfortunately, he had the wrong answers." I believe that the amelioration of Anna O.'s anguish arose from the emotional contact she had with Breuer. My interpretation of Anna's relief stands in sharp contrast with Masterson's (1984) suggestion that it arose from the transference relationship she had with Breuer.

My abiding interest in the case of Anna O. arises from the fact that it was the first dyadic psychotherapeutic relationship. It was the beginning of psychotherapy, which uses the relationship between the client and therapist as the basis upon which the work in growth of personality is founded. Slightly over one hundred years ago, stemming from the drama of human intimacy that was shared by a remarkable woman and her enthralled physician, a new kind of human relationship was formed. It was crude and ill defined, yet despite the limitations of human knowledge, that therapeutic relationship created modern psychotherapy. This historic interpersonal invention has expanded our understanding about human nature and has contributed to the alleviation of much emotional suffering.

Similarly, my work with a woman named Vivian furthered my education. With her, I learned more about the nourishing aspects of "emotional contact" that would help me understand the nature of the "hunger" that exists in the intimate human dyad (the two-person relationship).

Adventures with Vivian

Sometime after Karen terminated her therapy with me, Vivian, a grossly obese woman in her late forties, came into my office, making a totally unacceptable proposition. She suggested that I serve as her therapist with the goal of preventing her from committing suicide for the next six months. "Then," she said, "I'll kill myself." Vivian, who was also very pretty and bright, went on to declare that there was nothing that I could do to stop her. Vivian knew that I could have her hospitalized, but that would only delay her suicide by a few days. She had been hospitalized many times and knew how to behave to secure a medical discharge. She also knew that I was powerless to disrupt her plan, but she wanted my help in staying alive for six months.

Vivian had been informed by her attorney that if she remained alive for that time period she would inherit a large sum of money, which she wanted to pass on to her children. If she killed herself before the distribution of the estate in which she was a beneficiary, her children would receive nothing. Therefore, it was imperative that I help her stay alive for the next six months. She went on to say that if I tried to hospitalize her before the inheritance was distributed, she would kill herself prematurely. In that case, she reasoned, I would be responsible for denying her children their legitimate inheritance. She presented her case in such a clear, articulate, and matter-of-fact way that I found it difficult to refute her argument. However, I found her proposal emotionally repugnant, and I refused to work with her under those conditions.

Then, with barely concealed pleasure, she initiated to serious negotiations. I can still see her hunkering her gelatinous mass down as she prepared herself for a debate that she knew she would win. I, a hungry, young therapist, was duck soup for her. She had dealt with many of us in previous years of institutionalization for other suicide attempts. Vivian made it clear that she had never been psychotic and that her previous suicide attempts had been hysterical appeals for contact, not for help. She talked about how angry, lonely, hurt, and ravenously "hungry" for attention she was and had always been. Her inability to form a durable and loving relationship with a man left her confused and hopeless in the face of the unceasing agony of her solitude.

Upon giving me a verbal history of her suicidal escapades and hospitalizations, she struck a deal with me. She noted that I could, of course, retain my high-minded, but vaguely defined, therapeutic goals. Nonetheless, I should recognize that suicidal activity had been a longstanding pattern of behavior on her part. Therefore, I should not expect it to fall easily under voluntary control. Since that was true, I had to be content with her active participation in the therapeutic enterprise. Then, I suspect she said under her breath, "Each for our own purposes." I found her presentation, challenge, and "deal" irresistible.

Having agreed upon a contract of sorts, we settled down to the work of therapy. She told me her "case history," a story that she was quite accustomed to relating. She described herself as the only child in a wealthy Southern family, raised by absentee parents and a series of maids who treated her with varying degrees of indifference. She had a brief sojourn at a Catholic girls' school during her mid-adolescence, but she was expelled due to "flagrant" sexual misconduct. As a young woman, she had been very attractive and sexually active, and these attributes had brought her lots of attention.

With the hindsight of more than twenty-five years of practice, I can guess that it was almost impossible for her to permit herself to have sex in a loving context. I think that this was also true of Karen. Being unable to tolerate an adult loving relationship, Vivian resorted to "flagrant sexual misconduct" (she loved playing with that phrase) as a primary source of emotional contact. She craved attention and was relatively indifferent to the physical gratifications of sexual pleasure.

Although Vivian had an intense desire for contact, the pain and anxiety that she felt when she was in the midst of a loving relationship prevented her from experiencing love and sex in the same relationship. (Once again I was confronted with information about the pain of loving that I was not yet able to recognize.) In any case, Vivian escaped from her dilemma by gaining so much weight that most people avoided her sexually, although they were quite attracted to her considerable charm.

Well-planned suicide attempts also attract attention, so this type of destructive behavior replaced sex as the most meaningful activity in her life.

Our relationship was pleasant and playful. Vivian entertained and teased me. Knowing that I was wedded to the blank screen model of psychotherapy, she would delight in breaking through the role that I was playing and win tightly controlled expressions of pleasure, affection, and approval from me. Since I was never very good at being a blank screen, she would go to great lengths to get positive feedback from me or to embarrass me. Either of these reactions was equally satisfactory to her. I did not know it then, but now I realize that when she could not easily distract me from my analytic stance, she would feel anxious, throw herself at my feet, and hug my legs. That certainly drew my attention. Once when I protested that it was impossible for me to concentrate on the work of therapy with her hanging onto my body, she looked up at me and said, "I hope that one day you will learn how important touching is." I intuitively knew that she was right, but at that time I had no basis for thinking about the value of touching in psychotherapy.

In psychoanalytically oriented psychotherapy, touching is almost forbidden. For some therapists, any form of touching is tantamount to a violation of the code of ethics, but Vivian's appeal did not fall on deaf ears. I have often thought about her desire for me to learn about touching, and I did eventually overcome the prejudice of my early training and came to understand the significance of this powerful and much-maligned aspect of the therapeutic relationship.

Finally, Vivian received her inheritance. I did not see her again. There were no "good-byes," no heartfelt good wishes for the future, as there was no future for the two of us. Farewells would have been too heart-breaking. I received a final check for my services in the mail with a torn scrap of paper on which was written, "Thank you. Vivian." A few months later, I received a painful telephone call from her daughter, telling me that her mother's body had been found in the bathtub of a small deserted cabin in one of the remote canyons on the outskirts of Los Angeles.

My work with Vivian made me very aware of her hunger for contact and attention. She used me to fill herself up enough to live from one week to the next until her inheritance came through. During her six months of therapy, I was still attached to my idea of psychotherapeutic insight and was dedicated to helping Vivian see that her sexual preoccupations arose from the emotionally deprived relationship she had had with her parents. However, her many years of therapy had provided her with a system of explanations that were more than a match for those that I had developed in my all-too-brief tenure as a therapist.

The significant work that Vivian and I accomplished did not reside in the creation of insight; it was our emotional contact that was the most meaningful part of our relationship. This awareness crystallized my dissatisfaction with the way in which I worked in the therapeutic dyad.

By this time, the psychoanalytic role was becoming increasingly uncomfortable for me. Although I enjoyed the poetry of psychoanalytic interpretation, it did not seem very important. My work with Vivian focused my attention more sharply on the emotionality of the therapeutic relationship. Conversely, what is therapeutic about the emotionality of the relationship? I had a sense that emotional contact was important, but, as with other psychological concepts, I could not define it. The meaning of, and need for, contact were deeply puzzling to me. I had been trained to be a blank screen, devoid of any emotional contact with my clients. As with Karen, Vivian wanted and sought intense emotional contact with me in my office, but could not sustain it in a relationship with a man in her everyday life. It was not my sterling character or Hungarian charm that made me so appealing. The ease with which she was able to love me had to do with the way I was with these women in the office. Neither I nor any psychotherapist is a blank screen. Despite any intentional effort, no therapist is able to leave his or her character outside of the therapeutic engagement. So it was not simply transference that formed the basis of the love that emerged in our work. *I* had been meaningful. *I* had made contact. *I* facilitated learning and growth, to some extent. And I did not impose my personal needs on the clients.

Years later, I came to understand that without contact, emotional growth cannot occur. *Various* kinds of loving emerge from validating relationships, so personal growth is, for all intents and purposes, the essence of psychotherapy. It is the primary task of that relationship. Therefore, it follows that successful psychotherapy has to be a kind of loving relationship. I now know that my avoidance of the affectionate interaction I shared with Karen caused me to lose contact with her. Along with this loss, psychotherapy lost its value. Vivian helped me confront the importance of contact, but I had no way of knowing its significance in any human relationship, including psychotherapy.

Unfortunately, contact is not a simple, sweet elixir. It can create terrible dilemmas for both the client and the therapist. With some of my clients, the pain of contact—which is part of the pain of loving—was so difficult that they terminated treatment. What is there about contact that causes us to want and avoid it with almost equal intensity? Contact eases the pain of loneliness. At the same time, however, it makes us confront the awareness of our aloneness. *The very experience of the other also triggers an experience of our "selves." This awareness forces us to know that we are separate.*

To assuage the hunger of their loneliness, my clients needed both my *attention* and *approval*. Karen recovered dreadful memories of her childhood because I wanted her to, and Vivian entertained me and clutched my legs in order to maintain contact with me. Each of them transformed their feelings of loneliness into affection in order to get a validational response from me.

If a person has difficulty with, or is unskilled in, the experience and/or expression of one feeling, that person will involuntarily, automatically, use another with which he or she is more familiar. Joseph, Karen's husband, found it very difficult to express his anger toward her directly. Instead, he ejaculated prematurely and got even with her that way. I wish that I had been more secure in this knowledge then. Had I been, I would have engaged Joseph more actively and helped him to see that the expression of anger can be constructively used in a loving relationship.

Even though I had witnessed emotional transformation, my very brief sojourn with a man I will call James brought the transformational nature of feelings into sharp focal awareness. My work with him was both amusing and enlightening.

A Brief Encounter with James

James was an undergraduate student in political science at a university in Los Angeles. The efforts he made to avoid becoming an adult interfered with his academic endeavors and generated enough anxiety to compel him to seek help. Within the first few sessions of therapy, he quickly caught on to my interest in the expression of feelings. About five years into my practice, I had begun to focus more on my client's emotionality as a significant part of therapy. I was still operating within the analytic mode, but I thought that the cathartic principle, rather than insight, would be the curative process in therapy.

At that time, I was particularly enamored of crying. If a client shed tears, I assumed that significant work was being done. Observing my unspoken interest in crying, James would lie on the couch and cry copiously. He would shed tears about his poor grades, about feelings of abandonment caused by his parents' divorce when he was eight years old (in fact, neither of his parents had lost contact with him), and about a girlfriend who would not go to bed with him. All of these situations were cause for self-pity and tears.

This behavior went on for about eight sessions, during which time James's crying became very proficient. He was so task oriented that he would go directly to the couch, lie down, and cry. In the final session of this part of our work, he came into the consultation room, took a tissue, and carefully spread it on the floor at the end of the armless couch that I used. He then lay down on his stomach and contentedly watched the tears run down his long aquiline nose and drop onto the carefully placed tissue. All of this was done without a spoken word.

I was embarrassed and dismayed. I knew that he was responding to me in some way. I asked him to tell me what he thought he was doing. He told me that he had been following instructions. He believed that I thought crying would cure him. Like Karen, he was doing what he thought I wanted him to do. Therefore, he cried, and it felt good. He really enjoyed "treatment."

I was astonished. I had not intentionally instructed him to cry. Moreover, I thought that crying meant that he was in pain or sorrow. He was in neither. Crying brought him a sense of relief, but I suspect that this relief came from the emotional release of his tears and from the contact we shared. It was an interpersonal exercise, not an expression of sadness.

Unfortunately, a few months later he went to graduate school in the East, and our work ended.

My work with James brought to mind recurring themes. The expression of a feeling was a response to, or a manipulation of, me. He thought he was doing something that I wanted him to do. Now I understand that he was transforming his feelings of alienation and loneliness into tears to win my validational approval. When he cried, I approved of and validated him. My conventionalized understanding and expectations about feelings were wrong. There was something therapeutically meaningful about the sense of well-being he reported when he cried, even though his reasons for doing it were existentially absurd.

At this point, my adventures in psychotherapy raised serious questions about the nature of "cure." They shook what little faith I had in psychoanalytic theory. Unfortunately, I had no other theory with which to replace it.

Therapists need some kind of explanatory system to help them "understand" what is being said to them, and more important, to use as an intellectual "banister" to help stabilize them during emotionally tumultuous times. Therefore, I continued to try to function as a blank screen and to use other psychoanalytic ideas to explain my work as a psychotherapist. Yet, my interactions with Karen, Vivian, and James were dramatic experiences that eventually enabled me to realize the importance of the mutuality of the relationship I as a person was having with my clients. Karen and James followed my overt and covert instructions about how to do the work. Vivian added another dimension to my vision of the therapeutic relationship. Eventually, it became impossible for me to see my clients simply lying on a couch, free associating, and projecting transference images and wishes upon me. My clients were actively engaging me as a person, and I was responding.

At the time, I did not see my situation as clearly as I have just written about it. While my reliance on the blank screen was vitiated, I did not abandon it until I was supervised by Hellmuth Kaiser. He taught me more than any of my previous supervisors. My adventures with him turned me on to ideas about the emotional "dance" of the two-person relationship. These ideas illuminated aspects of the therapeutic process, which liberated me to engage my clients more actively.

He taught me that we danced to the tune of our dread of aloneness. Eric Fromm (1956) helped me to recognize the close relationship that exists among aloneness, love, and awareness. Love makes us confront not only an awareness of the other, but an awareness of our self. Self-awareness helps us face our separateness and aloneness—an anxiety-laden condition. Fromm describes it as follows:

> The experience of separateness arouses anxiety; it is, indeed, the source of all anxiety. Being separate means being cut off, without any capacity to use my human powers (p. 7).

However, I was too involved with questions and anxiety about the sexuality of psychotherapy to see the relationship between self-awareness and aloneness. Instead, I was concrete and practical and asked, "What function does the sexual experience have in psychotherapy? Where does psychotherapeutic love come from, and what relationship does it have to cure?"

In the following section, I will describe my work with Hellmuth and how it led me to see the triangular nature of the two-person relationship. My understanding of the dyad brought me closer to an understanding of psychotherapeutic loving, and it raised questions that help me develop this theory of personality.

A Sojourn with Hellmuth Kaiser

As I have mentioned, my early training as a psychotherapist was psychoanalytically oriented. While I loved working with patients, I was never enthusiastic about theory. During my internship in David Shakow's laboratory at the Illinois Neuropsychiatric Institute, I was voted the least psychoanalytically oriented member of the internship group. However, for reasons that I stated above, I decided that psychoanalytic theory would be the therapeutic model I would study and practice.

Shortly after I started my psychotherapeutic practice, I began my own personal analysis, and during those years I sought psychoanalytic supervision. At that time, psychoanalytic institutes refused to train psychologists as analysts. Therefore, I was forced to find supervisors who would bootleg supervision. When I heard that Hellmuth Kaiser, an analyst who had been a training analyst at the Menninger Foundation and at the New England Psychoanalytic Institute, had come to Los Angeles and was willing to supervise psychologists, I immediately sought out his services.

Four aspects of my relationship with Hellmuth turned my world (both personal and professional) upside down. I recall him as a wizened little man who sat far back in his lounge chair, watching and listening to me intently. He paid at least as much attention to the *ways* that I was talking to him, as he did to what I was saying. This made me very uncomfortable. When he commented on the way I was acting, my mouth went dry, and I felt tinglings of anxiety. Two of the four issues that changed my life had to do with Hellmuth's observations about the ways in which I was presenting myself to him.

I will never forget the dismay I felt when he observed that I said "you know" compulsively. I had been caught in a fraudulent act. I was being viewed in a way that was different from the one I had intended. He suggested that I was saying "you know" in order to covertly get him to agree that he knew what I did not know; therefore, if he colluded with me, I would not have to acknowledge that I did not know what I was talking about. He was right, of course, and I was suitably chagrined. My fraudulence had been exposed, and here I had always fancied myself to be an honest, open, and nonmanipulative individual.

The second issue had to do with the use of my person as a therapeutic instrument. At another supervisory session, I was deeply engrossed in describing a very elaborate dream interpretation that I presented to a woman whom I had seen earlier in the day. Hellmuth listened patiently for as long as I chose to talk. When I finished this long-winded description, revealing what I thought was my therapeutic acumen, I looked at him, expecting praise. But he was silent. When I asked him what he thought of my interpretation, he looked at me sadly and said, "You don't think that you are enough, do you?" A spurt of adrenalin charged my heart and raced through my chest. Damn, I had been caught again.

I had offered this complex interpretation to my client because I was feeling inadequate and wanted to impress her. I also wanted to hide that feeling of inadequacy from Hellmuth *and* myself by trying to impress him with my interpretive skill. I understood more when we discussed my use of interpretation as a way of convincing myself that I was a worthy therapist. Beneath my confident façade, I was insecure. I was more than aware that I had no therapeutic rudder. Furthermore, it had not occurred to me that my person was, could be, or should be a significant part of the therapeutic enterprise.

The third issue raised in my relationship with Hellmuth had to do with the nature of my emotionality. I was struck by the psychophysiological reactions that occurred within me when Hellmuth saw me hiding from feelings of inadequacy. This observation led to questions about the physiological nature of emotion. This was one of the questions I had studied in courses on Emotion and Physiological Psychology at UCLA and had forgotten about because they did not provide me with any meaningful answers. I was, now, ready to emotionally and personally confront this issue. This confrontation helped me begin my exploration of the relationship between the mind and the body. What relationship did my pounding heart have with the dismay that I felt within myself? I experienced my rapid heartbeat as a bodily reaction; I felt dismay as a feeling, a product of the mind.

The fourth issue with Hellmuth had to do with the therapeutic management of the fusion delusion. The fusion delusion was Kaiser's (Fierman, 1965) idea that we seek validation from one another to avoid the experience of aloneness. In my case, when I tried to manipulate Hellmuth into validating the illusion of myself as an insightful therapist, I was attempting to avoid the loneliness that I felt as a novice therapist at the beginning of my career.

The awareness of the fusion delusion helped me to find a therapeutic rudder and changed my understanding of the nature of psychotherapy. It was in the context of Hellmuth's observations about my presentations that he suggested that the feelings I was having about a client could reveal useful therapeutic information. He showed me, through pointing out my own manipulations, that it was reasonable to assume my client wanted me to feel the way I had been feeling. Why would I, or a client, do that?

Hellmuth reminded me of the ways that I had been trying to manage him. I remembered how I had tried to distract him in order to make him see me as a brilliant therapist. He went on to explain that this was a manifestation of the fusion delusion. If I could get him to collude with me in the delusion that he knew what I appeared to know (but actually did not), or if he would agree with me that I was a clever interpreter, then I would not have to come face to face with my confusion about myself as a person, a therapist, or a supervisee. At that point, I clearly understood how I was engaging in the fusion delusion.

Hellmuth also helped me see that the fusion delusion was a major defense that precluded me from seeing myself as separate and alone. This awareness led me to a deeper understanding of the nature of *affect hunger,* which I define as the brain's need for stimulation. I believe it is similar to the need that muscles have for exercise; that is, if we do not use our muscles, they suffer the atrophy of disuse. If parts of our brain are not exercised or used, psychological skills will atrophy, also.

The idea of affect hunger is a major hypothesis upon which my theory is built. It is the source of most of our motivation, and it also plays a powerful dynamic role in human interaction. Our need for contact arises from our affect hunger, as contact is a way of feeding this hunger. When it is not nourished by *validational feedback* from others, we experience loneliness. The fusion delusion enables us to escape from that experience. My clients were being fusional with me when they tried to arouse a feeling in me to avoid the experience of their aloneness. Vivian did this when she sat at my feet clutching my legs.

My understanding of the fusion delusion also forced me to confront the question of courage. "Do I have the courage to use the information of my emotional reaction to my client?" This was technically troublesome. How could I be sure that my clients wanted me to feel the way that I was feeling? I knew that I reacted to my clients emotionally. However, my feelings were so private that I was certain that they were the sole products of *my* madness. I was wrong. When we are with others, feelings are social phenomena. The feelings that we have are a product of the interpersonal moment.

I was vividly made aware of this issue as a result of my relationships with clients who happened to be beautiful women. My practice is, in many ways, exciting, rewarding, and dramatic. One interesting sidebar is that, having practiced in the core of the film industry, I have worked with some remarkably attractive women. There have been times when I would become sexually aroused by these women. Before Hellmuth suggested that I might use my feelings as a guide to what was going in my relationship with my clients, I reacted with a private guilt to any feelings of attraction that I had for them. However, as a result of his suggestion, I was struck by the fact that my arousal occurred only at certain times. I was not always aroused; therefore, mere physical beauty was not the trigger. I tended to become aroused when a woman would in one way or another signal a desire for my attraction to her. These erotic messages were usually covert—that is, they were not expressed verbally. However, subtle glances, smiles, and blushes would send shivers of arousal and embarrassment through me. It also became obvious when other clients wanted to provoke certain emotions in me as well. There were times when clients wanted to fight, or to make me feel sorry for them, or to feel defeated. Another client would question me about my fees in a scornful way, and I would become irritated. When I thought about it, the client was not really interested in the question of money; it was simply a convenient way of attacking me in order to elicit an angry response. This list could go on interminably. Clients, for the most part, unconsciously, are constantly in search of some kind of emotional feedback from the therapist, but this type of feedback is not always a pleasant experience.

Even though I knew from my own experience that I tried to manipulate the feelings of others, I found it difficult to see how I could apply my reactions to my clients therapeutically. I believed that it would be the height of *hubris* to suggest that a client wanted me to feel one thing when they were, in fact, talking about something else. However, when I screwed up my courage and responded to my clients by interpreting my feelings, in response to their manipulations, I became more relevant to them, and our work became decidedly more productive and exciting.

Could two things be going on at the same time here? Were my clients talking to me about one thing while simultaneously doing something else to me? Of course they were. We do it all the time. Actors call this interplay of communication "text" and "subtext." The text is the overt or manifest content of the communication. The subtext is usually the fusional process we use to obtain validational feedback. At times, it is a conscious manipulation to get what we want from the other. In psychotherapy, this duality is called content and process, where content is usually at the center of attention, and process operates in the background, usually outside focal awareness. Dialogue between people is like singing a song. The words of the text and the music of the subtext make up the song of human communication. Hellmuth saw that the fusional aspect of human interaction was so omnipresent that he called it "the universal symptom of neurosis."

This understanding taught me that I could use my feelings as a way of understanding what was happening between myself and my client, and I eventually came to see that I could use my feelings as a way of perceiving the therapeutic process. There is nothing new about this observation. Theodore Reik (1948) described it in his book, *Listening with the Third Ear.* I also became aware of why I felt that I was not enough for my clients. I was not using my feelings as a therapeutic part of the relationship. I was not enough because I was denying myself the use of vital information about what was happening "emotionally" between us.

Using my emotionality, I learned three psychotherapeutic skills: First, I discovered that I had to become more proficient in my ability to feel. The development of emotional skills enabled me to see what was happening between myself and my client. Second, emotional skill enabled me to stay task-oriented during intense emotional engagements with my clients. And third, these emotional skills allowed me to accept myself enough to admit my own fallibility. It is important for therapists to acknowledge that his or her interpretations or observations are not infallible dictates of a superior wisdom; rather, they are offerings of information that may be helpful. My insight about the operational use of feelings was the beginning of a long journey into my "self" during which I came to realize that both feelings and self are parts of the person.

These realizations occurred during the final phase of my own personal psychoanalysis. I became aware of the fact that none of these issues arose in my own analysis, and I ended this process with great ambivalence. I had not found the pot of gold at the end of my treatment rainbow; there was more to be learned. I was deeply disappointed with that realization, as I wanted to be finished with the search for more information about myself and luxuriate in the comfort of having completed my analysis. I wanted to "graduate," be "cured" and be finished with it!

My work with Hellmuth made me realize that analysis had not made me perfect. I had learned much about how my relationships with my mother and father had affected my relationships with women and work. However, I realized that it did not help me to learn much about developing emotional skills. This is a necessary part of a therapist's work for which psychoanalysis does not train the analysand.

My relentless ghost pushed me to pursue theoretical questions about the operational use of feelings, the dual process of dyadic interaction, and how feelings are used to influence others. These issues brought me to the triangular theory of the dyadic relationship, which I will describe in the next chapter. This theory provided me with the psychotherapeutic rudder I needed, and it changed my life.

Finding My Therapeutic Rudder

The Theory of Dyadic Interaction

I was as excited about the idea of the dyadic triangle as I was when I thought Karen would be cured by the recovery of the terrible memories of her parents' murder. I thought that I had the world by the tail. For the first time in my career, I had a sense of mastery. However, it turned out that I was not truly masterful, but I was a better therapist than I had been before. I also had a new understanding of the task of therapy. I believed that if I could help my clients develop better emotional skills, they could live their lives more competently. Remembering painful memories of the past had been somewhat meaningful, but, all in all, it did little to improve the quality of my clients' lives. The dyadic triangle gave me a rudder. And it gave me a clearer vision of the emotional destination toward which I could steer my therapeutic vessel.

The following discussion will describe only the simple structure of the two-person relationship. The emotional complexity of dyadic relationships will be described as the description of the person develops.

The simplicity of the idea of the dyadic triangle blinded me to the fact that before I could understand dyadic process, I would have to address three theoretical issues that had troubled me for years: First, I needed to be able to define what a person is. Second, I was confounded by the confusing nature of psychological definition, so I had to deal with that problem before I could define the person. Third, my attempts to solve the problem of definition drew me into the discovery that we have a doubly dichotomous mind. When I was able to articulate an understanding of these issues, my understanding of both personality and psychotherapy had been changed. Most of the ideas of my theory stemmed from my idea about the triangular nature of dyadic interaction.

The Dyadic Triangle

My concept of the two-person relationship arose from the simple observation that when we speak to one another we are doing two things at the same time. This is the beginning of the theme of duality that will continue throughout the rest of this description of personality. The dyadic engagement is like singing a song in which we respond to both the words and the music of our communication. We talk about things *and* we try to elicit validating responses from the other person with whom we are talking.

This observation enabled me see that dyadic interaction could b diagrammed as a triangle. In Figure 1, the *I* and *Thou* at the base angles of the triangle designate the members of the dyad. I have used *I* and *Thou* to acknowledge Martin Buber's (1970) contribution to my thinking about the dyad. The line of communication connecting I and Thou, the baseline of the triangle, specifies the covert emotional process that exists in the two-person relationship. The lines connecting the members of the dyad to the Subject at the apex of the triangle designate normal conversation.

The *subject* matter of our conversation can be the opera that we avoided going to last night, the truffles at the market that were too expensive to buy, my wish for the return of trolley cars on Main Street—it can be anything about which we share some purpose, knowledge, or interest. Here, the content of the subject matter is held in focal awareness (at the center of attention). Usually, when we are talking about something, we are relatively unemotional about the subject matter and speak to one another more or less reasonably. I refer to this kind of discussion as "talking through the apex of the triangle." In this mode, we talk with one another about some "thing."

While I am talking to another person about something, I may also be covertly soliciting some kind of validational feedback that may or may not be related to the *Subject*. I may want that person to like me and smile at me and think that I am smart and charming. I may also want to sell them a truck, or persuade them to spend Saturday night with me, or get them to do something else. The other person, likewise, is expecting and seeking a reciprocal kind of validation from me. When this happens, we are communicating on the baseline. Baseline communication (in Martin Buber's terms, I-Thou communication) rarely occurs in overt conversation; when it does occur, the members of the dyad are usually either very loving or angry with one another. I-Thou dialogue is emotionally arousing because the *automaticity* of personal presentations is interrupted. Automaticity and interruption will be continuing themes throughout the rest of the book. Talking through the apex and communicating on the baseline occur simultaneously. This is the duality that carried me through my journey into the mind.

The lines of the diagram that are perpendicular to the baseline designate self-presentations of the members of the pair. These are unspoken signals that we send to elicit validational feedback from others. Self-presentations initiate baseline contact.

The covert operations of the dyad, on the baseline, are expressed in the nonverbal characteristics of the self-presentation of the person. The smiles that we send to one another, the nods with which we signal approval to one another, the varied messages we send with our eyes, the ways we hold our bodies—these are the nonverbal expressions of baseline communication. They are expressions designed to transmit and/or elicit validating feedback between members of the dyad. When I speak of validating feedback, I am not only referring to positive experiences. Validation can also occur in unpleasant situations. The kind of valida-

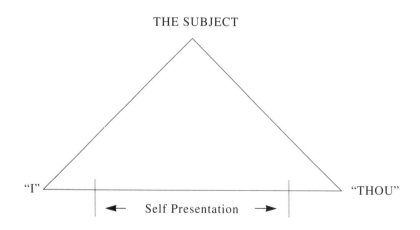

FIGURE 1
THE DYADIC TRIANGLE

tion that a person seeks depends upon the emotional structure of that person. Some are nourished by smiles; others are satisfied by a good fight.

The dyadic significance of validating feedback is most vividly experienced in its absence. When this occurs, the members of the dyad (1) lose interest in one another, (2) become angry, and/or (3) are unable to work or talk effectively—that is, they become alienated. *I believe that interpersonal validation is an equilibratory process that is almost as necessary to our survival as the food we eat. Equilibration* and *stabilization* are synonymous terms. Validation is a necessary ingredient in all loving relationships.

Baseline process is a primary source of the "food" that feeds our *affect hunger.* In the last chapter, I described the feeding of affect hunger as one of the primary biological/emotional dynamics directing our experience and behavior. It is for this reason that *baseline* communication is essential to the effectiveness and stability of the dyad. When both members of the dyad provide one another with validating feedback, they are in contact. Without it, the *pair* either stagnates or dies. Most of the fights that lovers have occur because they are, either knowingly or unknowingly, invalidating one another. The emotionality of the relationship arises from, and is primarily expressed on, the baseline.

Our personalities are volatile, shimmering constructions reflecting the enormous complexity of the brain. Our survival requires that the three-pound miracle of our brain be kept in its steady-state condition. Everything that we do or experience is at the service of this task. Every expression of personality has a stabilizing purpose. Feeding the affect hunger of our brain is the major internal work of our psyche. We feed this affect hunger by eliciting validational feedback from our work, play, and relationships with others. Internal and external stabilization make up the wings of our existence.

Not only are our personal and emotional expressions designed to influence others to supply us with validational feedback, but they are also used to stop others from doing things that are invalidating.

Apical and baseline communication can be compared to a picture where a central figure stands in front of a background. Apical communication occupies the center of attention in a way that is similar to our experience of the central figure. Baseline communication usually lies in the background of awareness. These two forms of communication form the content and process of the two-person interaction. Apical dialogue is about content, the subject matter. Baseline communication is primarily about the interpersonal process of the relationship. It is possible to alternate our experience of the interpersonal figure and ground nature of our engagement. One or both people in the dyad can choose to attend to the baseline process and ignore apical content. As I indicated above, this happens rarely in conventional relationships that are emotionally stable. However, I do it frequently in my relationship with clients.

We shall see in the next chapter that this practice had a dramatically effective impact on my clients. I do not do apply this therapy to normal social relationships, because doing so violates the normal social contract that people have with one another. The interpersonal figure-ground reversal is essentially the same thing that happens in the figure-ground illusion of Gestalt psychology. (See Figure 2, below.)

This figure-ground illusion can be seen as either a female face or a male saxophone player. In it, figure and ground can alternate in awareness. In other words, we can view the saxophone player on a white background, or our perspective can shift so we see a picture of the face of an attractive woman.

This phenomenon occurs in all psychological process and is not limited to visual perception. It occurs when we listen to a song; that is, we may be alternately more aware of its words or its music, and it occurs in the baseline and apical interactions that people have with one another.

Whenever we are talking to another person, our dialogue is overtly designed to help in the sharing of an experience or an action. At the same time, we want to influence this person to provide us with emotional goodies. As in the figure-ground illusion, we can alternate our attention to bring either baseline or apical communication into focal awareness.

When Hellmuth pointed out my duplicity, I recognized it as a familiar way of interacting. While I was embarrassed by being caught in a duplicitous act, I knew it as the usual way that people interact with clients, friends, lovers, and acquaintances. It is rare that a person communicates with another without engaging in some baseline manipulation, for without it, relationships tend to become boring and wither away.

The therapeutic dyad differs from the conventional dyad because the therapist speaks to the client on the baseline more than conventional pairs do. And the therapist's observations usually occur without emotional intensity. This creates a paradoxical situation because in this culture, at least, baseline interaction is usually dramatically emotional.

FIGURE 2

THE FIGURE-GROUND ILLUSION

Emotionality of relationships arises from our need for validating feedback from others. This need is expressed in the pleasure that we experience when others treat us well, or in the displeasure that we experience when we are invalidated by others. "Face" (a shorthand term for personal presentation) is an example of this. All human beings need to save face. The validation of face is a common source of feeding one's affect hunger. When we are insulted or disrespected, our personal systems are thrown into disarray, and we experience pain.

I introduced a kind and gentle woman into one of my therapy groups. She remained relatively quiet and observant for about three sessions. During the fourth session, she remarked that she was surprised at the respect and consideration the other members of the group had for one another. The group interpreted her observation as a criticism of them. They thought that she was saying that they were not doing enough emotional work. During the next session, a male member of the group told her that her comment had angered him and that if she wanted some action she could herself become more active, and he would be ready for her. Inadvertently, she had invalidated his sense of himself as a hard-working client. At the next session, she told me that it was all that she could do to keep herself from vomiting when he spoke to her. He had invalidated her presentation. She wanted to be liked and thought that she was expressing admiration and appreciation, not criticism.

We invariably project a range of painful and negative feelings on the person who is insulting us. We seek validating feedback from others to stabilize the structures of our personalities for the same reasons that we exercise our muscles to keep them in good operating shape.

As I mentioned above, the simplicity of the idea blinded me to the fact that before I could understand the dyad, I would have to address these three questions which had troubled me for years: What is a person? What is the psychological definition of a person? How can the problem of the doubly dichotomous mind be solved? The next three chapters will delve into the answers to the three questions. These solutions changed not only my understanding of the nature of the psychotherapeutic process, but they also changed my understanding of the nature of personality.

I had to spend a number of years exploring therapeutic and emotional ways of being, experiencing, and knowing how to use the theory of dyadic interaction before I could understand the person in its holistic unity. They were years of excitement, learning, and dismay. During this time, I became aware of the exquisite reality of the Theater of the Absurd and the paradoxical complexity of the person. The next chapter will describe some of my adventures on its stage, adventures which illuminated the nature of the person.

CHAPTER IV

Learning to Use
My Therapeutic Rudder

The idea of the dyadic triangle was exhilarating. I finally had an explanation that enabled me to make sense out of what my clients were doing. I had created another clinical tool. Not only could I use psychodynamic explanations about my client's history, but I also could see the emotional process that was occurring between us during a session, and I could use that information therapeutically. At that time, I believed that helping my clients become emotionally skilled was a major task of psychotherapy. As we proceed in this chapter, I will describe some other dimensions of the psychotherapeutic task, which unfolded as I pursued the task of emotional learning.

The acquisition of a therapeutic rudder changed the nature of my work. I spent increasing amounts of time on the baseline of the dyadic triangle with my clients, and I was able to use their feelings and my own to steer the ship of psychotherapy. However, I must confess that sometimes I found myself steering it in circles. In the early period, I found that my preoccupation with emotional skill training blinded me to the importance of the abiding pain of childhood confusions and abuse.

I left my position behind the couch. I no longer encouraged my clients to associate freely. I stopped thinking about transference and resistance as significant areas of therapeutic work. Instead, I responded to the personal presentations of my clients, as well as to the content of their discussion.

My person became an active part in the therapeutic process. I no longer hid behind the blank screen upon which my clients were supposed to project. Instead of being a sleuth in pursuit of hidden information buried in the past, I became more interested in the illumination of the process that was occurring in the present. I *split* the focus of my attention between the emotional and experiential interactions that occurred between myself and my client and the content about which he or she was talking.

The inspection of the "here and now" engagement reintroduced the past in a new and entirely different psychotherapeutic context. I found that if I shifted the focus of my attention from the content of what my clients were talking about to the way they were presenting themselves to me, I stirred up an emotional hornet's nest. Engaging the baseline manipulations of my client produced intense emotional reactions in *me*.

I had been partially prepared for these emotional reactions in light of the ones that I had in response to Hellmuth Kaiser. His observations about my "you knows" and my feeling that I was not "enough" had stirred intense feelings and emotions within me toward him. Furthermore, I found that if I did not become overwhelmed by the intensity of my clients' reactions to me, they would learn something about themselves and experience a sense of relief. Then, very often, they would have emotion-filled memories of relationships that occurred in their childhoods.

My clients found themselves both loving and hating me. I had looked past their presentations and had seen their naked, *unintentional* selves. Embarrassment became a common experience for my clients, and their personal presentations changed. They also became less anxious and less manipulative. My work with a man named Raymond exemplifies the nature of my work in this initial period of discovery and also illustrates some of the learning that occurred.

Dancing with Raymond

Raymond's father sent him to me from Florida. I believe that his father wanted to help Raymond; but he also wanted to get rid of him. When I first saw him, Raymond was teetering on the edge of psychosis. He was extremely depressed and complained with a snarling bitterness about a terrible pain in his stomach and a total sexual incapacity. He told me that my task was to rid him of his pain and enable him to have sexual relations with a woman. He stated these requirements contemptuously, indicating that he knew that I would fail him, as had his previous therapist. However, since he had little to lose, he would give me a chance.

At our first interview, I informed Raymond that I was going on vacation in three weeks. He had two choices. I could refer him to someone else, or we could see what progress we could make in the period before my month-long vacation. He felt that the following three weeks would give us enough time to evaluate the merits of our relationship. Then we would decide on our next steps. In the weeks that followed, we learned to know one another well enough to create a working relationship.

Raymond was somewhat surprised by me. I made contact with Raymond, startling him. Instead of taking a case history, I played with his personal presentation. He was a dreadful complainer. Everything was dark and distasteful. He was hurt, lonely, ineffectual, and everyone around him treated him badly. I read this presentation as an appeal for sympathy, so I responded to him with sarcasm. How could I do anything but feel sorry for him in his pitiful condition? He became furious, and I encouraged his expression of anger, which surprised him greatly. He found it unusual that someone would encourage him to express his anger and was also amazed to find out that this expression of feelings led to relief from his depression. He also experienced personal growth when he saw that my refusal to sympathize was meant to be constructive. I did not collude with his self-deprecating position, because sympathy would have validated his wretched self-contempt.

Before I went on my vacation, Raymond became worried and agitated about my leaving. He was afraid he might not be able to control his behavior while I was away. I told him that if he wished, I could put him in touch with a psychiatrist who would be willing to hospitalize him should he feel the need for it. That, too, surprised him. It had not occurred to him that he had any control over whether or not he should be hospitalized.

When I returned from my vacation, I eagerly checked in with my telephone exchange to find out how Raymond had fared while I was gone. There were no messages from him or from my psychiatric colleague. In high spirits, Raymond arrived promptly for our next scheduled appointment. He was delighted and relieved that hospitalization had not been necessary. Even more satisfying, he had experienced a psychotic episode without having to go to a hospital.

The psychotic episode had been a fascinating experience. He told me that while I was gone he had smoked his first "joint," which had sent him on a trip into outer space where he had been able to see the design of the whole universe. He had seen it as a magnificent, multicolored, and multidimensional geometric pattern. Within it, all of the answers to the problems of the universe were arranged in relationship to one another. When I pressed him for specifics, he could not relate them to me. I was eager to be let in on this wisdom, but he dismissed my desire as irrelevant. However, he expressed confidence that he could retrieve this knowledge when it suited him. At the end of both that session and the next one, he told me that he was very pleased with the work he had been doing with me.

The next six sessions were very different. In one of these sessions, he walked into the consultation room and looked down at me with a threatening and baleful expression. Since he was larger and stronger than I, I admit that I was uneasy. He sat down and said nothing. I inquired about his pain, the events of his daily life, and his anger toward me, all to no avail. When I pressed him for a response, he told me that he felt "shitty." Actually, I felt "shitty," too—anxious and helpless.

Just before our sixth session started, I was in my office waiting for Raymond, wishing that he would cancel his appointment. As I pondered this feeling of uneasiness, Raymond came into my office with a glowering demeanor. I realized that this performance was designed to push me away. I jumped up from my desk chair and sat down next to him on the couch. I put my hand on his shoulder and told him how delighted I was to see him. I informed him that rarely did I get a chance to be with someone who possessed so much charm and wit as he did. I went on to tell him how honored I was that he was willing to grace me with his presence. This was my first dance on the stage of the Theater of the Absurd. He turned, looked at me and asked, "Are you trying to drive me crazy?" I was not trying to do so, but I had to act crazy in order to make contact with him. I must admit that I felt a bit like Groucho Marx in this and other subsequent engagements with my clients.

Common sense had not directed my behavior. My departure from this traditional way of thinking had both clinical and theoretical significance. Clinically, it freed me to use my feelings as a source of therapeutic information. Theoretically, it enabled me to think about psychological process in the untraditional forms that I will be describing.

My absurdity enabled me to make emotional contact with Raymond, and it broke our therapeutic logjam. When we made contact, he explained that he wanted to hate me in order to be rid of me. His work with me had given him hope, and he was also experiencing feelings of affection for me, which were extremely disturbing to him. When Raymond found himself caring for me, images of my penis came into his mind, and he hated himself because he thought that he was a "faggot" and a "queer."

Raymond was the first person who put me in touch with cognitive transformations with respect to the pain of loving. For many, it is a deeply unsettling emotion as it was for Raymond. When I understood this, I empathized with his desire to be rid of me. While he disliked himself when he thought that he might be a homosexual, it became clear that homosexuality was not the real issue. It was an emotional transformation designed to cope with feelings about me. He was not sexually attracted to men; women were becoming increasingly appealing to him. His homosexual fantasies about me were transformations into a kind of loving that could be easily rejected, and they provided him with a "real" reason to get rid of me.

His thoughts of my penis or sucking on it were devoid of erotic feeling. It was the warmth and affection arising within him that created great anxiety and regression to a very early childhood period. When he found that he could not get me to do something despicable or to take his homosexual distaste seriously, his loving feelings were transformed into violent fantasies. At first, it was astonishing and disconcerting to listen to him snarl and shake his fists at me while telling me that he wanted to tear my body into shreds and drench the consultation room with my blood. When he expressed these feelings, a beatific smile of relief lightened his face. These were the only times that he smiled.

When the intensity of Raymond's feelings subsided, he recalled his adolescence, when he had had similar fantasies about his parents. Once in his father's workshop, he had had an almost irresistible impulse to smash in his father's head with a hammer. He had similar experiences with a knife when he was in the kitchen with his mother. These impulses occurred in moments of affection for them. We agreed to call his loving anguish "that place." When we first entered "that place," he suffered intensely. He wept, mucous dripped from his nose, and he held himself tightly to restrain his anger.

When rage could not obliterate the warmth of our relationship, he was overcome with nausea, tears, and anxiety. He became so anxious that if I moved closer to him or touched him, he started violently. I was shocked by the intensity of his reactions. He said that these responses were totally involuntary and astonished him as well. In the quiet moments after he recovered from these intense feelings, he recalled, as had Karen, that he had been abused when he was an infant.

Like Karen, Raymond's initial recollections were vague and inarticulate. I believe that the recall of abuse was murky, because he was remembering events that had occurred when he was either preverbal or when he was just learning to speak.

Raymond decided to confront his parents with his memories, and they admitted "slapping him around" when he was an infant. Years later, Raymond recalled sitting in his crib in the middle of the night, happily playing with his feces, when his father entered his bedroom. When he saw his son indulging in this play, he walked to the crib and hit him on the head with the back of his hand. Unfortunately, Raymond had no words with which to bind his memories into a form that could be verbally communicated.

Each time he recalled his father hitting him, his body became rigid, his arms tightened against his sides, his fists clenched, and his face flushed with rage. There were no words. On one occasion, after he relaxed from the exertion of this memory, he said that he believed the birthplace of schizophrenia was infant abuse. He went on to say that, after the child developed language, the mistreatment could cause neurosis instead of psychosis.

This is consistent with observations made by other clients, who have reported that they stopped experiencing feelings when their parents abused them. They say that their bodies became very rigid, and this stillness coupled with the obliteration of their self-awareness shut out the pain and rage that arose within them. These are the moments in the development of the individual where the fixation of infantile personal structures occurs.

The Psychotherapeutic Dilemma

Trying to stay within familiar bounds, while at the same time trying to change, created an exquisite dilemma for Raymond. On the one hand, I encouraged him to let himself experience painful feelings.

On the other hand, these are the feelings that had been structured to be automatically repressed, because they evoked sanity-threatening anxiety. I was teaching Raymond to love his pain.

Mammals are genetically structured to avoid physical pain, and systems of avoidance behavior are activated when this type of sensation occurs. Anxiety encompasses the experiential quality of fear, which is also structured to activate avoidance or flight behaviors. The avoidance of pain and anxiety is not resistance. However, psychological pain and anxiety are not physically threatening experiences. Reacting to these emotions as though they were physically dangerous destroys an opportunity to learn about important internal emotional processes. Experiencing psychological pain or anxiety is an opportunity for new learning and growth. Loving one's pain can liberate a person from imprisoning delusions of the past.

I reject the use of resistance interpretations for three reasons. First, they presume that the client has voluntary control over an emotional process that is involuntary. Second, they place the therapist in the position of blaming the client for doing something, or being, wrong. And third, they create a guilt process between the therapist and client that disrupts the baseline flow between them. The avoidance of painful feelings is an automated part of the client's character structure. There is nothing intentional about this avoidance, and to interpret it as resistance is to blame the client for doing something over which she or he has no control.

My work with Raymond caused me to shift from thinking that catharsis was a primary therapeutic principle to seeing that emotional training was the therapeutic path to follow. I did not yet understand what the functional value of emotionality was for the members of a dyad. When I tried to understand the nature of emotional process, I was faced with questions about the nature of personality.

As I was grappling with these questions, I formulated the idea that people, in their engagements with one another, are always trying to keep the experience of their emotionality within familiar bounds. This hypothesis prepared me to understand my work with Roger, the next client in my odyssey. It was with him that I came to see that feelings were anxiety reducing. I also saw that such emotions were a form of explanation. Then I began to understand that feelings are equilibratory/stabilizing processes. I came to realize that *emotion was the expression of disorganization* and that *feelings were stabilizing operations.* I learned much more about emotionality through my work with Roger.

Embracing Roger

Roger began treatment with me when I was practicing psychoanalytically oriented psychotherapy, and he terminated psychotherapy with relatively satisfactory results. When he started his treatment, he was having difficulties in his relationships with women and with his colleagues at work. At the termination of the initial period of therapy, he was getting married and was working effectively with his colleagues. Six years later he returned, seeking further help. In the intervening years, his marriage had matured. He and his wife had had two daughters who delighted him. On the surface, his marriage looked stable and gratifying. His work was progressing well, his children loved him, and his wife was dedicated to his well-being. She was also very worried about him.

At first glance, Roger seemed to be in excellent shape. After telling me how well he was doing, he confided that people at work were talking about him. In the company lunchroom, "they" would sit at a table near him, look at him, and whisper. "They" would stand outside his office door and discuss him in loud, derogatory terms. He knew "they" were out to get him. "They" had "bugged" his office and home with listening devices in order to gather incriminating evidence against him. It was impossible to have a private conversation with his wife, because "they" had listening devices outside his home. It was sheer desperation that permitted him to come to me, because he believed "they" had "bugged" my office, too.

Roger was infuriated with "them," but could not express his anger, even in the privacy of my office. He was terrified about what "they" might do to him. His fears were reinforced by newspaper stories about the Watergate affair and associated stories about the use of electronic listening devices.

After a few sessions, Roger informed me that, despite external appearances, his relationship with his wife was very strained. They were devoted to one another, but they could not communicate or work together without terrible misunderstanding and confusion. The overt focus of his complaint was their very poor sex life. He bitterly complained about his wife's sexual coldness and also about her inefficiency at home. However, he could not discuss any of this with her. It was clear that, while he was more skilled interpersonally, the same underlying processes that first brought him into therapy were still operating. The psychoanalytically oriented psychotherapy that he had with me left large areas of his character structure untouched.

Along with my new orientation to the work, I saw that Roger had great difficulty experiencing and communicating his emotionality. This blockage was transformed into his paranoid belief that listening devices were tuned in on his conversations with his wife. The breakdown of the baseline process of their dyadic triangle destroyed effective communication between them and prevented them from expressing their feelings to one another. I know now that they were furious with one another. His paranoia "explained" the mystery of his alienation from her. If they could have made emotional contact with each other, they would have had terrible fights, but they would not have been so anxious and alienated.

In many of his sessions, Roger would fall into a monotonic glaze. It was exhausting being with him. Our baseline contact had disappeared. He droned his complaints with an agonizing dreariness. When this happened, I complained that it did not seem to make any difference whether I was in the room listening to him or not. He barely noticed me when he told me that I was wrong. At one point, I reached over and shook his shoulder. The physical contact brought him out of his glaze. I recalled how Vivian had urged me to learn more about the importance of touching. I challenged Roger to show some feeling by teasing him about his resemblance to the computers with which he worked. After that, I frequently used touching to make emotional contact with him. I would grab his knee and shake it, tickle him, or pat him on the cheek. I also entered the Theater of the Absurd and spoke affectionately to him.

The Emotional Glaze

Emotional reactions to physical contact can be blocked if the receiving person resides behind an experiential wall—the glaze. Blocking the experience of contact permits the individual to avoid either intense psychological pain or paralyzing anxiety. The glaze is a major psychological tactic used to make life more manageable for many people who have been stunned in late infancy or early childhood. The concept of the glaze is one of the few places where this theory touches psychopathology. Anyone who has related intensely to schizophrenic patients or serious drug abusers is aware of the glaze and recognizes that it is the great impediment to making psychotherapeutic contact.

Glazing is an experiential operation. It occurs when the individual's focus is on an internal process. The glazed individual experiences engagement with the external world in the background of awareness. In a sense, glazing is an altered form of consciousness. In this condition, the normative state of awareness is reversed. Ordinarily, our awareness is focused on the external world. When two people are talking to one another, they (for the most part) keep one another at the center of their attention. In the background of their awareness, they may have an internal dialogue. Here again, I am referring to the figure-ground illusion. Recall that previously I described experiencing as being split into figure and ground displays of information.

Figural experiencing is the type of experiencing that we ordinarily have when our attention is focused. The object of our attention dominates our awareness, and background information is automatically processed—that is, outside of awareness. There is an emotional "stillness" when clients block out the pain of the abuse they experienced in childhood.

In the glazed condition, the internal object of focal awareness can be a wordless display of anxiety. For some it is displayed as an experiential "white noise." Others get lost in a wordy rumination about something in their stream of consciousness. Wherever the focus of attention may be, it is not on the other person, who is displayed in the background of awareness. This display of information permits the glazed individual to react in a linear, overlearned way to the generalities of the situation that is occurring.

When an individual is glazed, wiped out, or "spacey," she or he is out of contact. In terms of the dyadic triangle, little or no baseline information is being transmitted or received. The glazed person resides trapped and undisturbed in anomie. The other person, who is attempting to make contact, receives little or no validational feedback. His or her affect hunger is unassuaged in the encounter.

This condition has been an ongoing one in psychotherapy. I believe that the glaze is the condition that Freud recognized as resistance. When he accused a patient of being resistant, he engaged in a baseline encounter, and baseline encounters usually interrupt a glazed condition. This interruption may very well have led Freud to believe that the interpretation of resistance was therapeutically effective. Wilhelm Reich (1972) called the glaze "character armor." It has also been variously called the "glass wall" or the "bell jar."

Melanie Klein (1975) and John Rosen (1968) attempted to break through this "glass wall" with primary process interpretations. Their interventions were so powerful that observers of their work regarded them as talented, innovative therapists. I believe that the effectiveness of their interventions was based more on the baseline engagement that they used, rather than the shocking content of their verbal interventions.

Both of them vividly demanded that their patients focus attention on them in an "I-Thou" (baseline) encounter. It was in this way that they were able to make contact. Unfortunately, at times they did not know how to use their relationship with the patient. They did not recognize that an alternate personality had emerged, who, if attended to, could maintain them in the center of its attention.

Over a period of time, the glazed individual is able to adapt to the intensity maneuvers of the therapist. As a result, Klein and Rosen had to rely upon increasingly outlandish intensities to maintain contact. If the therapist uses only intensity as a way of making contact, she or he will be likely to engage in behaviors that violate the integrity of the other person. I believe that this is an aspect of therapist's behavior about which Masson (1988) complains.

Sexuality is one of the intensities that is commonly used to break through the "glass wall." This is true in everyday life as well as in psychotherapy. During the sexual revolution in the sixties, I saw a number of people who engaged in random, casual sex. The emotional contact of these sexual dyads was minimal and superficial, with little or no personal intimacy. Consequently, sexual interest as well as the relationships were short lived.

When the members of a pair are wiped out, there is little or no conversation. The relationship becomes starved and seeks a sexual source that will "feed" its affect hunger. Sex is a primary "nutrient" to feed affect hunger. In the conventional dyad, this use of sex creates confusion when sex is interpreted as love. When there is little or no emotional contact between members of the dyad, the baseline process between them is fractured. Loss of contact on the baseline creates a loss of sexual desire in the couple.

When therapists and clients engage in sexual intercourse, its primary function is to break the emotional glaze that exists between them. The results of this attempt to cope with the affect hunger of therapist and client are disastrous. Clients are misused and cheated. Therapists are tormented and confused.

Therapists, who are trained to believe guilt-laden explanations about their sexuality, such as countertransference, become phobic about its presence in relationship to their clients. Because of the sexual "bogey-man," psychotherapists are frequently admonished to refrain ever from touching a client/patient. I know therapists who are proud of never having physically touched a client! They justify this by righteously proclaiming that they do not wish to be seductive. For these and other reasons, there are therapists who avoid emotional contact with their clients. In doing so, they ignore the therapeutically destructive effects of the loss of contact caused by interpersonal coldness.

The psychotherapist's fear of being sued or called before an ethics committee has created an obsessive professional preoccupation with errors of commission. This preoccupation is so great that little or no attention is paid to errors of omission. These are the errors which, at best, severely limit the effectiveness of psychotherapy and, at worst, kill it. The anxiety about experiencing an emotionality, with which these therapists are unfamiliar and untrained, commits them to an explanation about psychotherapeutic learning that is patently untrue.

My work with Roger enabled me to see a door in the resistant, invisible wall. His presentation sensitized me to the emotional glaze that covers the "wiped-out" person. This is an experiential wall, sometimes so thick that contact with the glazed individual is impossible.

The glaze inhibits emotionality from emerging into awareness. The glaze of catatonic individuals illustrates this point. You can talk to them, touch them, and move them about the room; however, there will be no overt reaction to you. In the background of their awareness, though, you are recognized and experienced.

When I was a young intern at the Illinois Neuropsychiatric Institute in Chicago, a psychiatric resident invited me to sit in with him while he interviewed a catatonic young woman, whom he had injected with sodium pentathol.

Although the drug had an effect, the interview was rather dull. The woman responded to his questions, but her answers were brief and monosyllabic. After a tortured fifteen minutes, he turned to me and asked if I wanted to speak with her. I handed her a piece of paper and a pencil and asked her to draw a picture of a house. As she drew I commented that the roof line of her house reminded me of an English cottage. She agreed and said that she had always liked that house. I asked her where it was. She said that it was her childhood home. This led to a bright and charming discussion about her mother's multiple marriages, and her confusion about her stepfathers.

The interview occurred on a Saturday morning. I left there elated, convinced that she had been misdiagnosed. Instead of catatonia, I believed that she was suffering from a hysterical negativism. On Monday morning, I went up to the day room of her ward to witness more of her recovery. Seeing her standing alone in the corner of the day room, I walked over and greeted her. I was dumbfounded. She stood motionless and unresponsive to me. Then, after a moment, a smile and a wink flickered across her face. That was all. My diagnosis was wrong; the catatonic glaze had returned.

The ordinary wiped-out glaze is not so thick. In this condition, a person will say, "Sure, I hear every word you say," while watching the football game on the television. The person hears the words in the background of awareness, while the game remains in the center of attention.

The glaze looks efficient or skilled when a person is engaged in a repetitive, mechanical task. At other times, the glaze is totally inefficient. When individuals are wiped out, "spacey," or is "vegged out," their behavior is regarded as inappropriate and not to be trusted. People in this condition really do not hear you and cannot be relied upon to communicate with you. I have found that the glaze can be most effectively broken when I focus on the baseline process between myself and another person.

When LSD first became a popular recreational drug, a young man came into a group therapy session in the middle of his "acid" trip. He was bizarre, entertaining, and extremely disruptive to the group's work. As I began attending to our baseline engagement, his high subsided. When he came down, the group, including him, was able to return to its work. At the end of the session, I was concerned about the young man's ability to drive home safely. He reassured me in a way that led me to believe that the high of his acid trip was over. At that moment, he looked "straight" to me. However, at our next individual session, he told me that after he drove out of the parking lot, he returned to his "trip" and had a marvelous evening.

Return to Roger

When Roger fell into his glaze, I focused attention on our relationship (I went to the baseline of our dyadic triangle) and demanded that he attend to his feelings about me and what I was doing with him. This enabled him to express feelings about me. They ranged from whining complaints to anger to hesitant expressions of affection and respect. He left all the sessions in which he expressed feelings less anxious and with a diminished dread about "their" conspiracy against him. The improvement in his reality contact and his diminished anxiety reminded me of James, who expressed pleasure as a result of the amelioration of the anxiety that accompanied the shedding of his absurd tears. I also recalled Raymond's rage and the smile of relief that came over his face when he saw himself tearing me apart in his mind's eye.

One day Roger came into my office in an extremely agitated condition. He told me about listening devices that were directed at his house and asked me if any strange telephone company repairmen had come to my office. I put my arm around his shoulder and told him how much I liked him. He jumped and quickly pushed me away. "What are you feeling?" I asked.

He blushed and angrily demanded that I get away from him. I chided him, saying that he should not be afraid of my affection. The glaze enveloped him. He denied fear. Wanting to break through the glaze, I said, "Aw, come on, Roger, come over here and give me a kiss." He became furious, insisting that he was not a "queer." His paranoia either turned me into a homosexual or one of "them." After he told me how suspicious of me he was, he calmed down. When he saw that I was not upset and I was interested in him and his feelings, his trust in me returned.

At this point he was able to discuss his homosexual anxiety. He, like Raymond, transformed his love for me into a sexual experience that could then be logically denied or disavowed. After he was able to experience this, he saw his generalized sexual anxiety. This enabled him to accept some responsibility for the nonexistent sexuality of his marriage. At the close of the session, he was feeling much better. His fearful anxiety had been transformed into feelings of hopefulness.

Toward the end of the session, I asked Roger to tell me what he thought "they" were doing with the information "they" were getting from the listening devices. My question puzzled him. His anxiety had vanished, and he could respond aggressively by telling me that he wasn't afraid of "them." "They can go fuck themselves!" When I reminded him of his agitation at the beginning of the session, he became puzzled. Quickly turning away from his confusion, he immersed himself in thoughts of improving his sexual relationship with his wife. He was not at all interested in looking at the transformation of his feelings from anxiety to hope.

He had the same disinterest in his paranoid preoccupation that Raymond had in his "cosmic solutions." Roger was content with his release from anxiety and was preoccupied with the prospect of having a better sex life. It was a narrow focus, but he felt better, and that was enough for the moment. His paranoia diminished, and our work centered on his marriage. My work with Roger vividly demonstrated to me that the expression of feelings is clearly an equilibratory process. When a client can bring feelings to the surface of awareness and express them, she or he feels less anxious or depressed.

The Emotional Dynamics of Dyadic Engagement

At this point I was so enamored of emotional engagement as a therapeutic intervention that I believed that the sole task of psychotherapy was to facilitate the development of emotional skills. I believed that the experience and expression of feelings were the primary tasks of psychotherapy. Consequently, I carefully attended to the personal presentations of my clients and responded to the manipulative aspects of these presentations.

I am embarrassed to admit that I became a veritable Don Rickles of psychotherapy. I was sarcastic when a client asked me to collude with his or her self-deprecation. When a client fraudulently pleaded ignorance, I sardonically commiserated with their stupidity. If I saw my client using a dependent or fraudulent presentation that asked me to collude with a fusional and infantile position, I interpreted it as though it was the expression of an emotion that was crying out from infancy. This tactic was a constant source of anger and a means of learning for my clients. The expression of anger brought relief from depression and an awareness of self-defeating postures. My clients found these realizations to be both painful and useful.

In those days, my work could be likened to making paradoxical, hyperbolic interpretations or implosive interventions. Within a more psychoanalytic framework, they could be characterized as primary process interpretations. All of these terms describe a therapist's behavior interrupting and disrupting the usual expectations of the client.

Interruption activates emotional and cognitive re-equilibration and creates contact with the source of disequilibrium. As I learned more, I came to realize that one of the most significant parts of the confrontive engagement was the creation of contact. The psychotherapeutic relationship is unlike any other in the experience of the client. Patterns of emotional response to parents, friends, teachers, acquaintances, doctors, salespeople, and others are formed from early childhood on. The repertoires of reaction to people in these relationships become automated. In the psychotherapeutic relationship, however, there are no objects or external goals involved in the task of the relationship. Furthermore, the therapist (under the best of circumstances) requires nothing in the way of personal validation from the client. The uniqueness of this situation disrupts the automaticity that exists in other relationships and sets into motion equilibratory or stabilizing processes designed to restore a stable-state condition. The disruption of personal systems frequently creates intense emotional reactions.

When I engaged my clients on the baseline of our triangle, I disrupted their personal presentations, and they reacted to me with an intensity and vividness that was at times awesome. The willingness of my clients to endure the intensity of the pain and confusion of their reactions to my interventions astonished me. I came to realize that there were five components in these interventions that made them useful and enabled my clients to tolerate my provocations. First, I was neither angry nor self-serving with my clients. My interventions were not conveyed as insults. Second, I was respectful, because I was not colluding with my clients in a ploy that validated any pretense of their incompetence or ignorance. Third, my observations accurately reflected the interpersonal process that was occurring between us. Fourth, the emotionality that my interpretations evoked had an anxiety-reducing effect. And fifth, I was responsible. I did not back away from the anger that they expressed toward me. I admitted what I had done. I was not defensive about my intervention, nor did I deny the reality or meaningfulness of their complaints about me.

Learning about Emotional Skills

My immersion into the intense emotionality of psychotherapy enabled me to see that my clients and I had different emotional skills, the existence of which was brought to my attention in 1965, when I participated in my first Tavistock Group Process Learning Conference. There I discovered that I was not skilled in experiencing loneliness.

I heard about the conference in 1964 from Margaret Rioch, a professional colleague, who had recently returned home from her first experience with the Tavistock Group in England. The experience made a deep impression on her. Her description of the work of the consultants reminded me of my experience with Hellmuth Kaiser. I yearned for more of this type of experience, so I asked Margaret to send me an invitation to the next conference, which was to be held the following June at Mount Holyoke College in Massachusetts. .

The task of the consultants was to facilitate the learning of the groups, *not* of the individual members of the conference. In order to meet the requirements of this task, the consultants at *no* point addressed or spoke to individual members. When the consultant spoke, she or he made observations about the process of the group, including the way "it" was relating to the consultant. These observations were frequently seen as primitive or infantile emotional reactions to the consultant. In other words, the consultant engaged in a baseline interaction with the group.

The consultants generated intense stress and anxiety within the group in two ways. First, they made primary process observations about their relationship with the *group*, not the individuals. Second, in refusing to speak to individuals, while at the same time using the statements of individuals as though they were group feelings, the consultants disrupted (invalidated) both the expectations and the presentations of individual members of the group. The unexpected relationship that the consultants created with the membership of the conference prompted great and disturbing anxiety within some members of the conference. For others, the disorganization created an opportunity for reconstructing some of their personal systems and enabled them to understand themselves from fresh new perceptual orientations. I, myself, learned a great deal. The conference was very stressful, yet so beautifully managed that I felt as though I were swimming in shark-infested custard. It was both a painful and sweet, smooth experience.

At sunset on the second day of the conference, after our work had been completed, I walked along the edge of the lovely lake that nestled in the campus. I was embraced by both the beauty of the setting and by an acute pain that was both familiar and puzzling. I had experienced it at other conferences or conventions, and it confused me. It was not a physical pain, and I did not know why I was hurting.

My mind wandered. I thought about my sons, from whom I had been separated by a recent divorce. I was the only member of the conference who had come from Los Angeles. Most of the other members were either from Washington, D.C., or New Haven and had at least a nodding acquaintance with another member of the conference. Finally, it dawned on me. I was lonely.

As soon as I realized that I was lonely, the pain changed and diminished. I was still discomfited, but I knew what was troubling me. Now I had an explanation; when I realized that my pain could be explained as loneliness, I felt stupid. What was wrong with me that I had not recognized such a common and obvious feeling such as loneliness? I did not dwell on the question long. Like Roger and Raymond, I was more interested in ridding myself of the loneliness than in fathoming it. I went to the well-stocked bar provided by the conference, made friends, and got rid of my discomfort.

This was the first time that I remember consciously feeling loneliness. I later came to know it as a form of affect hunger, the major source of which is the absence of validational feedback from another person. We shall see in the following chapters how essential the "feeding" of this hunger is. From this experience of loneliness, I began to appreciate the power and importance of aloneness. It is not an abstract existential condition; it is an omnipresent psychophysiological condition. It involves both people's feelings and their physical well-being.

I was deeply moved by what I had learned at the conference and at subsequent conferences that I attended. The experience greatly contributed to my work as a therapist, and my understanding of the baseline process of dyadic interaction was also enriched by the Tavistock work. It confirmed my observations about the intensity of the emotionality and the emotional learning that the I-Thou engagement on the baseline evokes. Martin Buber was right. The I-Thou encounter is profoundly moving. I felt more confident that I was on the right track in my odyssey.

I was convinced that people were more or less skilled in the experience and expression of their feelings, and that becoming emotionally skillful put people on the high road to mental health. However, as time passed, I again had a sense of dissatisfaction. My clients, for the most part, found our work meaningful, and I was developing a good reputation in the community. But even though the work was exciting and seemed effective, I had a sense of running into another invisible wall that was not moved by therapeutic work as I was doing it. It would yield a bit when I hit it, but it did not permit me or my clients to pass through. So I searched for another door.

I recalled my work with Roger. When he first terminated therapy, he appeared to have accomplished the therapeutic goals that he had stated at the inception of his work with me. Yet it was obvious that the same debilitating character structures were still operating when he returned years later to therapy. My clients would become more skillful in experiencing and expressing their feelings, but parts of their self-deprecating, self-defeating, or self-destructive character structures continued to operate.

I saw this most vividly with clients who also were therapists themselves. They could both feel and see more of the emotional process within themselves and others, but they continued to have difficulties with loving relationships in their own personal lives. They were increasingly able to have loving, albeit stressful, relationships with their clients, but their relationships outside the consultation room were often conflicted.

As a matter of fact, I came to see that for most of my clients, loving was the most difficult emotion to integrate into their adult lives. This was particularly true when they were on the receiving end of a loving encounter. When confronted with being loved, they would experience various degrees of distrust and anxiety.

My work with Naomi helped me to see that the barrier I was encountering consisted of the childhood parts of the person. I learned that parts of the person could get "stuck" and did not change with the rest of the person as it matured within the individual. In psychoanalytic terms, parts of the person became *fixated* in childhood personal systems.

I came to see that fixated parts of the person ranged in complexity from simple emotional expressions to extremely complicated personal systems expressed as multiple personalities. At a simple level, an individual could be unskilled in the experience of a particular feeling, as I was when I learned to experience the feeling of loneliness. At a more complex level, there are individuals whose early childhoods were so traumatic that they invented "other" persons to cope with the intensity of their emotional distress.

These "personalities" became fixed parts of the overall personality of the individual, continuing to operate mostly outside awareness. However, some individuals find that these hidden "persons" operate outside the control of intentionality and occasionally pop out, much to their embarrassment and consternation. This was true of Naomi.

Playing with Naomi

When I opened the door to the waiting room to meet Naomi for the first time, I was greeted by a woman with a brisk, cheery vitality. After I said hello and introduced myself, she dazzled me with a brilliant smile, whisked past me into the consultation room, seated herself on a couch, and waited for me with expectation in her eyes. I was charmed and curious. I followed her into the consultation room, seated myself on the other couch, and asked her to tell me what I could do for her. Straightforwardly and without hesitation, she told me that she was having difficulties getting work as an actress, although she had been relatively successful some ten years earlier.

Furthermore, she worried about getting older. She was going to be thirty-five on her next birthday, and knew that she could no longer be cast as an ingénue. Furthermore, she wanted to get married and have a child, and here, too, she worried about her age. All this was conveyed to me in a no-nonsense, businesslike manner.

She presented a very neat, attractive package. Her issues were made to order for psychotherapeutic work. She stated them clearly and precisely. However, I had no sense of her feelings about these very real problems. Additionally, her inability to get work as an actress puzzled me. She knew the business. She was "in." She was talented, she had an agent, and her reputation was excellent. From my experience with other acting professionals, I knew that she was not working for reasons other than those that she expressed to me. I continued to be enthralled by her presentation, which I found to be more compelling than the overt content of what she was telling me about her life.

She paused and waited for me to respond to what she had told me. I said that I was terribly impressed by how pretty and talented she was. I went on to say that if I were a TV or movie producer, I would hire her in a minute. She blushed with pleasure and then got annoyed. She imperiously instructed me that it was my task to listen to her and discover what was impeding her progress. I was, then, supposed to tell her how to correct these deficiencies. She informed me that she had a set of problems that could be rationally understood and, therefore, should be logically explained and solved. She was so precise, orderly, and charming about her determination that I chose to respond to her presentation, rather than to her instructions. I told her how impressed I was by her ability to see issues and to state them with such delightful effectiveness. I declared that I was dazzled by the brilliance of her understanding and instruction. She again showed a flush of embarrassment, which quickly turned into a pout, followed by a tearful complaint that I was not doing what I was supposed to be doing.

The brittle, businesslike demeanor had cracked, and behind that façade, a hurt, confused, and adorable little girl emerged. This second personality was so sweet and injured that I sat next to her and held her comfortingly. She appreciatively cried on my shoulder. I gently told her that I was sorry that I had confused her. I also let her know that it was important for me to get to know this part of her. Now that I knew about the "young one," I could understand the torture with which she must have been living. She had been existing in an agony of never knowing which person would emerge in any given social situation.

My understanding placated her. In her baby voice, she talked about the auditions that she had had to cancel at the last minute for fear that the "young one" would inappropriately appear at the reading. She was terrified that this also might happen in the middle of a scene, when she was acting. Formal dinner parties were constantly problematic for the same reason. She had a few good friends who partially understood her dilemma and who were sources of counsel and comfort. They enabled her to have a rich and busy social life, but this life did not include close relationships with men.

In the following sessions, Naomi's "young one" and I became great friends. She was sweet and affectionate and told me about her family, who were all wonderful, delightful people. Her mother and father drank too much, but there were no major problems. She was the youngest member of the family, her parents and siblings loved her the best, and she made them all very happy. During the tenth session, Naomi acted especially sweet, displaying distinctly erotic behavior.

I was so touched by her "invitation" that I picked her up in my arms and swung her around in the middle of my consultation room to express my joyous appreciation of her proposition to make love and play. She was a very petite woman, which permitted me to do this. When I set her down, I asked if she really wanted to have sex with me. She became very shy, hung her head, and moved close to me. I held her and waited to see what she would do next.

In a few moments, she was transformed. I found myself sitting next to an adult speaking to me with a deep, guttural voice in a nonsense language. She was addressing me in earnest, but I had no idea what she was trying to say to me. I had a sense that she was being serious about something that was not terribly grave. I asked her if she could get someone to tell me what all this meant. Then the "young one" returned. She had calmed down and told me that the "old woman" would occasionally appear, but she did not understand her any better than I had.

I was still curious about her sexual invitation, so I used the ploy of telling her how attractive she was and that I was honored by her proposition. It was easy to see that she was a very sexy girl and that she liked me, but I did not see what having sex would do for us. At this point she curled up in my lap and began crying out for me not to hurt her. She grabbed the upper part of my arm and sank her fingernails into it with a force that made me flinch. I had black and blue marks on my arm for a week after that. Throughout this intense interaction, I felt that I was experiencing something that had been done to her, perhaps being pinched with the same force that she had experienced as a child. I believe that Naomi's sexual invitation was a ploy to distract both of us away from the physical abuse that a part of her was trying to reveal—shades of Raymond and Roger.

During the following year of therapy, I came to the conclusion that Naomi had been physically abused by her mother in the latter part of her infancy. She insisted that she could not tell me about this part of her relationship with her mother because she had promised that she would never tell anyone what had happened. She loved her mother and was loyal to her, so she never actually came out and told me about the physical abuse. However, I believe that her pinching showed me what had happened.

Naomi was the first multiple personality with whom I had the opportunity and privilege of working. Prior to that time, I was extremely skeptical about the meaningfulness of the concept of multiple personalities. Initially, I believed that the woman whose life was dramatized in the movie *The Three Faces of Eve* was not actually a multiple personality, but a product of her therapist's suggestions.

My work with Naomi and others has convinced me that multiple personality phenomena are a relatively common form of regression. We all have "young ones" within us, even though some of them do not have the clear characterological boundaries of distinct persons that "multiples" have. Instead, they have alternate personalities with highly differentiated emotional skills, self systems, and social beliefs and roles.

I began to understand that I had to develop an emotional relationship with a client's "young child" as well as a relationship with the person who presented her- or himself as an adult. It is all well and good to refuse to collude with a capable adult who is presenting a self as an incompetent, but it is downright insulting to mock and accuse a "child" of refusing to use capacities which he or she does not have. My use of sarcasm diminished. I found that it was necessary to work with my clients at the emotional age levels that were occurring at the moment of engagement. It was more meaningful to speak to the four- or five-year-old child, who was expressing him- or herself, than to reason with the forty-year-old body housing that child.

I came to see that people regressed to younger personalities when their adult personalities did not have the skill to deal with disturbing situations. For example, when a harried person is trying to hammer a nail into a wall and hits his or her thumb, the resulting emotion and feelings of intense anger and frustration manifest themselves in a childlike tantrum.

We fall back on childhood emotional expressions because they have been rehearsed and repetitiously reinforced for longer periods of time than our more adult feelings. We use these overlearned structures because their strength stabilizes personality structures more effectively than do newly learned ones.

A Walk Down Market Street

I vividly recall a conference I attended in San Francisco with a colleague who brought a client with her, a lovely young woman inhabited by several different personalities. My encounter with her showed me how an alternate person replaces the normative person when that person is unable to easily or automatically experience an emotion. Our noontime interaction illustrates this phenomenon. The memory of it touches me with warmth and sadness.

Three of us were walking up Market Street—on one of those shining, clear, joyous afternoons that endears San Francisco to me—looking for a place to have lunch. As we searched, I talked with the young woman about her college entrance examinations. I was delighted with her charm, wit, and intelligent clarity. We were having such a good time that I suggested we play "hooky" from the conference. I invited them to catch a cable car with me and go over to Fisherman's Wharf for lunch.

The instant I made the suggestion, the young woman was transformed. *He* bounced down Market Street, clapping *his* hands, squeaking with joy. In the midst of *his* delight, *he* turned and ran back to me asking for permission to ride on the running board of the cable car.

It was clear that the intensity of emotion and feeling generated by our pleasure with one another, and the prospect of play on the cable car, could not be contained in the person of the young woman. The "young boy" was coherent and consistent while the intensity of pleasure lasted. Unfortunately, my colleague persuaded us to be responsible and return to the conference. The intensity of our delight subsided. The person of the young woman returned, and we had a pleasant, albeit subdued, lunch. I found out later that the "boy" was eleven years old and had been sexually and physically abused for years as part of the rituals of a demonic cult.

In this vignette, we see the operation of a relatively "whole" multiple person. There are cases, however, with some people I have treated, in whom parts of an "alternate" also engage interpersonally. The alternate is not displayed in focal awareness; he or she functions in the background of awareness.

Another client very clearly demonstrates what I mean by an alternate person existing in the background of personal operations. All background processes have significant effects on adult personal relationships. In this case, the relationship is a marriage.

George and His "Little One"

George came into the session saying, "I hate her! She is such a pain in the ass." He went on to tell me about a vacation trip that he, his wife, and their two children had taken over a long weekend. He complained that his wife never let anything be simple. No, she had to take everything with her but the kitchen sink. He wound up feeling like a laborer carrying things out to the van. While he was telling me this, he had a big smile on his face, and he seemed to enjoy telling me about how wretched his wife was. I observed his pleasure and thought about how confusing it must be for him to experience delight in his hatred for her.

George admitted that he did not want to feel his wife's love for him or his own for her. I understood why a loving experience with his wife would have been extremely painful and confusing. His childhood had not prepared him for an adult, loving relationship. He was four years old when his mother, who loved him dearly, died of cancer. After her death, he was thrown into a maelstrom of confusing relationships that prevented him from mourning the loss of his mother.

His father, who also had lost *his* mother in early childhood, was devastated by the loss of his wife. He took refuge from his grief and despair in his work and in relationships with other women. Also, he was out of town on business for extended periods; this was another loss for George. One of his father's relationships turned into an impulsive and disastrous marriage, during which George was ignored and/or mistreated by his stepmother. That marriage was quickly dissolved and replaced by another, which endured. However, George was unable or unwilling to have a loving relationship with his second stepmother, even though she was dutiful and responsible.

As George talked, it became clear that he distrusted his father and did not want to identify with him. He saw his father as a sexually active, untrustworthy, and aggressive man. I then understood the sexual difficulties George was having with his wife. His concealment of his sexual desire was an avoidance of loving feelings. The experience of these feelings would reactivate the painful loss of his mother. The child in him could not accept the idea that any other woman would be able to make up for his loss. Also, the fixated child in him did not wish to be an adult.

His sexual orientation reflected a curious conflict. He wanted his wife to be sexually available and responsive as an expression of an indulgence to a child. At the same time, he could not show his wife any lustful or loving sexual desire; that would be too adult. To be an adult was to be like his father. To experience his lust for his wife was to be like his father. And to be like his father was to be abandoned. His childhood person did not trust the adult sectors of his personality to maintain the integrity of his being. He reacted to them with the same distrust that he had had for his father.

At this point, I understood that I was talking to a "child." The child within George was the "person" who controlled his intentionality. The child was and always had been the person in charge, and this was a child who did not trust adults to adequately care for him. Included in the scope of this distrust was the adult that he, the child, recognized as existing in his body, which was obviously not a child's body.

George, unlike my San Francisco friend, had a childhood formation that operated, for the most part, in the background of his personality. The adult aspects of his person operated extremely well in his business life. Nonetheless, he knew that this part of his person was a façade that concealed the child who governed his life.

George is not unusual. In my practice, individuals who were consistently misused or abused in early childhood have, as their primary task, the validation of their childhood formations. These formations stably reside in the background of their awarenesses. Figurally, they appear as adults; structurally, their persons are dominated by childhood formations.

There are within all of us childhood formations, which equilibrate the disturbances of our personal systems. When adult structures are unable to stabilize these systems, a childhood formation becomes operative. Usually, we are only briefly aware of our "child" operating. It emerges into awareness momentarily and then quickly retreats to an unnoticed place in the background of the hustle and bustle of our lives. Even though it resides unnoticed behind the scenes, it is vigilant and easily injured.

While the "child" has an equilibratory function, it has its own affect hunger that needs feeding. It, too, requires validating feedback to maintain its own steady-state condition. Childhood validations are similar to the validational needs of adult systems, except that they operate as background processes, outside focal awareness. This requirement is the foundation of the irrationality of our immature behavior. As it is with all the other systems of the brain and body, it reacts to invalidation as do the other systems that make up the person. It activates behavior that will feed this need, and the meeting of this need is an essential interpersonal ingredient in the establishment of contact between people.

This idea about contact drew me further into the theory, and I pursued my learning about this concept, leading to a deeper understanding of the nature of affect hunger. When I saw affect hunger as a physiological need, my attention was again drawn to the brain, where I discovered the neurological ego. The next chapter describes this part of my adventure.

Chapter V

Contact, Affect Hunger, and the Neurological Ego

Most of the important work that is accomplished in psychotherapy arises from the emotionality of the relationship between the therapist and client. This belief and my work with Hellmuth Kaiser enabled me to see the triangular nature of the dyadic relationship. Understanding the baseline process of the dyadic triangle helped me more clearly understand the nature of interpersonal contact. This is the heart of psychotherapy, for without contact, psychotherapy is either destroyed or severely impaired.

Contact occurs when the affect hunger of each member of the dyad is being fed in their relationship. As I learned more about affect hunger, I realized that it is the central psychobiological process that guides our existence. From there, it was a short step to realizing that what is ordinarily called the ego is a neurological system, not the psychological one it is commonly assumed to be. This chapter will describe my clinical and theoretical adventures with contact, affect hunger, and the shimmering neurological ego. I will expand upon ideas about the neurological underpinnings of personality to which I have alluded in previous chapters. They are the central hypotheses of my theory, and they enabled me to create an integrated and interrelated set of psychological definitions about the person.

Contact

I will begin the definition and description of contact with a story about my relationship with Ben, a fellow therapist. I first met him at a blackjack table in Las Vegas. We were relaxing after a dull day attending a convention. He was a great storyteller, and beneath his rowdy exterior was a sweet, sad man for whom I felt affection. At the close of the meetings, we exchanged phone numbers as a gesture of friendship, knowing full well that it would be unlikely we would see one another socially in Los Angeles. However, six months later, I received a call from him. He wanted an appointment to see me professionally.

His voice on the telephone was mournfully deep and balefully monotonic. When I saw him the next day, he looked like a raw, bloodless wound. Rarely had I seen a person as acutely and painfully depressed as he. His voice sounded as though it were coming to me from the depths of a dark cavern in a faraway place. He started speaking about a malpractice suit that had been brought against him. The complaint sounded trivial, and my superficial inquiry convinced me that he had handled it effectively and that his practice was not seriously jeopardized. I told him that I knew there were other reasons for the pain that brought him to see me.

He agreed and told me that a colleague, with whom he had shared a practice for twenty years, had died recently. Then he stopped talking, and I felt incomplete and suspended, watching him held in the grip of a motionless ache. I reached over to him, put my hand on his knee, and asked, "Is everything lost?"

His face convulsed, tears rushed from his eyes, and he wept. After a time he looked up at me, relieved, and said that it had been years since he had cried. Then he was able to tell me that his wife was dying of cancer. The malpractice suit, the death of his dear friend and colleague, and his wife's cancer left him feeling helpless and unable to cope with the deluge of injury and loss with which he was confronted. After he cried, he became furious , thinking about the injustice of his patient's malpractice suit. The release of this feeling enabled him to mourn the death of his friend, which blended into grieving about the impending loss of his wife.

Anger emerged from the agony of his anticipated loss. Ben loved his wife, but he was also furious with her. He blamed her for the emotional and sexual deprivation that existed in the marriage. Yet, he was not the victim he believed himself to be. He treated his wife in ways that were bound to turn her off sexually. For him, loving had to be laced with discontent. His complaints about his wife were accompanied by feelings of terrible loss and anger when he thought about her dying, but it was difficult for him to openly experience these feelings. Everything emotional within him was shut down. This emotional isolation and loneliness caused the deep and acute depression that precipitated his call to me.

The contact we made in Las Vegas enabled him to call me. It permitted him to share feelings that he had never shared before. Contact is one of the principal interpersonal means by which we feed our affect hunger. It is among the basic "foods" that nourish our souls. The arts "feed" us. Play and work are also powerful "nutrients." However, physical and emotional contact are the emotional "bread and butter" of human interaction. Contact assuages the pangs of affect hunger that we experience as part of the loneliness of our everyday lives.

Contact is a magical and paradoxical psychological phenomenon. At times, it can heal the anguish of sorrow, depression, and loneliness. In other instances, it can be unbearably painful, as when it breaks through the barriers of emotional isolation. This happens when *incongruent personal systems* are triggered. By incongruent personal systems I mean childhood personality systems that, for reasons I will explain in chapters VIII and IX, did not mature as we grew older. Childhood structures become stable and enduring parts of our characters, and they are activated when more mature adult systems fail to perform their equilibratory function.

Recall the torture that Raymond felt as he experienced loving feelings for me when I reached out to touch him. His mother had punished him for crying while he was in the midst of his infantile love for her. During adulthood, he automatically reacted to my desire to comfort him with the same fear and rage he experienced when his mother beat him. The personal transformation of Naomi is another example of a childhood personality formation becoming operative when an adult structure is unable to equilibrate the emotionality of the moment.

My relationship with Raymond is a dramatic example of the conflict that can occur when the childhood personality structures that endure within the adult person take over. Furthermore, it illustrates the deeply moving psychological effects of physical contact. Emotional contact also has major physiological effects, though. The tears that Ben and Raymond shed, the blushes of embarrassment that shine on our faces when we receive unexpected praise or love, and the sexual arousal that accompanies infatuation are all examples of the physiological effects of emotional contact.

In terms of the dyadic triangle, interpersonal contact is, principally, a baseline process. On the baseline of our triangle, Ben was asking for comfort and understanding. He moved me, and I wanted to comfort him. I responded positively to his pained signals for comfort by doing and saying things that were meaningful to him in the context of his despair.

I had made contact with him in two ways. I put my hand on his knee, and I let him know that I understood his pain. I comforted him with my compassionate touch and made contact verbally by saying things that were congruent with his pain. I "understood" him. One of the richest kinds of interpersonal feedback relieving psychological pain is understanding. What I said and expressed "matched" both the emotional and the feeling processes that were going on within him. My physical touch expressed the warmth and understanding that he was seeking.

Vivian, in her appeals for physical contact, and Ashley Montagu (1971) were right: Knowing about touching is profoundly important. If I had misunderstood Ben, I may have made contact, but it would not have been for long. The invalidation of my misunderstanding would have ended our relationship. He would have turned away from me.

The contact that Ben and I made enabled him to experience the pain of his loss, his rage, and the aching isolation of his life. A chronic, unfulfilled affect hunger lay at the bottom of his loneliness. He had lived with emotional deprivation for so long that it had become an automatic part of his personality structure. He would have dismissed any thought of escape from it as futile. Our contact enabled him to bring into awareness feelings of anger, loss, and hunger. Experiencing these feelings released him from the grip of his suicidal depression, which led to a renewed sense of hope and an increased ability to think and cope.

Ben had been alone and isolated for as long as he could remember. Neither he nor his wife could bridge the emotional chasm that existed between them. They could be affectionate, but they had great difficulty touching one another in the deeper childhood parts of their personalities. They had lived for many years in an agonizing and chaotic emotional isolation. When they were not fighting, they wiped out (glazed) emotionally and watched television.

I have chosen to tell the story of this part of my relationship with Ben because it illustrates both the interplay of physiological and psychological phenomena when contact is made and the emotional glaze that prevents contact. His tears, his flushed, convulsed face, his depressive exhaustion, and response to touching were all physiological expressions of the profound emotional disturbance that had incapacitated and depressed him.

The psychological difficulties involved in denying his grief about the loss of loved ones, and his anger toward them, made up the psychological side of the mind-body interaction. If I touch you physically or if I "touch" you emotionally, similar physiological and psychological reactions occur. In either case, your blood pressure will rise, and your heart rate will increase (cf. Lynch, 1977); these occur on the physiological side. On the psychological side, you will experience feelings, and I will be centered in your attention.

Physiological reactions arise from the neurological ego's—the core brain's—inability to automatically process a response to contact. The feelings and experiential focus on me when I touch you are psychological responses to the core brain's disturbance. This description of contact underscores the central importance of emotional contact in the immediate existence of the individual. The stability of the core brain is essential to our survival.

As I have indicated above, contact is not simple nourishing "honey" that everyone should unambivalently seek. It can also unleash sanity-threatening anxiety and pain. It is not uncommon for the emotional glaze, which I first described in my work with Roger, to descend over the awareness of the individual in order to shield her or him from it.

The glaze may help a person avoid painful emotional contact, but this avoidance has psychological costs. First and most common among these costs is loneliness. The avoidance of contact prevents the glazed person from getting validational feedback, leaving the person's affect hunger unrequited. In the following discussion, I will more specifically define affect hunger and describe its other psychological and neurological effects.

Affect Hunger

I first came across the phrase "affect hunger" a number of years ago, while reading Sandor Ferenczi's (1956) description of his patients' need for contact. He was one of the first analysts to focus on and explore the disturbing emotionality of the psychotherapeutic relationship. The idea of affect hunger made intuitive sense, as it fit experiences that I had had in my practice.

Vivian most physically and vividly illustrated the effects of affect hunger in our relationship. Unless the demands of her affect hunger were met, she did not think that she could remain alive long enough to pass her inheritance on to her children. At first, I thought of affect hunger as a purely psychological phenomenon. However, when I read Platt's (1972) insights regarding the constant "search for invariance" of living systems, it illuminated the psychobiological significance of affect hunger for me.

The idea of affect hunger helped me to see the purposiveness—that is, the biological adaptiveness—of the baseline dynamic of the dyadic triangle. There is no intentionality implied in this term. It simply means that an action serves some biologically adaptive purpose (cf. Granit, 1977).

I realized that, within interpersonal relationships, people are constantly seeking validation from one another. Validation is the term I use to denote the process of providing invariant feedback between people. Like Snow White's stepmother, we look into the eyes of others wanting them to tell us that we are, indeed, the "fairest one of all." Each of has our own meanings for "fairest." The definition of "fairest" is determined by our character structure. It can mean the kindest, the wisest, the most understanding, the ugliest, the meanest, and so on. The list is endless. The meaning of what is validating is determined by the ways that the stable-state condition of the person/neurological ego relationship has been organized.

The effects of the absence of validational feedback on personality functions have been dramatically documented in research on sensory deprivation. Haggard (1964), in his survey of this literature, reports the following:

> The dramatic effects of "just doing nothing and having nothing happen," even for short periods of time, have been reported by the subjects both during and after isolation. In most cases, the subjects reported a variety of sensory, sensory-motor, affective, and cognitive changes during the experience. Although the reported disturbances are not the same in all cases, there appears to be a general deterioration and lability (often unpredictability) of the usual mental processes and functions. More specifically, reported changes include such perceptual disturbances as the spontaneous appearance of partial or full-blown visual, auditory, and somatic illusions, hallucinations, or delusions, color anomalies and distortions of tactual experience, body image, and the time sense. Affective disturbances, includ-

ing spontaneous bursts of affects as fear, anxiety, and anger, or reactions involving restlessness, boredom, agitation, and a sense of depersonalization were frequently reported. As for cognitive processes, some subjects reported a rapid disintegration of their ability to attend, concentrate, or think in a directed and sustained manner, to solve abstract problems, or even to carry out such simple tasks as serial counting (p. 435).

The importance of validation is seen in the discomfort most of us experience when there is silence between ourselves and another significant person. Our tolerance for silence is variable. Some individuals are comfortable with it, but these people are rare. Many others cannot stand it. The power of blank screen psychoanalysis arises from the absence of validating feedback from the analyst. That and his/her encouragement of a therapeutic regression creates an emotional intensity that disrupts normative patterns of personality process. The disruption of old patterns of feeling and explaining are more the sources of personality change than are interpretations of the meaning of childhood relationships. The absence of validating feedback in the psychoanalytic therapy hour disturbs the baseline process of the therapeutic dyad. When this happens, silence is a common and painful occurrence. Karl Menninger (1958) encapsulated this feeling in the following couplet.

> Sticks and stones may break your bones,
> but silence will break your heart.

People normally do not supply one another with validational feedback when they sit in silence. I have seen people writhe in discomfort as a result. The pain of silence or the absence of validational feedback manifests itself in heart-breaking loneliness. James Lynch (1977), in his book *The Broken Heart,* documents the "medical consequences of loneliness." His work in the clinic and research laboratory demonstrates the disastrous medical effects, frequently resulting in premature death, of the unmet needs of affect hunger.

Cannon (1942) in his study of "Voodoo Death" describes the life-threatening effects of social isolation (the absence of validational feedback). Kohler (1959) interestingly speculates about the neurological effects of social isolation in a way that is congruent with my concept of affect hunger. He asks:

Could it be that prolonged lack of social contact and, as a consequence, of sufficiently interesting "objects" establishes a particular condition in the nervous system, and that, in a general way, this state is comparable to lack of food, water and so forth? (p. 177).

Contact (validational feedback) has long been recognized as a significant human need. My theory incorporates this recognition in its concept of affect hunger. The absence of validational feedback disequilibrates "hungry" neural structures; information that does not match the information-processing characteristics of a neural system invalidates it and disequilibrates it as well.

Invalidation is most likely to occur when the person receives feedback that cannot be automatically processed, or when expected congruent feedback is not forthcoming. Most people express the need for validational feedback in their desire to be liked. When these individuals are confronted with criticism or expressions of dislike or disapproval, they experience anxiety, pain, and/or depression in various combinations and intensities. The varieties of reaction to invalidation are dependent on the relationship, context, and ego strength of the individual.

The concept of affect hunger freed me from relying upon common sense as the information base upon which I would build my theory. I began to think about personality as an equilibratory or stabilizing process, instead of trying to explain the phenomenal appearance of emotionality, motivation, or self. I began searching for an understanding of the purposiveness of our experience and behavior.

I knew from my experience with Hellmuth Kaiser that I wanted him to see me in particular ways, but that information alone was not sufficient to explain my attempts to manipulate him. Why was his approval so important? Furthermore, I knew that he was not the only one that I was trying to manipulate. It was obvious that I, myself, and others went around spending inordinate amounts of time and money seeking approval. Approval, then, was the feedback for which I was looking. I eventually realized that my desire for approval was the psychological manifestation of an underlying neuropsychological need.

When I understood this desire, I came to appreciate Hellmuth's concept of the fusion delusion. It is so omnipresent in interpersonal relations that he believed it to be the "universal symptom" underlying neurosis. The delusion is based on the need to have a stable, continuing source of validating feedback from another significant person.

I came to realize that affect hunger is the brain's need for invariant stimulation. The brain is the most complex organ of our body; some estimate that it is composed of 100,000,000 neurons. Not only is it the most complex, but it is also the most volatile of all of our body systems (cf. Burns, 1968). Our sensory systems (vision, audition, etc.) require constant exercise on the invariant stimulation of the external environment to maintain their normative operating conditions. If they are not used, their efficiency is impaired. The same holds true of the brain. The homeostatic requirements of the unstable brain are incredible. Repeated studies of brain growth show that its use and effectiveness are highly correlated with stimulation, activity, and use.

Experiments on sensory deprivation (cf. Zubek, 1969) experimentally validate this observation. Furthermore, experimental work on the neurological deficits that accompany the absence of sensory stimulation, and experiments on neurological enrichment that occurs when creatures are raised with abundant sensory stimulation, enabled me to see the neuropsychological implications of validational feedback, which I define as the feeding of affect hunger.

Restak (1984) summarizes the evidence of studies showing that neural growth and the complexity of neural relationships are increased by the richness of stimulation from the external environment. Of this phenomenon, he writes:

> Increases in the number of synapses are associated with corresponding increases in the complexity and number of dendritic spines. This process is dependent on *environmental stimuli*. If the brain is deprived of environmental stimulation, the number of spines and, by implication, the complexity of synaptic connections is reduced. For instance, raising an animal in darkness reduces the number of synapses in the animal's visual (cortical) area. Even more dramatic are the differences in brain organization that can be found between animals raised in deprived vs. enriched environments. Merely adding a few toys to play with, or mazes to run through, leads to an increase in the number of synaptic contacts as well as a thickening of the animal's cerebral cortex. A similar relationship can be found in the wild: Domes-

ticated animals have thinner cortical layers compared to their counterparts in the forest, an observation first made by Charles Darwin (p. 47) (Italics inserted by author).

Invariant stimulation of the brain tunes and stabilizes its fragile, unstable and volatile neural structures. Stabilization occurs when a neural system automatically processes information that "matches" (cf. Edelman, 1989) its structures, just as exercise tunes and maintains the integrity of muscles. When this happens in the brain, the person has a sense of either being validated or of doing something satisfyingly familiar.

In its simplest form, then, *invariant validational feedback* is the "exercise" of living structures, like muscles and neurons, on the relatively hard and stable objects of the external environment. In its more complex forms, invariant validational feedback occurs in our interpersonal engagements. When we smile and nod at one another, we are mutually "feeding" our affect hungers.

This theory, being constructed within the context of twentieth-century science, is fundamentally different from psychoanalysis, a theory that used the closed-system paradigm of nineteenth-century science. The closed-system model of equilibrium was based on the notion that stillness was the ideal condition of equilibrium. Psychoanalytic theory, therefore, hypothesizes that stimulation is to be avoided.

This basic assumption of Freudian theory (cf. Bowlby, 1969 and particularly Holt, 1989, for an extended discussion of the relationship of this idea to the tension-reduction concept of motivation) is at variance with twentieth-century biological knowledge. Freud was raised in the neurophysiological tradition that conceived of the brain as a passive receptor of unwelcome stimulation. In "Instincts and Their Vicissitudes" (1915/1957), he states as a basic assumption:

> The nervous system is an apparatus which has the function of getting rid of the stimuli that reach it, or of reducing them to the lowest possible level; or which, if it were feasible, would maintain itself in *an altogether unstimulated condition*" (p. 120) (Italics inserted by author).

His model resembles a balanced, motionless seesaw as the metaphor of equilibrium. The model of seesaw equilibrium, as a closed, self-maintaining balance, was the norm for nineteenth-century science. Bowlby (1973) discusses this part of Freud's theory in relationship to the psychoanalytic model of motivation:

> The basic postulate, or model, referred to by Freud in his every discussion of metapsychology, and the one that underlies his "economic viewpoint" has as one of its corollaries that *no external object is ever sought in and of itself, but only in so far as it aids in the elimination of the "incessant afflux" of instinctual stimulation* (p. 79-80) (Italics inserted by author).

In light of present-day science, we know that the *opposite* is true. We know that without exercise, living structures deteriorate and that this is particularly true of the brain, which houses our personalities. It is now common knowledge that the brain, and for that matter, all living tissue, is in constant movement and requires perpetual stimulation.

My theory makes the assumption that the brain is a volatile, open system, requiring continual internal regulatory maintenance—that is, homeostatic regulation and stabilizing, validating feedback from the external environment. This engagement with the external environment exposes the individual to the need for incorporating increasing amounts of information. In this model, growth is a means of accommodating increasing amounts of information, and, in doing this, it facilitates the maintenance of the steady-state (homeostatic) condition of a living system. I will be using the terms *homeostasis, homeorhesis,* and *autopoiesis* interchangeably, to refer to active, open system regulatory processes that maintain the stable-state condition of neurological systems.

Affect hunger is an *underground* stream of neurological process that is neither directly seen nor felt. Its effects take on different forms of behavior and experience, depending upon which part of the brain is in need of feeding or stabilization. For example, should a part of the septum in the neurological ego (core brain) require validational feedback, the person is likely to experience sexual arousal or desire.

I have chosen to label this underground stream "affect hunger" for two reasons. First, the "hunger" part of the phrase has experiential and behavioral effects similar to those of food hunger. I believe that this similarity led early psychologists to use food hunger and its gratification as the model to explain all of motivation. Like food hunger, affect hunger is essentially a physiological need. It, like other neurological processes, can emerge into awareness psychologically. Similar to unsatisfied hunger for food, affect hunger preoccupies the attention of the individual until it is satiated; then it loses its pressing significance.

When this need is not fulfilled, it is transformed into behavior and experience that can still the pangs of affect hunger. Curiosity and exploratory actions are manifestations of stimulus-seeking behaviors. These behaviors are manifestations of what Platt (1972) called the "search for invariance." Berlyne (1966), a psychologist who studied these behaviors, recognized that searching or exploration in animals was not only directed toward external goals, such as food or sex, although he did not specify what internal processes might be operating to arouse these behaviors. I suggest that they were exercising on the hard objects of the external environment to satisfy the affect hunger of their sensory and nervous systems. In our everyday lives, we can see the restless search for the satisfaction of our affect hunger in the popularity of theme parks, rock concerts, prize fights, the theater, or any activity that elicits a high level of emotional arousal. Battegay (1991) describes some of the medical and psychiatric consequences of affect hunger deficits in his description of "Hunger Diseases."

When the affect hunger of a particular system is chronically unfulfilled, behaviors and/or experiences will be activated within the individual to satisfy that hunger. These behaviors or experiences may or may not be psychologically or socially adaptive. Nonetheless, they do have a biologically functional purpose.

Affect hunger is frequently interpreted or explained as nutrient hunger. The people in my practice who suffer from eating disorders are also emotionally deprived. They binge in a metaphoric attempt to satisfy the affect hunger that arises in their core brains and persons.

Roth (1982), in her book, *Feeding the Hungry Heart,* recognizes that "food is a metaphor" for the loneliness of bulimic individuals. She describes "nonphysical hunger," which I have labeled affect hunger, in the following passage:

> Most of us walk around hungry; some of us will die hungry. Subtle in its manifestations, nonphysical hunger can take the form of a vague disturbance, an amorphous dissatisfaction, a feeling that there has to be more to life than what we've known or had. If we interpret the hunger literally, we can use food or drink to satisfy it, or, more to the point, to dull it. Nonphysical hunger

is difficult to tolerate because it is uncomfortable to feel. If our attempts at avoiding it are unsuccessful, the inner gnawing grows, and the discomfort gets more and more unbearable. (p. 94)

The following condensed transcript of a session that I had with a heroic and unfortunate young woman with an eating disorder clinically illustrates the experiential transformation of her affect hunger into nutrient hunger.

Irene's Desire to Binge

This interview occurred when a woman I will call Irene was in the throes of the break-up of the only significant love affair of her life. Her other heterosexual relationships had been isolated, secretive affairs. They were primarily sexual encounters in which neither she nor her companions had much emotional contact with one another.

This relationship had been different, though. The two met and were accepted into one another's families. Friends and colleagues at work knew and socialized with Irene and her boyfriend as a couple. Yet there was a serious limitation to the emotional growth of the relationship. Irene's lover, Gene, refused to have a monogamous sexual relationship with her, and he would not consider the possibility of living together. At the time of this interview, he was preparing to leave Los Angeles. In anticipation of her impending loss, Irene increased her binging behavior. During the interview, I focused my attention on the loneliness of her eating disorder in order to call her attention to the emotionally isolated nature of her binging.

Zoltan: I do wish you'd let me watch you eat sometime.
Irene: Are you serious? I can't imagine. I've been having big binges.
Z: Why don't you invite me over?
I: Zoltan! You're crazy.
Z: I don't understand. Why do you think I'm crazy?
I: Do you watch her eat? (She was referring to another bulimic client I was seeing and about whom she was very jealous.)
Z: I'm sure I would if I wanted to.
I: You mean something about me is unique. And not identical with her. I'm not putting you down.

Z: (Laughter.) You're very funny.

I: I don't think this is funny. I'm relieved that you're not mad at me for saying that.

Z: I would like to watch you eat.

I: I'm amazed. I thought he's probably done the same thing with her. You know. Fuck.

Z: I would like to watch you eat.

I: She'd get jealous. (Wishing to avoid the topic of my being with her during a binge, she made jealous references to her "rival." This led to a discussion of her painful love affair with Gene. She described how she teased him about his other love affairs. She recognized that she had changed the subject.) I feel so ashamed when I think of you seeing me eat.

Z: What is so shameful about letting me watch you eat?

I: There is something very sexual about what you are doing with me.

Z: Really! That's interesting.

I: No. Maybe not.

Z: No, no, please pursue that. What's so sexual about my watching you eat?

I: It's your willingness to do it. Persistence.

Z: It's not willingness. It's a desire.

I: (Laughs.) I want to throw up. That's not sexual? This is getting gross. It's making me nauseous.

Z: What's nauseating about it?

I: Reminds me. (Talks about conference where she was asked to recall early childhood experiences with food and eating. She recalls saying that "my father was a dietitian and he forced it down our throats.") I thought, my God, that's my throat thing. My throat's hurting a lot. Because the thing is that you only eat when you're hungry and I'm not that hungry often. I'm really not. But my throat. That's part of the problem with a commercial diet program, you do get hungry. Well, there's other foods I could eat. Vegetables and stuff like that. I love you, Zoltan. It's hard to tell you that.

Z: What's so hard?

I: Because you're doing something. What is this reminding me of? You're doing something in the past very potent and poignant right now. Something very intense we've done. I can't remember it. It was another life in therapy. It's like another book. It was so far away. We're definitely starting another book. Does that make sense? I haven't spent a lot of time thinking about you and therapy. But now that Gene's gone. . . .

Z: He's changing. Gene isn't gone. He'll never be gone. He's changing.

I: In me?

Z: Yes. And it's lovely to watch. But I wish you'd stay with food and me. You won't let us get together.

I: You're being so intense and soft and giving. It's too difficult to get near you. It does remind me of something in the past. It's so touching. (Confused) Say it again. I'm getting dizzy, Zoltan. I can't understand what you're saying. I'm spinning. No. You're doing too much of it. Nobody treats me this way.

Z: What way?

I: I don't know. You touch such empty spots. I don't want to get addicted to it. To you. I can't look at you. I want to hit you. Arrrgh. Hit you. Hit you. Hit you. How much more time? I feel bad. Aaah. What are you doing, Zoltan? I feel like an asshole. Nobody talks to me this way. They're always mad at me.

Z: Sorry you find it so hard to look at me.

I: Because you do something. You're tender. I can't concretize it. The way you deal with me is something I've never had before. (Relates me to the understanding and acceptance she feels with her sister. She describes her avoidance of the pain of loving.)

Z: You're talking here about a core conflict you have. This is why you've never been able to have a man in your life.

I: I guess because I can't take much.

Z: (Laughter.) Give me a hug. Would you give me a hug now?

I: No way.

Z: Aah, come on! Be a friend.

I: (Laughs.) Don't guilt trip me. You know what happens. Is our time up?

Z: No, we have fifteen minutes more.

I: I'll throw up.
(I return to the topic of my watching her eat. I tell her that she can call me when she is about to binge, and I will come over and be with her then.)

I: It wouldn't work anyway. Binges put me to sleep. The two are exclusive things. Food versus sex and Gene. Love and sex on one side and food on the other side.

Z: That's interesting. Can you tell me more?

I: Oh, it makes it so easy to leave Gene when I have food. I don't want him around when I have food. I don't think about him. I can get rid of him. He can't hurt me. It's a pleasure.

In this interview, Irene expresses many of the major manifestations of affect hunger and its fulfillment that I will be describing in the rest of this book. Her deeply rooted *alienation from the loving experience* and her *loneliness* are expressions of unrequited affect hunger. Her desire for my attention and jealousy of my other client are fixated, childlike attempts to fulfill this hunger. Yet the *pain of loving* causes her to find my desire to be with her during the emotional intensity of a binge *nauseating*. When I touched the deeper parts of her loneliness, she *loved* me and was fearful of becoming *attached*. To defend herself from the anxiety generated by loving contact, she *transformed* it into a desire to *hit* me. The experiential parallel between nutrient and affect hunger was part of her bulimic fixation. Irene's affect hunger was also *fused* with food by her intense love for her father who was a fanatic about healthy eating.

Remember, the first reason for using the phrase "affect hunger" referred to its similarity to nutrient hunger. The second reason for using this phrase arises from the word "affect." It is a term denoting emotion. As we shall see in chapter VIII, emotion arises when the neurological ego is destabilized. When it is not sufficiently validated, it suffers from affect hunger. The disturbance of the neurological ego is caused by either insufficient validation or by invalidating feedback.

Affect hunger is the biological underpinning of our dread of aloneness. Aloneness, when it is experienced as loneliness and alienation, stands next to love in psychological importance to the individual. A major explanatory tradition about the meaning of love describes it as a refuge from loneliness (cf. Fromm, 1956).

David Levy (1937), more than anyone else, experimentally and theoretically, recognized the significance of affect hunger. He wrote:

> The term affect hunger is used to mean an emotional hunger for maternal love and those other feelings of protection and care implied in the mother-child relationship. The term has been utilized to indicate a state of privation due primarily to a lack of maternal affection, with a resulting need, as of food in a state of starvation. . . . The use of the term, affect hunger, rather than affection or love hunger, opens the possibility of hostility,

though this has yet to be investigated. . . . I am not using the term to apply only to individuals who have suffered lack of maternal love in early years of life (pp. 643-644).

I define affect hunger structurally—that is, it is a biological need that has psychological consequences. The need of neurological systems for validational feedback is a more general description, which can encompass a greater variety of psychological phenomena than an experiential or behavioral description. Levy recognized that the term could have a more general application than the deprivation of maternal love. I share this belief.

A dictionary definition of *affect hunger* can be found in Hinsie and Campbell (1960). They define it as the following:

> *Indiscriminate* and *insatiable* demand for attention and affection, seen often in children who have suffered *emotional deprivation* (q.v.). Affect hunger frequently takes the form of aggressive, hostile, antisocial behavior with an inability to accept limitations or recognize the needs of others (p. 345) (Italics inserted by author).

This definition implies that affect hunger is a psychologically pathological condition. Instead, I believe that it is a normal and necessary biological activity that underlies all living process. Aside from this difference, my definition of affect hunger is similar to that of Hinsie and Campbell.

As in their definition, I agree that the appetite of affect hunger is, indeed, *insatiable!* As long as we live, this hunger persists. It is a manifestation of life. The satisfaction of our affect hunger contributes to keeping us alive. It is *indiscriminate* in the sense that physiological processes do not discriminate.

Validational feedback from the external environment is essential for optimal growth and development in the individual. *When we have any kind of relationship with a consistent source of validational feedback, we develop a loving relationship with it.* Validation leads to growth and stability, so we develop loving attachments to sources of validation. This is as true of our explanatory systems as it is of the *people* whom we love. The satisfaction of affect hunger underlies our love of both sensation and cognition. (We are crazy about both Disneyland and explanations.)

The ways that we think and feel about ourselves also provide us with validation, invalidation, or deprivation of feedback for our affect hunger. We love, hate, or isolate ourselves. The methods by which an individual seeks or avoids "supplies" that "feed" affect hunger shape the uniqueness of the individual's personality.

The hypothesis of affect hunger as a physiological process redirected my attention to the core brain. I saw within it structures from which our emotionality emerges. Emotionality is where the body and its mind most intimately meet. Then it occurred to me that many of the functions usually attributed to a psychological ego would be better explained as a *neurological ego.* The theoretical implications of this idea changed my understanding of human nature. Many of the axioms that I had unquestioningly accepted became absurd, and I rejected them. For example, the concept of affect hunger replaced the idea of the brain as an inert receptor of stimulation. Along with that replacement, my theory was liberated from the confusion of ideas of tension reduction, drives, needs, or energies (cf. Holt, 1989). In their stead, I propose that the affect hunger of the neurological ego and its personal equilibratory systems are the bases of both the motivation and the emotionality of the individual.

The Neurological Ego

Years ago, when I was trying to decide on the topic of my doctoral dissertation, lobotomy operations were in vogue. At that time, I also had the good fortune to be serving my internship at the Illinois Neuropsychiatric Institute, an exciting and internationally renowned neurological research center. Psychological research during this period was unable to pinpoint any intellectual impairment resulting from the lobotomy operation.

I could not believe that no deficits could be attributed to an operation that disconnected major portions of the frontal lobes from the core brain. My curiosity was piqued, and I decided to do my dissertation research studying the effects of the frontal lobotomy operation on learning and perceptual transformation.

At that time the metaphor of the "black box" was used to indicate an awareness of the brain as a significant but unknown part of the stimulus-response system, which was thought to be the underpinning of personality. The black box was described as a literal box. As I indicated above in my discussion of Freud's conception of the nervous system, it was axiomatically thought to be a relatively inert system, seeking nothing for itself. It, in and of itself, never activated movement to serve its own needs. It was likened to an inanimate telephone system. Messages were put into it, and it responded by sending messages out. There were no clear ideas about what the system did to affect the messages. Nor, like a telephone system, did it have any needs of its own that generated either thoughts or behavior.

However, an affect-hungry neurological ego—that is, fundamentally self-serving—is a reasonable idea, which fits the facts of brain function and personality. It also bears the merit of giving my theory of personality three major explanatory dimensions. First, it provides the theory with an explanation of psychological movement. The unending movement of thoughts, dreams, fantasies, and ideas that flow through our minds correlate with constant equilibratory processes that occur in our brains. Second, it enables the theory to explain both responses to the external environment and responses to internally motivated conditions. My theory therefore escapes the ignorance of a black box that simply responds to external stimuli. Third, this kind of a system enables my theory to more explicitly explain the eternal, anxiety-producing conflict that exists between our intentional self and the more powerful, mysterious, and anxiety-provoking presence that exists within us.

This presence, which I have personally described as my ghost, activates the experience and behaviors that violate the desires of the self. With the concept of the neurological ego, we no longer need to rely solely on the "unconscious" voice of the past to explain this mysterious conflict. Also, it goes a long way toward ridding us of the need to appeal to mystical or supernatural forces within us to explain the mysteries of our complexity (cf. Eccles and Robinson, 1985).

I attribute to the neurological ego three characteristics a neurological system easily accommodates. First, it has the centrality that is usually assigned to a psychological ego. It resides at the center of the individual. The core brain is certainly the center of our existence and is the ultimate homeostat that keeps us alive. Second, the traditional conception of the ego is that it is the power center of the person. When a person is self-serving, he or she is said to be "ego-oriented," "egotistical," or "egomanical." Third, the neurological ego more readily accounts for that internal presence within us that operates outside the control of our intentional self, the "I." Both the "I" and the ego are commonly experienced, but they have different experiential characteristics. The "I," which I identify with myself, can be described with a clarity, specificity and vocabulary that is absent with the experience of the ego. When I describe my "I," I know it as the agent that governs my actions; I am the source of my "free will." I have a self-concept, within which my "I" is central. Surrounding it are attributed a number of characteristics that uniquely identify "me." However, the experience of "I" raises the enormously difficult question of what motivates it. What causes it to act, to move, and for what purposes?

The idea of a neurological ego is attractive because it solves the major theoretical problem of explaining what moves the human system. Instead of resorting to explanations of vitalism or mechanisms (cf. Holt, 1989), the concept of the neurological ego as a homeostatic structure and process relies upon the movement of living process. By doing this, the theory also escapes the difficulties encountered by relying on a concept of energies to account for the dynamics of experience, behavior, and personality (cf. Bateson, 1972). Although there are no definitive scientific explanations about the nature of living process, approaches to it are being made by Prigogine (1980) and others.

Unfortunately, the mystery of what motivates the "I" and the experiential vagueness of the neurological ego have made it extremely difficult to describe and define. This vagueness is exemplified by Ryle's (1949) and Koestler's (1967) descriptions of it as a "ghost in the machine." The formlessness of the experience of the neurological ego is accurately depicted in the metaphor of the ghost. The visualization of ghosts is usually illustrated in vague ways. Actually, most of our knowledge about the ego does not arise from direct experience—that is, it is not displayed in awareness.

For the most part, our sense of the ego arises from inference. I infer its existence by observing behaviors and experiences of myself arising outside my ordinary experiences of an intentional or sentient self. Previously, I introduced my ghost as an ongoing system of my brain, which operates outside self-awareness. It affects me in ways that exist beyond my reason and awareness. When I am inspired by intuition, processes of psychological classification, and organization (cognition) operate outside any sense of intentional control that is associated with my "I." Naomi felt totally out of control when her personalities shifted. Raymond was rocked with tremors and nausea when I touched him affectionately. Roger's paranoia vanished with emotional contact and arousal.

The neurological ego, unlike the "I," is not affected by the conventions of social life. In the examples mentioned above, the neurological ego is a self-serving part of the individual that overrides the experience of an intentional self, the "I." That clinched it for me. The idea of a powerful central self-serving system within the individual enabled me to explain the mindless, irrational, and self-destructive behaviors of the individual.

When I formulated this idea, I was reminded of a professor of mine who challenged us to locate the person in the brain. Of course, we could not. However, he used our ignorance as a reason to encourage us to avoid trying to bridge the theoretical chasm that exists between the mind and the brain. It is obvious that I was not obedient; I was challenged. To meet this challenge, however, it was incumbent upon me to locate the ego within the brain. As I have indicated above, it is the core brain.

In the center of the brain are highly unstable neurological systems that serve as the highest centers of homeostatic regulation keeping us alive. These systems have been variously called the "core brain," the "old brain," the "paleomammalian brain," and/or the "hypothalamic-limbic system." I call it the neurological ego. Edelman (1989) describes it as being made up of

> the hypothalamus, pituitary, various parts of the brain stem, amygdala, hippocampus, and limbic system (p. 94).

These structures require, as do all other living systems, validational feedback in order to maintain the integrity of their structures and functions. In addition to its role as the prime physiological regulator of the body, there are *centers within it from which all our basic emotions arise.* This combination of neuropsychological facts validated my perception of the core brain or the hypothalamic limbic system (cf. Weil, 1974) as the "ego." This, then, is the "neurological ego."

Revisiting neurology after a forty-year absence has been an exciting adventure. In that period, neuroscientists have illuminated what had previously been dark parts of the brain. In the early 1950s, the structures of the paleomammalian (core) brain were known, but their relationships to one another and to the cortex were shrouded in ignorance. Now, in the 1990s, neuroscientists are not only able to map the neuronal relationships between the core brain and various parts of the cortex, but they are beginning to talk about a "self" and consciousness as emergent properties of these systems.

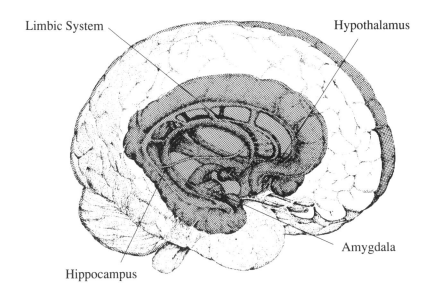

Limbic System

Hypothalamus

Amygdala

Hippocampus

FIGURE 3

THE NEUROLOGICAL EGO

Edelman (1989), LeDoux (1989) and Eccles (1991) describe the neural relationships between various parts of the core brain, the brain stem, and the cortex (particularly the frontal cortex) in sufficient detail to support the hypothesis that a regulatory relationship exists between them. As I learned about the core brain and its relationship to the frontal cortex, it made more and more sense to me to think of the core brain as the ego and the cortex—the prefrontal and the frontal lobes of the brain—as the neurological dwelling place of the person.

Consistent with this position is Luria's (1973) observation:

> The *human frontal lobes* are much more highly developed than the frontal lobes even of the higher monkeys; that is why in man . . . processes of programming, regulation and verification of conscious activity are dependent to a far greater extent on the prefrontal parts of the brain than the processes of regulation of behavior are in animals (p. 93) (Italics inserted by author).

The structural complexity of the frontal cerebral cortex correlates with the psychological complexity of human personality. *The affect hunger needs of neural structures is similarly correlated with human psychological needs for stimulation.* The regulatory functions of the prefrontal lobes are associated with behavior, consciousness, and the structures of the hypothalamic limbic system. The prefrontal lobes regulate the emotional structures of the neurological ego. Luria's (1973) description of the function of the prefrontal lobes and the evidence from lobotomy operations are congruent with my hypothesis that the person is the autoregulatory system of the ego.

Gerald Edelman (1989), writing from the neuroscientist's perspective, recognizes a central brain system that he calls the "self." *Self* is one of the many psychological terms that have varieties of different meanings. My theory describes the self as a part of the person. His "self" is, within the nomenclature of my theory, the neurological ego. He writes:

> I shall use the terms "self" and "nonself" in a strict biological sense, not in the personal or psychological sense of "self awareness" or in the social or philosophical sense of "personhood" (p. 94).

While reading his description of "consciousness" as a property of the brain and his concepts of "categorization" and "matching," an image arose in my mind of neuroscientists and psychologists reaching across a chasm of ignorance that separates our understanding of the brain and its mind. In this fantasy, I had a sense of our fingertips touching, but we could not firmly grasp one another's hands. I do not believe that we will be able to do this until we achieve three different kinds of knowledge.

First, we must have a deeper understanding of the nature of the ways that the cortex of the brain regulates the systems of the core brain—particularly those parts of the cortex that underlie what we now call cognition. Second, neuroscientists need a psychological theory that contains a self and emotionality. Current mind/brain model builders are limited to either behavioral or cognitive psychologies when they attempt to discover neural correlations to psychological processes. These psychologies are inadequate—due to their definitional imprecision—to interface with brain models of experience and behavior. There are crude, metaphoric approximations of a "self" in the mind/brain models of Edelman (1989) and Powers (1973). Unfortunately, no theory of self exists that is clearly or specifically defined to enable the neuroscientist to discover systems of neurons from which a self and/or an ego could emerge. Without a self and/or ego, no complete mind/brain model can be built. Third, we need a psychological theory with a vocabulary that is usable by both psychologists and neuroscientists.

I am hopeful that the theory I am describing in this book will contribute to the second and third needs. In the next chapter, I will present a way of escaping from the trap of definitions of psychological terms based on common sense. This will contribute to bridging the conceptual gap that exists between psychology and neuroscience. Even though the idea of the neurological ego turned my understanding of human nature upside down, I have found that dealing with the ego as a neurological system, not a psychological one, was what enabled me to arrive at a whole theory of personality.

Like the psychoanalytic ego, neurological ego is a centrally important concept. Unlike the psychoanalytic ego, it has characteristics that make it look more like the Freudian Id than a rational, mediating ego. My neurological ego is a mindless, self-serving system without a personal "self." There is no homunculus hidden within it. It is not a psychoanalytic "executive." It has the same relationship to pleasure that it has to pain. Its only purpose is the maintenance of its own steady-state condition, and this purpose is the motivational center of our being. It seeks nothing and has no purpose other than to restore itself to its homeostatic steady-state condition. In serving its primary purpose, the neurological ego, as the body's last court of homeostatic appeal, keeps us alive.

Ego is an old word that has usually been thought to label a psychological phenomenon. Calling the paleomammalian brain the ego gives it a new meaning. Shifting the meaning of the ego from a psychological thing to a neurological one creates the paradigmatic shift of this theory. While the new meaning requires us to alter our familiar understanding about what moves us, it enables the theory to account for the movement of personality and motivation in a conceptually neater way than we have been able to do before.

For me, the neurological ego is a mindless tightrope walker. It stabilizes itself on the high wire of its existence with a balancing pole that has a mask and a bag of tricks tied to each of its ends. The mindlessness of the walker refers to the fact that there is no homunculus in the brain organizing, intending, or doing anything to control the conduct of the individual.

To stretch the metaphor a bit, the balancing pole represents the bimodal equilibratory process of homeostasis. *The affect hunger of the neurological ego is fed by information from both the external and the internal environments of the individual.* We seek stabilizing information from the external environment, which we bring in through our sensory systems, *and* from our internal environment, which is displayed as our psychology.

This is the fundamental dichotomy upon which our existence is built, and the two ends of the balancing pole represent this dichotomy. The bags of tricks at the ends of the balancing pole are metaphors of the mind; the masks are the personal presentations we use to elicit validating feedback from others to assuage our constant affect hunger. The dichotomy emerges from the two sources of validational feedback that stabilize the brain—the external world and our own inner psychology.

The mind, our psychology, has traditionally been thought to be the center of our being. Freud, following the platonic tradition that placed *pure reason* at the center of the universe, and called our rationality the "Ego." It was thought to be our essence, and the body was only its servant. My theory inverts this hypothesis. The mind serves the core brain, a part of the body. We are directed by the requirements of our brain, rather than by the experiences of self and feelings. Herein lies the paradigmatic shift of this theory from traditional theories of personality. In effect, I, like Alice, had stepped into Wonderland. Unlike Alice, though, I did not recognize the new world I was looking at until I understood why defining psychological phenomena has been so difficult.

The idea of the neurological ego forced me to reluctantly try to conceptualize the way that the mind was related to it. Frankly, I was afraid to tackle that problem because I thought it was too big for me. I tried to ignore it, but I was confronted by it whenever I sought to define any of the major terms of the theory. There was no escape from the problem. Whenever I tried to define the person, emotion, or cognition, I ran into it. And I could not continue my pursuit of the theory without defining those terms. When I came to understand that the mind formatted information in doubly dichotomous ways, then I could understand why I—and others—had so much difficulty with psychological definition. That understanding enabled me to articulate ways of knowing about personality that are different from past learning and assumptions.

However, when I reached that understanding, I departed from the familiarity of common sense and began looking at personality in a strange new way. The next chapter will describe the mind, its formatting systems, cognition, and consciousness. These descriptions will then allow me to present an alternative to common sense as the explanatory foundation of personality.

The alternative enabled me to use functional definitions in much the same way that biologists were able to functionally classify living systems. When they learned about metabolic and reproductive systems, they could escape from the trap of basing their classifications on the visual appearance of plants and creatures.

After I concluded that the ego is a neurological system, I could look past the phenomenal appearance of psychological process. Instead, I was able to think about the different ways information was used to tune and stabilize the neurological ego. In a sense, I had pulled back the psychological face of human nature and looked at the "machinery" that lay behind it.

CHAPTER VI

Sea Monsters Populated the Oceans When the Earth Was Flat

A Description of the Mind

When I thought about the ego as a neurological system, I became engrossed in the theoretical maze that has confounded philosophers and psychologists for ages. Altering my understanding of the ego as a psychological entity or process to that of a neurological one forced me to confront universally tangled conceptions about the mind, its relationship to the body, consciousness, and the person. These are the most profound mysteries of our existence. Our compulsively inventive minds enshroud these enigmas with fantastic explanations, which often compound our mystification. To free ourselves from the anguish of this confusion, we invent religions.

When we thought that the earth was flat, we concretized our anxieties and the fear of our ignorance about the oceans with delusions that saw the seas inhabited by atrocious creatures—monsters and dragons. We have done the same thing with the mysteries of our love and sexuality. In the face of ignorance, we inject these feelings with debilitating fantasies that give birth to mental and emotional incapacity. However, delusions and fantasies only momentarily relieve acute anxiety. They become forms of explanation that function merely as temporary tranquilizers.

The recognition of the ego as a neurological system had the same effect on me that the realization of the roundness of our planet had on ancient navigators. Our understanding of the global nature of the earth encouraged us to explore it and to rid our minds of fantasies about horrifying sea monsters. Similarly, I hope that an understanding of the neurological ego will help us to love more freely and happily.

As I expanded my understanding of the implications of the neurological ego, I found that I could define the mind, consciousness, and the person more clearly. These became the paths that took me out of my theoretical maze into my theory of personality. I have found that any theory of personality must encompass a description of these terms *and* their relationships to one another; otherwise, it is flawed and limited.

This chapter will describe a mind with doubly dichotomous cognitive systems. It is the balancing pole of the labile neurological ego—my mindless tightrope walker. From this equilibratory engagement, a person emerges and is displayed in consciousness. The description of these concepts and their relationships will lay out the conceptual foundations of my theory of personality. This chapter also sets the stage for the next, where I will discuss the mind/body relationship. Then I will be able to present theories of the person and its subsystems, which include self, emotionality, and reality.

When finally I caught a glimpse of the nature of the mind, I found that I had stepped out of a maze into a strange new world. I again felt like Alice in Wonderland. I was in an environment with familiar places and street signs that led me to unusual and surprising destinations.

Ordinarily, consciousness, the mind, the ego, the person, emotionality, and cognition are randomly scattered throughout the fields of philosophical and theoretical literature, yards apart from one another. While there are superficial acknowledgments that relationships exist among them, little attention is paid to their specific nature.

As my theory took shape and I began to truly understand the relationships that exist between these concepts I felt as if I were a guest at the Mad Hatter's Tea Party. There I saw these relationships crowded around the end of the tea table chattering together so intently that I had a hard time differentiating one from another. Only when I discovered that the neurological ego served as the Mad Hatter did I realize how the previously estranged conceptions of human nature are intimately related to one another. Then, all my dearly held assumptions about what the "person" is and what it does in our lives were turned upside down.

Conventional wisdom suggests that the person and its intentionality rules the individual's universe. This wisdom is not only untrue, it is the source of much of the confusion that we have about our psychology. Belief in the power and supremacy of the rational mind extends back at least to Plato. His devotion to the symmetry of pure reason and the Golden Mean is more a statement of his attachment to equilibration than it is to a wise observation about human reality. Freud, to his eternal credit, challenged this belief with his concept of "unconscious motivation"; unfortunately, he could not abandon this ill-founded proposition. He restored it to its customary place in our thinking by making *his* Ego the rational mediator between the Id and the Superego.

Implicit in the axiom of the existential priority of pure reason is the assumption that the "I" of the self is the governor or the possessor of that reason, and a corollary is the belief that the "I" is the manager of conduct. The "I" in Western civilization is ordinarily presumed to be the center of the person's universe. This maxim is similar to the old belief that the earth was the center of the universe, and it is equally erroneous.

However, first I want to describe an underlying way of thinking about the mind that is both unusual and unconventional. I had to rid myself of the erroneous assumption that the mind is an operating system that does psychological things. Instead, I realized that the mind is the *label* we place on the experiential display of the operations of complex neural systems. In other words, "the" mind as an operating system is an illusion. The "the" creates the illusion that the mind is an "it" that does something. My "mind" is not a reified thing. "It" does not do anything. The mind is an emergent phenomenon—that is, it emerges into experience out of the operations of the brain. The experienced mind is like a holographic display of the operations of the brain that actually does something. The brain keeps us alive. (I will define experiencing or consciousness later in this chapter.)

The Illusion of the Mind

The idea of the neurological ego was conceptually upsetting to me. It took me some time to escape from the psychological/neurological dualism that I had been trained to axiomatically accept. On the one hand, it is logical to realize that the mind emerges from the brain. Yet I found myself thinking about psychological process as though it were the mover of my behavior. I thought that my feelings were the source of my conduct. I believed that if "I" felt angry, envious, aggressive, or whatever, these feelings caused me to do what I did in their presence. This kind of thinking that excludes neurological process is a simplistic omission of the most significant motivational variable directing our behavior. It is also obedient to an erroneous illusion—that the "I" is the conductor of the emotional symphony that exists within us.

I now know that psychology is simply an experiential display of neural process. In and of itself, psychology has no direct operational power. Once I escaped from this dualism, I found it easier to develop my theory. Finally, when I could accept the ramifications of the illusory nature of the mind, I was able to arrive at this definition:

> The mind is a word that denotes all of the neurological activity that *emerges* into experience as psychological phenomena. This activity is biological information processing. Information is anything that causes change between systems. Three sources of information activate the neural systems that emerge as the mind. First, information is imported from the external environment (sensory perception). Second, information arises from within the body, including the brain itself (nonsensory perception). Third, information is generated within systems as affect hunger. Information is stored (memory), retrieved (remembered, recalled, or recognized), classified (cognition); cognition transforms information into different forms such as words, symbols, ideas, images, dreams, and explanations. Finally, there are neurological operations that *display* both sensory and nonsensory information (consciousness). When these various information-processing operations are displayed in awareness, they are classified as operations of the mind.

Much of what is called the mind has its residence in the cortex of the brain. The classic research of Cannon, Luria, Masserman, and others demonstrates that this area of the brain is a regulatory system of the core brain. The cortex encompasses the thin layer of cells covering the bulk of the brain. We also know that the cortex is, among other things, the home of cognition, the queen of psychological systems. Clinically, it is evident from the need for, and comfort that we get from, explanations (a product of cognition) that cognition is an equilibratory process. In other words, *psychological process is the experiential display of the regulatory activity of the brain.*

The core brain without the regulatory controls of the cortex can activate wild and unrestrained behaviors. This line of reasoning enabled me to realize that the person that emerges out of the prefrontal cortex of the brain represents the display of neurological activities designed to regulate and nourish the neurological ego. The person is an expression of equilibration, rather than the ruler of the individual's universe. The most obvious line of evidence for this hypothesis about the neurological locus of the person comes from the effects of lobotomy operations and clinical observations about people suffering from damage to the pre-frontal cortex.

Our humanity is an expression of the dazzlingly complex interaction of the cortex and the core brain. Kagan's (1989) work on temperament experimentally demonstrates the relationship between the core brain and personality. He convincingly argues that a relationship exists between temperament and operations of the amygdala, a neurological structure in the core brain—the neurological ego. "Temperament Emotion," as he calls it, is the temperamental orientation that people have toward their world and their relationships in it. In some respects, Kagan's Temperament resembles Jung's (1983) introversion-extroversion dimensions of personality. It is an overall emotional template that determines whether we are freely outgoing or internally oriented in our relationship to the world at large.

This is the beginning of an explanation of the relationship between the person and emotion. The movement of the core brain creates the bodily activity that we call emotion. We have always intuitively known that *emotion* and *personality* are related to one another, but these are such poorly defined terms that we have never been able to theoretically define the nature of this relationship. However, when we recognize that the person can be described as a cortical (cognitive) system and emotion as the movement of the core brain, then we have the beginnings of an understanding of the relationship that exists not only between the person and emotion, but between the mind and body relationship as well.

Before I could fully grasp the ramifications of this reversal of my understanding about the mind and the neurological ego, though, I had to be able to define *emotionality* and *personality;* I wanted to know what relationship they had to the brain. Since the mind emerges from a bio-logical system, its information-processing activity has a biological pur-pose. It occurred to me that it sustains the life of the individual. That is, the mind is the display of equilibratory systems whose primary task is the maintenance of the steady-state condition of the core brain and the cortex.

Herein lies the drama and the dilemma of human existence. The cortical operations of the mind, in their homeostatic mission, respond to the neurological ego. In turn, they are homeostatically regulated by the neurological ego that they serve. This moebius strip metaphorically illustrates the elegant, involuted transformations of the regulatory arrangements that exist between the core brain and the cortex.

These regulatory systems are intricately developed throughout the course of our lives. This complexity invariably creates conflicting systems. At times, they produce deadly destabilizing events in the brain. There is no death instinct in this theory. Instead, there are structurally mismatching neural systems, which can cause the individual to commit suicide.

Describing psychological phenomena in these terms *does* raise the question of reductionism, as some could argue that I am reducing psychological operations to neurological ones. However, my theory does not attempt to simple-mindedly cram psychological process into undefined neurological concepts, or vice versa. Instead, I am presenting a way of thinking about *both* psychological and neurological process within a single, congruent descriptive system.

This is part of the paradigmatic shift of this theory. It creates a descriptive frame of reference including both psychological process and neurological operations. The theoretical stance of this theory is not reductionistic. In a limited way, it describes both neurological and psychological phenomena within the same theoretical frame of reference, without assuming that they are operationally the same. The theory does not attempt to describe the neurological operations that create the experience of the mind. However, concepts of consciousness and emergence enable me to describe the relationship that exists between the mind and the brain. In this way, we can cut the Gordian Knot that has confounded our understanding about the mind/body relationship.

This radical conclusion makes me uneasy. Despite the fact that it is logical and reasonable, it puts me at the side of B. F. Skinner (1990). He was a man whose creativity I have respected and with whose theoretical asceticism I have disagreed throughout my studies in psychology. At the 1990 American Psychological Association Convention, he said:

> So far as I am concerned, cognitive science is the creationism of psychology. It is an effort to reinstate that inner initiating-originating creative self or mind which, in scientific analysis, simply does not exist (p. 6).

This is precisely what I am saying. Neither the self nor the mind function as operating systems. They exist only as experiences of neurological operations to which we have attached the labels "mind" and "self." In this regard, I stand shoulder to shoulder with Skinner and the Buddhists. Both regard the mind and self as illusions. Since mind and self are psychological phenomena, other experienced psychological information processes have the same illusory characteristic. I believe that Skinner had the same distaste for the limitations of commonsense definitions and explanations about psychological process that I have. However, this put me into the difficult position of being both a theorist and a psychotherapist. I abandoned common sense as a primary way of thinking about personality and psychotherapy. Having done that, what could I substitute for common sense?

Entering the Gardens of Wonderland

If all of psychology is illusion, psychotherapeutic interventions and explanations about personality, theoretically and psychotherapeutically, have to be cast in a new light. At this point, the loss of common sense became theoretically meaningful as well as being psychotherapeutically effective. When I rid myself of common sense, I could see my clients and myself in a productive new way.

In the early days of my practice, when I was exploring the baseline of the dyadic triangle, I experienced conflicting emotions about the fun I was having playing in the Theater of the Absurd. I enjoyed myself, and my clients were learning much more about themselves than when I was making insightful interpretations from behind the blank screen. Still, I did not understand what I was doing; I could not explain how the dyadic dance worked.

Eventually, I came to understand that psychological interventions and explanations can and do provide disequilibrating (invalidating) input into ongoing neurological systems. I found that logical, linear explanations were among the least effective psychotherapeutic interventions. It became obvious that emotionally involving engagements are most effective in facilitating personality change.

Later, I learned that personality change results from breaking up old emotional habits or patterns. Habituated response and cognitive systems take on an automaticity that can be altered only when they are forced to integrate dissonant or mismatching information. Characterological (habituated personality) systems are basically emotional systems and, therefore, are relatively unaffected by logical thought.

To escape the unproductiveness of linear interpretation, many therapists use metaphors, paradoxical interventions, and personal engagement to make contact with the emotionally organized static structures of the client's personality. This line of thinking enabled me to understand how I could work with clients without having to conform to assumptions about psychological process as operating systems.

Understanding the illusory nature of psychological process, though, did not inhibit my work as a therapist. Rather, it liberated me to intervene in the emotional process of psychotherapy using metaphor, paradox, and the active presentation of my person. Engaging my clients emotionally helped them to de-automate inappropriate response and experiential systems. The following transcript of an interview with a woman I will call Katherine illustrates what I mean by being released from the limitations of common sense. The following interview occurred six months after treatment began.

Getting Katherine's Attention

Katherine came to see me, suffering from incapacitating anxiety. She could not work, rarely left her apartment, and devoted herself totally to the care of her seventeen-year-old daughter. At first glance, she looked like an android. Her face was finely carved alabaster—wrinkleless and expressionless. Her lips and eyes were carefully made up, and her hair was stiffly and impeccably coiffed. Long scarlet fingernails attested to the fact that she spent endless hours grooming herself to create a flawless appearance.

Katherine described an utterly mad childhood and adolescence as though it were an ordinary, all-American story. Her mother was the center of her existence, and she was her mother's obsession. Rights and wrongs were clearly spelled out. There was a rule for everything, and her mother knew all of them. Instead of being guided by feelings, the routines of Katherine's life were determined by correct adherence to the rules.

Katherine's father earned his living as a grifter. When he was at home, he served as the enforcer of her mother's view of the kind of life the family was supposed to live, but he abused his son, who was older than Kathy. Brother Ted was devoted to the traditions of the family, and taking care of Katherine was one of the primary requirements of family life.

Katherine was also a devotee of family tradition. After she graduated from high school, she married, had a daughter, was divorced and returned to her parents' home by the time she was twenty-one years old. Katherine's daughter was brought up just as she had been, dominated by both her grandmother and her mother. They trained her to live within the framework of their realities.

Shortly after Katherine returned home, her mother developed abdominal cancer and convalesced for the next ten years, ruling the family from her bedside until she died. All this occurred without any experience of the feelings that are usually present in intimate relationships. Katherine never developed a sense of her own autonomy and was totally dependent upon her mother's reality as a guide to her existence. An undercurrent of suppressed fury was the cornerstone of the raw alienation that estranged the family. Katherine constantly looked for explanations that could provide her with instructions on how to conduct herself and to obliterate any awareness of the pain that resided behind her anger.

Unfortunately, Debbie, Katherine's daughter, also began to experience the same rage that her mother did. Debbie began separating herself from her mother's reality and domination by becoming obsessed with her own lover. By the time Debbie was about to graduate from high school, she and her mother were engaging in prolonged, mutually insulting fights about this young man. Katherine continued to treat her daughter as though she were a five-year-old. Debbie found herself alternately adoring and hating her mother. Finally, she exploded, fled from her mother's apartment, and sought asylum with her father. The transcript that is excerpted below occurred the day after Debbie's departure.

The initial part of the interview centered around Katherine's asking me either to tell her how to get Debbie back or to coach her in ways to manipulate Debbie into returning home. During that part of the interview, I suggested that she would be in a better position to relate to her daughter if she had a clearer sense of what she was feeling about Debbie's departure and about how she might have participated in the outrage that caused her to move out. However, these suggestions fell on deaf ears.

Trying to get Katherine's attention, I suggested that she find another therapist who would be more willing to help her develop a strategy for getting Debbie back. She dismissed what I said as though it were totally irrelevant and relentlessly pursued her monologue about how to get Debbie back. I fruitlessly tried to get her to attend to her feelings of loss and the possibility of grief if Debbie did not return.

I finally realized that Katherine was entrenched behind a glaze that blocked out all her feelings. She was focally riveted on developing strategies to remain in control. The first part of the interview illustrates my attempts to try to get to her feelings; then, after I realized the depth of her glaze, I tried a new tactic.

K: I was fine at Jane's (a friend) Monday and Tuesday. I came home Tuesday night, was okay, and woke up Wednesday, and was just a basket case. Sick to my stomach and just getting crazier each day.

Z: Tell me about getting crazier each day.

K: Keep thinking did I do the right thing?

Z: The right thing?

K: Yeah.

Z: You couldn't have done anything else.

K: Do you think she loves me?

Z: I know she does. But you make it very painful to love you when you don't see her. When you are off on your own track. When you don't validate her reality.

K: But her reality is so unrealistic.

Z: I don't mean by agreeing with her. Just acknowledge that she has said something without judging her. If you keep trying to correct her, you will lose her.

K: I'm just trying to help her.

Z: That kind of help is poison. Correcting her is destructive. You'll kill the relationship.

K: How do I help her then? If I don't do it by correcting her, how do I help her?

Z: Have you thought of dating any men?

K: Yes.

Z: What kind of man would you like to date?

K: Oh, a rich lawyer. (Laughs.) I don't know. Someone nice. Not phony. (Long silence.) Understanding. The kind you can bond together. Not this new way of living that everybody lives. 'Cause I just can't get behind it.

Z: What's this new way of living?

K: You know getting married and everybody going their own way and doing their own thing. I don't understand the point of it.

Z: You're very lonely.

K: Yeah, I know that. That's why it was really strange seeing the three of them together. (Debbie, her father and his new wife) I mean. Like I was the outsider. But I didn't feel I was the outsider. His (her ex-husband's) wife felt like the outsider. Not me. The three of us were laughing and joking. And even though she's as sweet and as nice as can be, I will tell you I never talked to anybody sweeter. And Sunday at 10:30 I was sleeping, but she called Jane at 10:30 to see how I was. I mean very considerate. Very, very sweet. And I called her back the next day, to thank her for calling, for being concerned. And I said to her how about one day next I'll come into town and we'll go to lunch. Jane said, "Don't make that a habit. Start getting too close." I said, "No I don't intend to." But she is living there with my daughter. Being very sweet to her. And I do want to be on good terms with her. I don't see where that would be wrong. Is that being wrong?

Z: How's Ted (Katherine's brother) doing?

K: He doesn't want to know from any of it. He's through with it. He said, "David did you the biggest favor. Now she's out of your hair, off your hands and now you can live your own life." I was thinking of going down there this weekend, but I don't think I'd be ready this weekend to hear his lectures. I'll probably go next weekend, because it's his birthday. I was only going to go only because I wanted to get out of the house instead of going crazy at home, but I don't think I'll go this week. Because I know that as soon as I get there I'll just want to be home again. I'll go next week, just because it's his birthday, just for the week. I just don't want to go hear his lectures about what a great favor he did me. "Now you're free." Now, kid, I'm not free, she's my daughter. Am I wrong?

Z: You're very lonely.

K: 'Cause it was real strange. Because it wasn't like I was an outsider with them. It's like his wife was. And she didn't catch on to things real quick. And it was a very strange feeling. Would I be wrong, going to having lunch with her or should I just not make . . . ?

Z: Have you thought about your mother recently?

K: Only once. I thought if she were here this would have never happened. She would have straightened her act up in no time. But no, it's yesterday's news already. You got live for today and tomorrow. That's history already. (Lengthy silence) Or maybe I'm afraid Debbie's going to like Nan (ex-husband's wife) better than me. I mean I know this is going to take time. I just don't, I don't know (silence), I just don't know if I should take it in my own hands and this is the way it is. I always think about things afterwards, I never think about things before they happen. I always think about things afterwards. Yet I know this is good for her. It's good for her to get to know her father. It's good for her to . . . to see family she hasn't seen in ten years. Get to know them. I mean I know all this will be new and good for her. I'm sure she's not happy about not seeing Jim (K's daughter's boyfriend) every day or anything, but she'll never let him know that. She wouldn't open up to him, at least at this point, like she would to me. I don't know, I guess, just not knowing. I'm surprised I haven't heard from her.

Z: When are you going to get a job?

K: Maybe this summer, I'll go back to work. The last thing she said to me, before I left, she said, "You're not mad at me, are you?" And I said, "Well, I'd be lying if I didn't say I'm disappointed. But I'm not mad."

Z: Did you notice what I have been doing to you for the last five minutes?

K: Just letting me talk.

Z: Not true.

K: What?

Z: What's happened every time you've asked me for advice?

K: You've given it to me. (Zoltan laughs.) I think you have.

Z: That's really weird. First you ask me about calling Debbie, and I ask you about your brother. Every time you've asked me for advice, I've changed the subject.

K: And I haven't heard you.

Z: That's right.

K: Didn't seem that you were changing the subject to me.

Z: When you started asking for advice about anything.

K: You asked me about Ted.

Z: Very consistent. The last five minutes, I said to myself I'll do to you what you do to me and others. And a . . . hello!

K: Yeah, I'm just laughing at myself. I know what you're saying.

Z: See how little attention you pay to what's going on?

K: I pay so little attention to things. Then why do I hurt so much?

Z: Because you don't have any feelings.

K: If I didn't have any feelings, I wouldn't hurt.

Z: No, no. If you had feelings, you wouldn't be hurting. If the emotional process doesn't get converted into feelings, it can be experienced as pain.

K: Don't feelings hurt, too?

Z: Some of them do. Some don't.

K: Isn't being angry a feeling that hurts?

Z: No. Whenever you're angry, you don't hurt. Anger sometimes masks hurt. Rarely does it cause hurt.

K: Well, I guess I'm just scared.

Z: That's a lot of anxiety. Pain, anxiety, and depression are words that are used for emotion that cannot be expressed as feelings.

K: Going back, can I ask you a question? The psychologist we're taking Debbie to said I should call her every couple of days and not lose contact.

Z: Have you ever tried being a blonde? (Laughter.)

K: Come on now, please don't change it. Do you agree with that? I was going to call her last night, and I fell asleep.

Z: This is the fourth time I have agreed with that.

K: But you won't, you won't. . . . But should I call her or should I not? Should I wait for her to call me?

Unfortunately, I was only able to hold her attention for a brief moment. To the best of my knowledge, Katherine and her daughter are still estranged. This vignette is another illustration of my departure from a commonsense orientation to my clients, where I responded primarily to the content of their talk. It also helped me see a way of working with people without believing that psychological systems had direct effects on behavior.

I came to see that much of my engagement with clients took them out of their habituated ways of experiencing and responding to me. From this change they experienced altered ways of understanding themselves. I again had the uncomfortable sense of standing in the shadow of B. F. Skinner.

However, the impersonal and mechanistic aspects of Skinner's conception of psychological process were abhorrent to me, and I avoided thinking about them. Furthermore, he was totally disinterested in trying to fathom the mysteries of that "black box," our brain. I, on the other hand, have had a long-standing interest in it and in playing the theoretical game. Despite my aversion to Skinner's theoretical orientation, I came to believe that his idea about "reinforcement schedules" was relevant to the validation and invalidation of personal presentations in which I engaged with my clients.

While it is true that we do not know much about the complexity of neurological regulation as it emerges into psychological phenomena, we do know enough to build a theory of psychology around it. Ideas about equilibration, inhibition, facilitation, matching, orientation, tuning, skill, habituation, and adaptation have a long history in psychology and a rich experimental literature. These terms are also congruent with neurological process. Furthermore, they are much more easily defined than drives, needs, libido,, or intentionality. Unfortunately, psychoneurological terms have not yet been conceptually linked to theories of emotionality or personality. This is what I will be doing in the following chapters.

I have defined the mind. Having defined it, could I now describe a mind that has both the characteristics of common sense and the madness of emotionality? That is the unavoidable task I had tried to dodge before I entered the theoretical maze, which began with the theory of dyadic interaction. When I entered it, I was instantly thrown into theoretical adventures, which were awesome. Fortunately, they turned out to be rewarding, and they changed the way I understood myself and my work. Then, to my surprise and delight, I discovered that I understood some aspects of the difficulty of psychological definition. I also discovered to my dismay that I had departed from comfortable and handy ways of explaining who we are and why we do what we do. The recognition of the duality of the mind put all of psychology into a new light for me, and it provided me with a way of describing both reason and madness in the same frame of reference.

The Doubly Dichotomous
Formatting Systems of the Mind

The theory of dyadic interaction, where both apical and baseline interactions occur simultaneously, turned my attention to the duality of the mind. As I pursued this thought, I learned that duality has been a long-recognized and much-explained phenomenon. From the ancient Chinese concept of the yin and the yang to the present-day knowledge of split-brain operations, the mind has been seen as a dichotomous information-processing system. Orenstein (1975) presents a lengthy list of the many ways this dichotomy has been classified. However, the linear/nonlinear duality we see emerge from the left and right hemispheres of the brain do not account for all of the dichotomies listed by Orenstein. The idea of formatting came from the description of linear and nonlinear information processing described by researchers of the split brain operations (cf. Kinsbourne, 1982).

This formatting concept enabled me to see that logical or analytic thinking, common sense, intuition, and feeling were displays of differently formatted ways of conceptualizing. My recognition of this fact allowed me to see more of the iridescent complexity of the brain's operations, which give rise to the mind. To avoid the awkwardness of constantly referring to the neurological process that emerges as psychology, I will simply use common psychological terms, with the understanding that they refer to the underlying neural process.

Formatting refers to the internal neurological organization of information before it becomes what we ordinarily call psychological process. It is never directly displayed in awareness; we experience only its effects. All cerebral information processing is formatted. Consciousness, perception, and cognition are formatted processes. In the following discussion, I will be concerned primarily with the description of formatting as it applies to cognition—the classifying systems of the mind—because personality is, largely, a cognitive product.

The double dichotomy can be inferred from the ways in which we think, perceive, and experience ourselves and the world. Common sense, scientific thought, intuition or poetic thinking, and feelings are all forms of thinking, classification, or explanation. However, thoughts about self and feelings are experienced differently from logical, analytical, or commonsense forms of thinking. Common sense and logic have a neatness and orderliness that does not exist in the thinking that occurs in our emotionality or personality. Emotional and personal operations are fluid and shift about in ways that do not occur in logical thought. Regardless of these differences, they are all cognitive, equilibratory processes.

In addition to the linear/nonlinear dichotomy of cerebral information processing, it is evident that our thoughts about physical objects are shaped by our sensory experience of them. It is also apparent that the experiences we have of ourselves, our feelings, our thoughts, and our intentions arise from nonsensory sources within the body/brain. When one reflects upon sensory and nonsensory phenomena, one is struck by the differences in the experiential qualities existing between them.

Linear, sensory experiencing has the hard, sharp boundaries and stability that exist in the physical objects one visually sees in the external environment. When one thinks in an analytical or commonsense mode about repairing a motor, the experience of thinking is stable, and the parts of the motor are laid out in a linear, systematic way. Unless the repairperson is emotionally upset, attention will remain stably focused on the problem of repair. The boundaries of the issue at hand will remain relatively intact.

On the other hand, nonlinear, nonsensory experiencing is fluid and flows with the movement of the equilibratory process that is oriented toward stabilizing the person and the neurological ego. The fluidity and movement of this kind of thinking are most vividly seen in our dreams, which flow with the movement of both internal equilibratory process and external events occurring in the environment of the dreamer. Dreamers will incorporate the ringing of an alarm clock or the heat of the room into the fight that they had with a lover earlier in the evening, frequently an internal source of the dream.

These ideas were the beginnings of an understanding of the double dichotomy of the mind—the linear/nonlinear and sensory/nonsensory dichotomies. These underlie all mental processing. Doubly dichotomous information processing occurs without regard to the content or the kinds of information that it structures. The figure/ground process occurs in visual perception, in dyadic interaction, in music, and in motion picture production. The mind/brain formats sensory information arising from the external environment, as well as nonsensory information arising from within our brains.

A Description of Doubly Dichotomous Formatting

Our mind is blessed with doubly dichotomous formatting systems. McLuhan (1965) succinctly describes it in two sentences:

> *A Passage to India* by E.M. Forster is a dramatic study of the inability of oral and intuitive oriental culture to meet with the rational, visual European patterns of experience. "Rational," of course, has for the West long meant uniform and continuous and sequential (p. 15).

Within the classificatory scheme of the double dichotomy, "European patterns" are formed from linear, sensory formatting. "Rational" is "sequential." They are words that denote linearity. And, of course, visual means sensory. This kind of thinking has been a formidable tool in the solution of mechanical problems that arise from the arrangement and relationships among physical objects, where either the objects or the relationships between them are stationary.

It is obvious that a still, physical object is different from the evanescent movement of cerebral/psychological information processing. The essence of this movement is the stabilization of relationships between highly unstable living systems. The thinking that works for one stable thing at a time is not too effective in classifying relationships between complex, unstable systems in constant flux.

Human beings have the greatest cerebral skills with single, stationary objects that can be seen, although even relationships between still things are not easily conceptualized. It was not until the twelfth or thirteenth century that perspective drawing was created. It took human beings that long to develop the conceptual and visual skills necessary to create perspective in their drawings. Relationships and patterns of objects remain difficult for the human intelligence to describe. It is much easier to draw a picture of the arrangement of furniture in a room than it is to describe it verbally.

Ivins (1953) presents the interesting hypothesis that the Industrial Revolution was made possible by the invention of graphic printing. Information about the relationships between parts of machines was much more readily conveyed by pictures than by words, dramatized by the homely cliché that "a picture is worth a thousand words." Western civilization has great skill with, and love for, visual information. This Western visual predilection is expressed in another misleading aphorism, "Seeing is believing."

The eighteenth-century philosophical tradition of empirical enlightenment was based on this premise (cf. Becker, 1932). If one could not see, taste, touch, hear, or smell information, it was denied as being worthy of thought. Furthermore, philosophers during this period of enlightenment also passionately denounced emotion as a disastrous impediment to productive thought, and they were not at all sanguine about it. In fact, they became so emotional about this belief that they violated their own injunctions to be rational. Unfortunately, feelings, self, consciousness, the mind, or any other psychological process is displayed in experience without the benefit of vision or any of the other exteroceptive senses. It was for this reason that academic psychology, from the 1920s to the 1960s, for the most part, banished personality and the mind from being meaningful areas of study. Fortunately, this prejudice is now being overcome.

Linear formatting emerges as logical thought when it analyses things by taking them apart bit by bit in a sequential way, a kind of thinking called logical or analytic thought. Nonlinear sensory perception formats the *relationships* of physical objects that exist in the external environment. Intuition is a form of nonlinear thought. Logical thought, when it is wedded to sensory perception, is common sense.

The left hemisphere is frequently described as the part of the brain that organizes information into linear formats. The figure/ground illusion is an example of the linear/nonlinear duality in the experiential display of visual perception. The figure is the linear organization of the subject at the center of attention. The ground is the nonlinear organization of information about the relationship of the figure to its surroundings. The linear/nonlinear dichotomy is abundantly described in the neuropsychological literature. Linear structure enables us focus on information about the thing, as in the subject of the dyadic triangle.

The right hemisphere of the brain is considered the cerebral structure that organizes information into nonlinear formats. Nonlinear formatting organizes information about relationships that exist between things or processes. Information about relationships is the essence of nonlinearity. Emotionality is a nonlinear process. Consistent with this observation is the fact that emotionality is largely a right hemisphere function (cf. Tucker, 1981).

I can now, at last, fully introduce you to my ghost. "He" encompasses the nonlinear, nonsensory, cognitive aspects of my mind. He is a sleepless, omnivorous, unintentional, automatic, nonlinear organizer of information. Even though I describe this part of my mind/brain as a little homunculus governing me, I do so only metaphorically. As I noted before, there is no need for a homunculus in this theory. However, since I have learned to enjoy this part of my mind, I affectionately anthropomorphize it. It is not identified with my *self,* nor does it have a self. It is different from the "me" that I experience as the constant companion of my being. Yet it is a powerful, demanding system of the mind that intrudes upon the well-groomed order of my intentionality. The mysteries of this part of our mind are the roots of spirituality and religious tradition.

Tao, the Kabbala, Zen Bhuddism, Sufism, and Christian gnosticism are concerned with fathoming and mastering the power of the nonlinear, nonsensory process within us. The experience of my ghost bears a striking resemblance to the experience of Tao:

> Look, it cannot be seen—it is beyond form.
> Listen, it cannot be heard—it is beyond sound.
> Grasp, it cannot be held—it is intangible.
> These three are indefinable;
> Therefore they are joined in one.

> From above it is not bright;
> From below it is not dark;
> An unbroken thread beyond description.
> It returns to nothingness.
> The form of the formless,
> The image of the imageless,
> It is called indefinable and beyond imagination.

> Stand before it and there is no beginning.
> Follow it and there is no end.
> Stay with ancient Tao,
> Move with the present.
> Knowing the ancient beginning is the essence of Tao.

(Lao Tsu, p. 16)

If something can be seen, heard, or grasped and does not move, it is readily comprehensible. If something provides no sensory data and is constantly moving, it is a mystery. As stated in the above quote, the experience of Tao is nonsensory, as are the unceasingly moving, nonlinear, nonsensory aspects of the mind—my ghost. The operations of these systems have been eternally mysterious. They can be interpreted as the parts of the brain that are most receptive to spirituality or spirituality, can be regarded as the product of the classifactory imperative of cognition. In other words, the nonsensory, nonlinear process of the brain can be thought of as being the receptor site of spirituality. Or, the experience of nonsensory, nonlinear process can be classified as being spirituality in the same way that Jaynes (1976) describes the origins of Greek mythology, as explanations for personal motivation.

Regardless of how one interprets the nature of spirituality, it is interesting to note that the sensory/nonsensory duality, like the linear/nonlinear duality, is also geographically represented in the brain. As I mentioned above, linear and nonlinear information processing generally occurs respectively in the left and right hemispheres of the brain. The sensory/nonsensory dichotomy occurs in the front and back parts of the

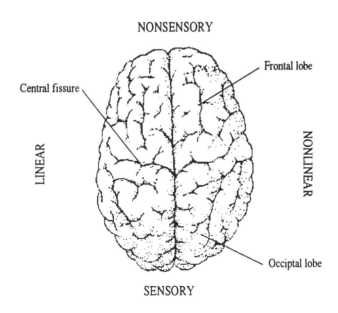

FIGURE 4

THE DOUBLY DICHOTOMOUS BRAIN

brain. The cortex of the back (posterior) part of the brain is largely devoted to organizing sensory information, primarily visual information. The front (anterior) part of the brain (the frontal lobes) organizes information within the brain in preparation for action. It is here that much of the integrating, synthesizing, and planning functions of the mind occur. Personality, for the most part, also resides in this part of the brain.

These four ways of organizing information underlie all of the different ways that we think, feel, perceive, and experience ourselves as persons. We think in sensory, linear ways; in nonsensory, linear ways; in sensory, nonlinear ways; and in nonsensory, nonlinear ways. As I said above, common sense is a sensory, linear way of thinking. Scientific analysis is frequently a nonsensory, linear form of thinking. Poetry is often a sensory, nonlinear form of thinking. Feeling that emerges from emotion is a kind of nonsensory, nonlinear thought. As I became familiar with the idea of formatting, I began to understand cognition in a new way. The following definition of *cognition* lays the groundwork for the definition of the person, which I will present in chapter IX.

A Functional Definition of Cognition

Cognition is a multipurpose term used to denote a variety of psychological processes. For the purposes of my theory, I will describe cognition as the automatic categorizing or classifying process of the mind/brain. Cognitive classifications emerge into awareness as thoughts, ideas, or explanations. This is one of the major hypotheses of the theory. This never-ending classifying process underlies all psychological dynamics. Whatever the source of information—be it from clouds we see in the sky to the movement of the hypothalamic limbic systems of our paleomammalian brain—which we experience without the benefit of the sensory systems—cognition attempts to classify it.

Up to this point I have described what cognition does with information. This kind of information management also has a biologically adaptive purpose or function; that is, classification equilibrates the neural systems that are required to process information. If incoming information arrives at a "matching" neural system, it will automatically be processed.

"Matching" simply refers to the situation where neural structures transmitting incoming information "fit," are congruent with, or "match" neural (cognitive) structures that classify information (cf. Edelman, 1988,

1989). When this happens, neural structures remain in their steady-state (homeostatic) condition. If there is a "mismatch," the neural systems involved become disequilibrated. Disequilibrated (disorganized) neural structures emit "error signals" (cf. Powers, 1973), activating a regulatory process to restore the steady-state condition. Cognition is one such regulatory system. It operates to reorganize either information or cognitive classifications of information to create a "match." This is another way of describing Piaget's (1970) concepts of assimilation and accommodation. Immediate recognition is a psychological example of this. When we see something familiar, there is a "fit," and we know how to react to it. If it is insignificant to the situation in which we are engaged, it is dismissed and passes almost instantaneously out of awareness.

Psychologically, the regulatory process of cognition emerges into awareness as the need for explanation, one of the major sources of satisfaction of our affect hunger. Explanation, like all other cognitive operations, stabilizes our neurological ego. I will discuss this way of thinking about explanation shortly.

Doubly dichotomous formatting underlies all cognition and consciousness. It is the foundation upon which classification or categorization is built. The ways that information is classified depend upon the formatting skills of the individual. Sensory, linear formatting produces the simplest form of classification, placing immobile things into categories of sensory similarity. The most complex form of classification is the nonlinear, nonsensory form of classification. Recognizing patterns displayed in awareness in the incessant movement of our brains is the essence of nonlinear, nonsensory classification. In other words, this kind of classification organizes moving, nonsensory systems into a single category. Various elements or things are organized into a category describing their relationships to one another.

For example, I classified logic, scientific thinking, intuition, and feelings into a single category—explanation. They are all words describing different kinds of cognition, but they all have the same functional property of explanation: they equilibrate the core brain and its mind. Categories unify diversity. The experience of this unity has been a reason for believing in the unity of the mind (Marks, 1981).

More detailed discussions about the nature of psychological classification, to which I have been referring, can be found in the work of Margolis (1987) and Lakoff (1987). In its simplest form, common sense enabled us to classify whales as fish. They look like fish. They swim in oceans, as do fish. They even swim in a pod in a superficially similar way to the way that fish swim in schools. From a linear, sensory formatting position, whales and fish reside in the same classification. On the other hand, when we observed that whales suckle their young the way we humans do, we inferred and observed that whales have bodies with the same organ systems that mammals have. They, like us, are warm-blooded creatures. Their metabolic systems are different from those that exist in fish.

This is functional classification. Mammalian metabolic activity is the classificatory principle. Metabolic activity describes between-system relationships that usually lie outside sensory awareness. Therefore, from a nonlinear, nonsensory formatting position, whales are now classified as mammals.

There are similarities between these two ways of classifying information, which enable me to use the same words to label psychological phenomena. I can refrain from creating new words to label and describe my theory. Instead, I can use common words such as *personality, feelings, emotion, mind,* and *consciousness.* Rather than labeling *psychological process* as it is displayed in experience, I classify it according to its functions. In other words, I define it by how it contributes to the maintenance of the biological integrity of the person, not by how it "looks."

Commonsense classification of psychological phenomena is based on how these phenomena are displayed in awareness, on the "look" of processes. Linear classifications of things do not consider the relationships that exist between objects or processes. Definitions of emotion are based on cultural meanings attributed to the experiential qualities of different emotional processes. They are not conceptually related to other psychological processes. For example, commonsense definitions of emotions have little or no conceptual relationship to the person or consciousness. In this theory, definitions are based on the equilibratory relationships that exist between different processes, as in the case of whales being classified as mammals.

The term *common sense* usually refers to popular or conventional ways of thinking about phenomena. It also has connotations of being a reasonable and rational way of conceptualizing things and processes. As such, it is an efficient and meaningful way of thinking. Many forms of common sense are based on linear, sensory formatting. In the following discussion, I will use the phrase "common sense" to denote linear, sensory thinking. This usage is a shorthand way of referring to the unfamiliar operations of a kind of cognitive formatting.

The idea of the fourfold formatting systems of the mind enabled me to understand the linear sensory bias of conventional psychological definitions. That liberated me from the confusion of commonsense definitions.

The Loss of Common Sense

Comfortable though they may be, traditions of belief based on the ignorance perpetuated by common sense keep us enmeshed in tragic prejudice. There has been a long-standing advocacy for the use of common sense as the data base within classical research-oriented social psychology (cf. Heider, 1958). He recognized that

> while we may use commonsense psychology to advantage in the development of hunches and concepts, simply classifying the common sense we discover will not give us a psychology of interpersonal relations. (p. 7)

It is evident from what I have said before that I am in agreement with the last sentence in his quote.

Despite the almost universal recognition of the limitations of commonsense-based theories of psychological process, there is a continuing defense of its use. Lazarus (1991) argues that

> the most important rebuttal to the denigration of folk psychology [common sense] is that if one believes, as I do, that the way an individual evaluates the personal significance of encounters with the environment is a cause of emotional reactions in that individual then this is precisely the low-level and concrete explanatory theory psychology must have for the emotions. . . . The main downside of this position is that sometimes people don't know and can't describe what is in their minds, which could produce distortions of what researchers infer is happening. (p. 15).

The fact the ". . . people don't know and can't describe what is in their minds" is central to my argument that a commonsense data base for developing a theory of emotionality is flawed. My reading of the research literature on emotionality has convinced me that the emotionality researched in the psychological laboratory is a different phenomenon from the emotionality encountered in the consultation room.

The emotionality studied in the laboratory, as opposed to the emotionality worked with in the consultation room, are classified as separate entities. Lazarus (above) and most other academic theorists speak of "the" emotions and then attempt to define or describe them as static entities with universally stable meanings. The emotionality of the consultation room, on the other hand, is equilibratory process, where the experiences of feelings shift and alter their meanings to restore the person to her/his stable-state condition. For example, anger can be used to mask embarrassing sexual arousal; affection is used to mask anger; joy conceals depression. The transformational process of emotionality is at the center of psychotherapeutic engagement. The movement of emotionality is more congruent with poetry than it is with common sense reality.

Furthermore, I found that I had to be wary of the underlying biases in thinking that the use of common sense creates. It is not a data base to use uncritically. The interaction between common sense and ordinary language creates dreadful misconceptions about human nature. Common sense is a form of thinking to which most of us pay thoughtless allegiance. For the most part, it classifies everything into categories of the senses, primarily vision.

Common sense thinking attempts to classify information based on the visual similarities that exist between the things it attempts to organize. That is, if things look alike, they are put into the same category. It also analyzes problems by taking them apart piece by piece. In our search for the fundamental piece of a phenomenon, we easily lose sight of the patterns of relationship that exist between its "elements." The essence of our humanity exists in relationships—the moving relationships between neural systems, people, and social institutions. Deciphering the nature of relationships is much more illuminating when it comes to personality process than is the analysis of mechanistic "pieces" upon which personality is presumed to be built.

Analytic thinking is largely accompanied by words, which are based on the experience of our senses. It is a kind of thinking that is wonderfully powerful when we think about physical objects we can see. However, physicists (cf. Capra, 1975) have long recognized that they run into the same problems using common sense that have plagued psychologists. Both sciences have been confronted by phenomena that are not visually perceived and are not physical objects in the sense that tables and chairs are.

Common sense-based theoretical explanations are created from the skewed information of experience. Piece-by-piece experiential information is linearly arranged into an explanatory pattern designed to preserve our comfort or to avoid anxiety. I learned early in my career as a therapist that we (both my clients and myself) are not primarily interested in the truth of our explanations. We are most interested in preserving a sense of security, which is an experiential signal that our personal systems are in or near their steady-state condition. I have, with pain, learned that my sense of security is only casually related to truth.

The wonderfully funny conversation that Alice had in Wonderland while playing croquet with the Duchess illustrates the absurd lengths to which our love of common sense explanations can take us. The following quote is from the discussion the Duchess was having with Alice. Being a bright girl, Alice was puzzled by the way the Duchess related to her.

"How fond she is of finding morals in things!" Alice thought to herself.

"I daresay you're wondering why I don't put my arm around your waist," said the Duchess after a pause: "the reason is, that I'm doubtful about the temper of your flamingo. Shall I try the experiment?"

"He might bite," Alice cautiously replied, not feeling at all anxious to have the experiment tried.

"Very true," said the Duchess: "flamingos and mustard both bite. And the moral of that is—'Birds of a feather flock together.'"

"Only mustard isn't a bird." Alice remarked.

"Right, as usual," said the Duchess: "What a clear way you have of putting things!"

"It's a mineral, I *think*," said Alice.

"Of course it is," said the Duchess, who seemed ready to agree to everything that Alice said: "there's a large mustard-mine near here. And the moral of that is—'The more there is of mine, the less there is of yours'" (Carroll, 1965, pp. 132-134).

The Duchess mindlessly classified "bite" and "mine" in totally inaccurate pairs, because the letters of the words are the same. She classified the "bite" of a flamingo and the "bite" of mustard as the same thing. The mustard "mine" is treated the same as the "mine" of possession. In some respects, this kind of confabulation is similar to that which confounds psychological definition and thinking.

Common sense-based theories emerge from the immediate sensory experience we have of things. We are most skilled, experientially and cognitively, with sensory information. We love the immediate visual experience of things, like lamps and bottles and soup spoons. It provides us with the comfort of believing that we know where reality is, even though that belief may be delusional. Sufi tales, such as the one which follows shortly, tell about the absurdities that occur when our thinking is dominated by common sense. Much psychological theorizing is still hobbled by this limitation (cf. Morton, 1980 and van Holtoon and Olson, 1987).

The experience of feelings is not as secure and familiar as the experience of tea cups and coat hangers. We do not see anger, desire, or atoms. Furthermore, unlike physical objects, nonsensory phenomena are in constant flux and are changing their relationships with internal parts of themselves and with other systems with which they interact. They are not like still objects and, therefore, cannot be classified or thought about in the same way. In other words, the thinking that is most appropriate and productive in these areas is nonlinear and nonsensory. Common sense is a very clumsy cognitive tool with which to construct psychological theories or explanations because it does not organize information about patterns or relationships that move.

I first came to realize, as have other thoughtful psychologists, that the words we use to label psychological phenomena are all vaguely and variously defined. Psychological definitions arise from the ways common sense is organized. They are the labels that are applied to the experiential displays of nonsensory neural process. That is, we have a feeling or a thought or an experience of self, and we process it as though it were the experience of a wheelbarrow. Common sense-based definitions cast volatile psychological processes into classifications designed for still, physical objects that are visually experienced.

The labels and definitions of psychological processes that I use match the conceptual characteristics of this theory. The labels are similar to conventional usage, but their definitions differ from everyday meanings. Instead of using definitions constructed from common sense; I will use a functional frame of reference. The definitions of psychological processes will be based on how they *use* or manage information. The distinction that I am making between common sense and functional description is similar to the distinction that Lewin (1935) made between *phenotypic* and *genotypic* description. Instead of labeling and describing the phenomenal appearance of psychological operations, I will be labeling and describing different psychological functions. To help keep these definitions in mind, see the glossary at the back of the book.

Second, it became apparent to me that most of the common sense axioms about the nature of motivation and of psychological process were either wrong, or were, at best, half-truths. For example, psychological pain is not the deterrent it is commonly thought to be. Love is not the ultimate goal everyone seeks, and love and sex are not the same thing. Although many of the misconceptions we have about sexuality are painful and perpetuate human misery, we preserve them because they allow us to escape from the anxiety of not knowing how else to experience them.

Among its other characteristics, common sense tends to be extremely literal in its classifications and in the meanings derived from them. It makes us believe that things are what they appear to be or what we think they should be. The distinction between literal, linear cognition and nonlinear, relational cognition is illustrated in the "Unsolved" Sufi tale told by Idries Shah (1977):

> Two worthies of the Land of Fools heard that someone called the Polite Man was visiting their capital. Desiring to meet him, they went to the city's main square. Here they saw a stranger sitting on a bench. "Do you think that it's him?" one asked the other.
>
> "Why don't you go and ask him?"
>
> The first man went up to the stranger and said: "Excuse me, but are you the Polite Man?"
>
> The stranger answered: "If you don't leave me alone, I'll smash your face in!"
>
> The inquirer went back to his companion. "Well, was he the man we're looking for?"
>
> "I don't know—he didn't tell me!" (p. 69).

Linear cognition, being unable to encompass relational phenomena, omits nonlinear information. The first man in the Sufi tale was so literal and linear that he could not use the information given by his relationship with the stranger. Therefore, he could not tell whether or not the stranger was the Polite Man. As I said above, we tend to be as literal about our feelings as our Sufi friends were about the Stranger.

The same kind of literal interpretation or attribution occurs in interpersonal relationships. For example, I know a man who married a woman who was used to being treated like a queen. Unfortunately, he was not as wealthy as his wife's previous husband. On a trip to France, he found himself embroiled in fights with his wife about his casual, spontaneous way of traveling. She was dissatisfied by his unwillingness to create detailed itineraries; he was puzzled by her querulous nitpicking. He in fact, was willing to have her plan the itineraries and to participate with her in them, so her complaints did not make sense. Then he realized that he had not been taking her to first-class hotels and five-star restaurants. When he became aware of this dilemma, he better understood his wife, felt less confused, and vowed to become a wealthy man. He so loved his wife that he had compassion for her dissatisfaction.

The confusion that this man experienced is similar to that which confounded our Sufi friends. This man was so caught up with discussions about itineraries that he could not see that his wife was disappointed because he was not taking care of her as well as her previous husband had.

In both stories, the people could not process information that was being presented on the baseline of their engagements in their explanations of what was happening. I have frequently referred to the significance of explanation as an equilibratory phenomenon. The following discussion will elaborate on this issue.

The Nature of Explanation

Explanation is another of the major concepts in my theory, and my definition of explanation is an example of how meanings derived from commonsense analysis expand and change. Sometimes I use *explanation* as it is ordinarily used. However, it means more than the simple linear-descriptive or clarifying process we normally understand it to be. In addition to being a logical description of phenomena or relationships of things to one another, explanations are also metaphors, analogies, dreams, and *feelings*.

As I have suggested, explanation is an equilibratory process. Like other psychological systems, it is the display of the stabilization of neurological structures that underlie both cognition and the neurological ego. This is the emotional function of explanation. When we are in a situation we cannot explain, we are tense and uneasy until we find, or are provided with, an explanation. Then, depending on the nature of the explanation, we relax. Since they are unfamiliar, my explanations about human nature are disturbing to some.

As psychological processes, explanations have a functional purpose. They serve to equilibrate and stabilize the core brain or the neural structures that underlie the person. As intellectual operations, explanations communicate understandings about the nature of phenomena and our relationships to them.

These understandings, however, should not be equated with truth. This is an important distinction to make. If an explanation is being used for equilibratory purposes, it is not necessary to know that the explanation is truthful. Stabilization fulfills the biological purpose of the explanation. If, however, the purpose of the explanation were to create knowledge, then truth would be an essential criterion in measuring the meaningfulness of the explanation.

Both sex and explanation are omnipresent human preoccupations, because they are biologically and psychologically stabilizing processes. Of the two, I am inclined to believe that explanation is motivationally more potent than sex. One has but to observe the anguished confusions that exist about sexuality as a result of psychologically misbegotten explanatory systems to see the power of explanation.

Human beings are omnivorous explanation eaters in their attempts to satisfy equilibratory needs and insatiable affect hunger. We are especially partial to explanatory traditions that arise from sensory information. The most familiar ones use visual information or metaphors of vision. In everyday conversation, we say "I see" to convey the idea that we understand. When I was preparing to write this book, I was constantly enjoined by my friends to liberally use visual images to illustrate my concepts.

The changing forms of Western religion also illustrate the profound importance of explanation as a human need. Aside from their theological purposes, religious systems are explanations of the relationships that human beings have with one another and the world within which they live. As human beings have developed a more complex consciousness of themselves, the focus of religious belief has shifted from explanations about the nature of the external environment to explanations about emotional processes. That is, the explanatory focus of religions changes from attempting to describe the physical world within which we live to creating theories of personality.

Greek mythology described the earth as a flat, circular structure, which was divided east and west into two equal parts by the Mediterranean Sea. The River Ocean flowed around the earth from south to north on its western side and in the opposite direction on the eastern side. The gods had dominion over the sea, the earth, the atmosphere, the sun, and the moon. The movement of these phenomena occurred because the gods willed it. Control over the forces of nature was sought through prayer and sacrifices to humanlike gods (cf. *Bulfinch's Mythology*, 1978).

I have been enthralled by Jaynes's (1976) fascinating hypothesis that the early Greeks explained their motivations by projecting them onto their gods. In other words, Mycenaean man believed that his motivations were directed by the wishes of a god. When confronted with the mystery of his internal emotional processes, he explained them in terms of external phenomena that he came to believe were "real." When an ancient Greek was confused or ashamed of what he did, he would say that Zeus or some other god "made me do it." The early religion of the gods became an explanatory system to give meaning to the confusion of internal emotional processes, as well as of the forces of nature over which he had no control. (I have used Greek mythology as an example of polytheistic explanation because it is familiar.)

To carry this argument one step further, I believe that the Hebrews were unfulfilled by the explanations of social conduct used in the mythology of their time. They dismissed a panoply of the gods, and, in its stead, created a single God who had authority to decree a set of rules to *explain* and govern social conduct. The confusion that human beings had and continue to have about emotionality required them to invent a stable, external, eternal, all-knowing and powerful entity to establish a system of rules governing interpersonal commerce. Human beings have always required a conceptual banister of external rules of conduct upon which to stabilize our evanescent brains.

Primarily, religions, in these terms, was still externally oriented. It prescribed what we should and should not do in various circumstances. However, it provided little or no explanation or guidance about the mysteries of emotionality, particularly the anguish of our love and sexuality.

Christianity was the natural outgrowth of the need for explanatory systems about the nature of internal emotional and personal process. I believe that the reason that Christianity was and is so powerfully appealing is that it concerns itself with explanations about the bewildering and painful emotions of love and sex. Elaine Pagels (1989) quotes Jesus Christ, who was described in *The Gospel According to Thomas,* as saying:

> If you bring forth what is within you, what you bring forth
> will save you. If you do not bring forth what is within you, what
> you do not bring forth will destroy you.

How much more psychotherapeutic can you get?

The point of this discussion about religion is to illustrate the psychological and social importance of explanation as a stabilizing and/or a cognitively clarifying process. Unfortunately, they can be, and often are in many ways, destabilizing processes as well.

On a personal level, explanations are descriptions of the relationship of self to the situations within which "self" is operating. We experience relief and understanding when we are able to make cognitive connections between our "selves" and parts of a system. *An experience of relief occurs when a cognition is related to an experience of self and is displayed in awareness.*

This is the major reason for our devotion to awareness as a curative process. Both explanation—particularly psychotherapeutic interpretations—and awareness are anxiety-reducing processes. Most forms of psychotherapy are based on the beliefs of these properties. Experiencing and cognition are so intricately interwoven that we cognitively blend them.

When this happens, we do not differentiate between thinking and awareness.

When new information that is relevant to the person impinges upon him or her, he or she will either try to explain it in old terms or try to invent a new set of explanations. Explanation is one of the most powerful equilibratory systems that preserve the sanity and integrity of the person. Explanations emerge not from the psychological systems that Skinner, rightly, decried, but from the neurological ones that underlie our psychology and make up our cognitive systems.

To this point I have been using the words "aware," "experience" or "conscious" without defining them. The following definition of consciousness is central to understanding the operation of the mind and its relationship to the body. As I pointed out above, they are different words about the same thing, but have different definitions. It has been an extraordinarily difficult phenomenon to define. The following definition will functionally define it.

A Definition of Consciousness

There are many reasons why *consciousness* is difficult to define and describe. I will discuss four of them. First, consciousness is a nonsensory process. It has no sensory referents, and phenomena that have no sensory referents have always been difficult to conceptualize. Nonsensory psychological phenomena have been experienced as long as human beings have been sentient. We have tried to explain and define them using sensory metaphors, the most common of which have been religious ones. They are the spirits and the ghosts and the gods who operate outside our intentional control. As we progress in the description of the person, we shall see that intentionality is unreliable and unpredictable when it is applied to nonlinear/nonsensory personal process.

Jaynes (1976) recognized this when he observed that the ancient Greeks were only just beginning to develop a sense of self—that is, they had difficulty experiencing a motivating self. Jaynes pointed out that even their language was just beginning to develop personal pronouns. Because they did not clearly experience their "selves," they had difficulty articulating and conceptualizing their motivations. Instead, they attributed their motivations to gods. He describes how Menelaus, Ulysses, and the other Greek heroes believed that they did what they did because some god wanted either to save or to punish them. It is a tradition that continues into the present. You may recall that I introduced you to my "ghost." Our dependence on scientific, linear, sensory formatting makes it difficult to categorize nonsensory, nonlinear process.

The second reason for our difficulty in defining consciousness is our continuing inability to identify the neural systems that underlie consciousness. While there is evidence that the ascending reticular system of the brain stem is related to consciousness, the neuroscientist is unable to describe the neural systems in the brain that give rise to it. When we develop clearer definitions of consciousness, neuroscientists will be more specifically guided in their search for these neural systems.

Third, as I mentioned above, consciousness has also been defined as experience or awareness. This definition is circular because awareness is not conceptually defined. Rather, it is defined by the way that it is displayed in consciousness—that is, we are aware that we experience. Experiencing is a form of consciousness. In other words, we have three words referring to one another without specifying what the psychological phenomenon of consciousness/awareness/experiencing does.

Fourth, consciousness is frequently experientially and conceptually fused with other psychological phenomena. The meaning of consciousness is often blended with other psychological processes. As a result, it has been difficult to recognize that it has a separate and unique information-processing function. As a matter of fact, perception, awareness, knowing, and understanding are treated as though they were synonymous (cf. Dennett, 1991). It is for this reason that consciousness is defined as a kind of knowing. Here, classification and display are fused. When we want to let another person know that we know something, it is not unusual for us to say, "I am aware of it." Consciousness is also confused with perception, as in the case of a person saying that he or she is aware of something because she or he has "seen" it. Consciousness is also fused with personal process, as in self-consciousness, which is one of its most frequent definitions. Both Edelman (1989) and Jaynes (1976) define consciousness as self-awareness.

One of the most common fusions of consciousness with other psychological functions is the intimate but unexplained relationship between the "I" and consciousness. Hofstadter and Dennett (1981) describe this intimacy and the dilemma it causes by asking and partially answering the following question:

What makes you you, and what are your boundaries? Part of the answer seems obvious—*you* are a center of consciousness. But what in the world is consciousness? Consciousness is both the most obvious and most mysterious feature of our minds. . . . How can living physical bodies in the physical world produce such a phenomenon? Science has revealed the secrets of many initially mysterious natural phenomena—magnetism, photosynthesis, digestion, even reproduction—but consciousness seems utterly unlike these. For one thing, particular cases of magnetism or photosynthesis or digestion are in principle equally accessible to any observer with the right apparatus, but any particular case of consciousness seems to have a favored or privileged observer, whose access to the phenomenon is entirely unlike, and better than, the access of any others—no matter what apparatus they may have. For this reason and others, so far there is no good theory of consciousness. There is not even agreement about what a theory of consciousness would be like. . . .

The mere fact that such a familiar feature of our lives has resisted for so long all attempts to characterize it suggests that our conception of it is at fault (pp. 7-8).

I hope my definition will correct this "fault." The following definition is introductory and partial. I will limit myself to the discussion of the consciousness of ordinary waking life. For simplicity's sake, I will be using experiencing, awareness, and consciousness synonymously. I will not consider the consciousness of dreams, psychoses, or other altered states (cf. Fischer, 1971 for a more detailed description of other kinds of consciousness).

In my theory, experiencing means *the display of information*. Consciousness, using a visual metaphor, is like a biological television screen, or like a hologram (the three-dimensional illusion that Disneyland uses so effectively). When a television set is turned on, information is displayed on the tube. This definition is composed of visual analogies. But, obviously, other kinds of information are also displayed in awareness. Smell is displayed when the olfactory bulbs are stimulated. Sound is heard when the semicircular canals in the middle-ear are disturbed. Emotion is experienced when the hypothalamic limbic system in the core brain is out of its steady-state condition, and so on. Similarly, *when the person is confronted with information that cannot automatically be processed, it is displayed in awareness with an associated sense of self.*

I am indebted to Robert Orenstein (1973) for this part of the definition. It was he who observed that experiencing did not occur when information was processed automatically. From that observation it was an easy step for me to see that experiencing was a display function.

The experiential display system is turned on when we cannot process information automatically. When we are very skilled, familiar with, or habituated to anything, we do not experience it. When we drive a car over a familiar route, we do not experience much of the ride. We automatically stop, avoid other cars or obstacles, and turn corners without experiencing (displaying an awareness of) anything. A few moments after entering a perfumed room, we stop smelling the fragrance. Skilled tennis players react brilliantly without experiencing any conscious thoughts about what they should do when the ball comes over the net. They automatically go for it.

The Ditchburn-Riggs (1960-70) experiments on visual perception also verify the fact that when the individual adapts to information, it falls out of awareness. In these experiments, a tiny beam of light is cast on a single spot on the retina of the eye. The light is adjusted so that it moves with the saccadic (small, involuntary) movements of the eye. Therefore, the light consistently stimulates only a single spot on the retina. After a relatively short time, the subjects of the experiment report that they no longer *see* the light. In other words, they are no longer conscious of the light that is shining on their retinas.

At the personal level, the experiential shut-off mechanism plays tricks with our personalities. We all have characteristic ways of presenting ourselves. There are the "jovial gladhanders," the "dour melancholics," the "darling good guys," the "sexy sweethearts," and on and on. These presentations are learned early in childhood and are practiced and rehearsed throughout the rest of our lives. They become so automatic, and we become so skilled with them, that we use them without being aware of them. Many of these mannerisms were first formed in early childhood when they served a meaningful purpose. Unfortunately, some of them persist into adulthood. When this happens, we engage in idiosyncratic behaviors and are embarrassed when they are brought to our attention.

The kinds of information we experience about our person and our behavior are incomplete and warped. Experiencing is not like looking through a clear glass window, which permits the light of the world to enter into the dark inner space of our being. Experiencing one's self is like looking into a funhouse mirror at the amusement park. All information that is personally relevant is shaped to keep or return personal systems to their steady-state—that is, to their normative condition. "Experiencing" is a dynamic, stabilizing process that impacts cognition in three ways.

First, it holds information steady or in place when it is not automatically processed. Information is held in the display mode until it is classified, and then it can be automatically processed, and we experience a sense of relief. We usually experience classification as an explanation, and it is for this reason that we love explanations; they are tension-reducing.

Second, consciousness facilitates information storage (remembering). While it is true that we do remember things that we have not experienced, such as the drive over a familiar route, the memory of the trip is very poor. On the other hand, when we bring things into focal awareness, we more readily recall them, as focal awareness facilitates cognitive classification. When information is structured into a classificatory scheme, it is more easily remembered.

I accidentally encountered this phenomenon in my doctoral dissertation research. As part of my study, I had two groups of subjects learn the configuration of the Sequin Formboard, which contains ten simple forms such as a square, triangle, circle, etc. The board was covered so that the subjects could not see it, and they had to learn the board's configuration and forms in the board from their sense of touch and movement alone. I instructed one group to try to remember what the formboard "looked like" as they were putting the forms into it. The other group did not receive this instruction. They were simply asked to put the forms into the board. When they had completed the task, I asked both groups to draw a picture of what they thought the board looked like.

To my surprise, I discovered that the incidental learning group of normal (unimpaired) control subjects—that is, the group I had *not* asked to remember the board—was able to recall significantly more forms than was the comparable intentional learning group. I was dismayed.

Most of the psychological literature documents the fact that intentional learning is superior to unintentional learning. How could I explain this discrepant finding to my dissertation committee? I struggled with it for weeks, until I remembered that the subjects of the incidental learning group talked more during the course of their drawing. I took meticulous and voluminous notes at the time, so I went back and studied them. I was relieved to learn that I had recorded everything that the subjects had said about the forms as they drew them. I counted the forms they named. Of course, the incidental learning group named significantly more of the forms than did the intentional learning group. I speculated then, and still believe, that I had unwittingly set up the intentional group to try to directly visualize the shape of the form from their tactile experience of it. This translation is difficult for most people, who are primarily guided by vision. Most people do not have preexisting classificatory structures to facilitate the touch-to-vision translation. On the other hand, the incidental group had the freedom to transform the experience of their touch into a word, and then to draw the word. Here, preexisting classifications are abundant. Most of the words of our language are visual metaphors. They did not have to make the touch-to-vision translation. There are numerous other studies validating the idea that structure facilitates recall, and consciousness facilitates cognition.

Third and last, as I described it above, consciousness is also formatted. You may recall that in the discussion of the dyadic triangle, I described how the subject at the apex is displayed in focal awareness, and the baseline process resides in the background of experience. I likened the experience of the dyad to the figure/ground illusion that has been extensively studied by the Gestalt psychologists (Kohler, 1959). In my discussion of the dyad, I only considered the linear/nonlinear aspects of consciousness in the dyadic experience.

I believe that consciousness differs on sensory/nonsensory dimensions as well. Since there are no research studies exploring consciousness within this conceptual frame of reference, I can only speculate from clinical experience. I will repeat the observation that I made above when I described the formatting systems of the mind. The consciousness and cognition of sensory information has hard, firm boundaries, whereas the consciousness and cognition of nonsensory phenomena are much more variable and are subject to equilibratory movement occurring within the brain. I will discuss the fluidity of sensory and nonsensory experiencing more completely in the next chapter.

In this chapter, I have covered the mind, its relationship to the neurological ego, consciousness, and cognition. I also described the equilibratory function of explanation. These are conceptual foundations that are necessary for a description of how the mind emerges from the brain. Once that relationship is clarified, I can discuss emotionality and the person.

CHAPTER VII

Building a
Conceptual Bridge

In this chapter, I will build a theoretical bridge across the psychological chasm that separates the body from its mind. When it is built, we will cross it to reach our destination—a place where we can construct preliminary definitions of the person and emotionality, which will occupy the remainder of this text. This bridge is a description of how cognition, consciousness, and neurological processes combine to produce the experience of the mind. Neurological operations of the brain are transformed into cognitions about the neurological ego, which emerge into awareness as a person with a self, "reality," feelings, and emotion. In addition to theoretically describing the emergence of the mind, I will also describe why we have traditionally thought about the mind and brain as though they were two different "essences" or things.

We do not yet know enough about the equilibratory codes and the information-processing relationships in the brain to describe a structural system that could explain the emergence of psychology from brain process. Instead, I will describe a way of *thinking* about the relationship of consciousness to brain process, rather than attempting to outline the actual neurological structures from which psychological phenomena emerge.

Before we step onto the bridge, though, I want to further describe cognitive transformations, which were mentioned in chapter IV. An understanding of this process will enable me to describe why the experience of the mind and the brain are different and how these different experiences have led us to confusing conclusions about their relationship. Cognitive transformations make up the mercurial magic of our minds. They are the dances of our dreams, creativity, and delusions. They represent the balancing pole used by the mindless tightrope walker.

Cognitive Transformations

As I approach the bridge, I feel myself to be at the fantastic transition that Cortázar (1969) described in a story about a visitor at an aquarium. The visitor was studying an ancient Mesozoic fish, who was, in turn, watching him. As he observed the fish peering at him, he gradually began to experience the fish's perception of him. He was able to experience himself in the tank observing himself on the other side of the glass. When this happened he "saw" himself intently watching a two-legged creature looking at him as he swam a safe distance away from that strange human being outside the glass walls.

Cortázar's story vividly illustrates the bewitching transformational capacities of cognition. *By cognitive transformations, I mean the categorical reorganization of information. Cognitive transformation reorganizes information to match the equilibratory requirements of disequilibrated neural structures.* The fluid equilibratory structures of cognition move and change categorical classifications of information into every imaginable form. When information disequilibrates either the person or the neurological ego, it activates the cognitive system to reorganize itself or the disturbing information to match the equilibratory requirements of the destabilized system.

In the case of Cortázar's observer, his empathic capacities enabled him to move into the tank and to transform himself into the experience of being a potentially dangerous creature. The every-night experiences of our dreams are vivid expressions of the transformational process at work in the imagery of our personal systems. In our dreams, we transform the most mundane objects of our lives into fantastic images.

Transformational operations occur in all cognitive process. Transformation is applied to everything we sense in the world and everything we experience within our bodies. It is applied to the skies and to the movement of the neurological ego, which is experienced as emotion. In chapter IX, I will describe some of the transformational operations of emotionality, where anger masks sex; sex masks anxiety; embarrassment masks the anxiety of unfamiliar personal exposure, and on and on in the creative multiplicity of our spellbinding cognitive capacity.

Hellmuth Kaiser's (Fierman, 1965) concept of the fusion delusion describes the most confusing, painful, and devastating of the cognitive transformations within our personalities. The experience of attachment, within a childhood personality structure, is cognitively transformed into a desire and belief that a oneness (Silverman et al., 1982), a unity (fusion), exists between the individual and the other loved person, thing, or belief system. The combination of an unstable neurological ego and its affect-hungry attachment to a fusional belief creates intense anxieties when that belief is invalidated. In my practice, I have found that most people seeking psychotherapy do so because of the pain engendered by fusional loss.

When the person is comfortable in a familiar setting, well-established cognitive structures maintain the steady-state condition of the neurological ego. However, when a person is upset and is confronted with disturbing information, he or she will transform it or him- or herself to restore the neurological ego to its steady-state condition—that is, to restore a feeling of comfort.

An example of cognitive transformation in psychotherapy occurred when I was talking with a young movie director who had won a significant award for his work in prior years. Since that time, he had been working well, but in an undistinguished manner. The industry thought of him as competent but rather mundane.

During the course of our therapeutic work, he would tell me about aspects of professional projects on which he would be working. Occasionally, I made comments that he found useful; he incorporated some of my ideas into his work. In our conversation, he discussed the progress of a new project about which we had previously talked. It received a much better reception than he had expected. It was like old times. As he was reveling in the restoration of his success, I said, "I hope you are appreciative of the help that I gave you on it." He became outraged and told me how disgusting I was. He saw me as hungry and needy in my demand for recognition. He questioned my therapeutic integrity because I imposed my need for recognition on him. He expressed resentment at the "fact" that I always wanted to take all the credit.

I said that I was sorry that he was angry with me and that I had not intended to take all the credit. I simply wanted him to acknowledge the help that I had given him. Again, he was upset with me for being so "piggish." I was puzzled and asked him to explain to me where I had been "piggish." He told me that I looked terrible when I acted so hungry for his gratitude. I remained curious about what was so distasteful about my hunger, which I readily acknowledged. I told him that I wanted to be recognized for my good work, and that I failed to understand why he found that to be so revolting. As I pressed him to tell me more about my disgraceful conduct, he began to see that he was very uncomfortable about letting anyone know his own desire to be appreciated. Then, he realized that in the past several years he had been instrumental in helping others receive awards. As he saw that I was reflecting hidden and unacceptable parts of his self, I became less ugly to him. When he recognized his conflict about exposing his desire, he was less nauseated by me.

While the director experienced an emotional form of cognitive transformation, others shape the nature of reality and truth. Whatever form the transformation takes, it is at the service of stabilizing the neurological ego. Having described the fluid creativity of cognitive transformations, I can now start building my bridge.

Building a Bridge Between the Mind and the Body

This bridge has three spans. The first span describes the emergence of neurological process into the experience of psychology. The second span is built upon the fact that differently formatted information is experienced differently and is, therefore, cognitively transformed in a variety of ways. The third span of the bridge is composed of the relationship of the "I" of the self to the experience of phenomena. When we have crossed the bridge, we will understand why the body and its mind are experienced as being unrelated and varied phenomena.

Emergence

The concept of emergence (cf. Robinson, 1980) proposes that psychological process *emerges* from operations of the brain. Emergence, however, is described in a multitude of ways depending on how consciousness is understood. Robinson (1980) describes "emergentism" as follows:

> In psychology, it was the Gestalt psychologists, rejecting the reductionism of the empiricists, who emphasized the emergent properties of perception. A triangle, for example, is perceptually more than and different from three lines; it has a form, a cohesiveness, a "truth" that cannot be deduced from a knowledge of straight lines. Consciousness, that gray figure who has haunted

la Mettrie's machine for two centuries, would seem to be a condition that emerges from the neural mix of which our brains are made. It appears to be more a fact than a thing. In this respect, it is not unique in nature. Gravity, relativity, time—these are facts. They are conditions of nature that transform matter without being matter (p. 143).

I disagree with Robinson. While both Robinson and I recognize that brain process emerges into consciousness from a "neural mix of our brains," his conception of consciousness is very different from mine. In the last chapter I defined consciousness as the display of information, not as a ghostly presence. In this sense, it is an information-processing function of the brain. The display experientially and cognitively transforms neurological information into psychological process. When this happens, the mind emerges into awareness. Consciousness is not a "fact" that "transforms matter without being matter." It displays cognitively transformed neurological information into the experience (display) of psychological process.

The idea that brain process emerges into consciousness conforms to the findings of neuropsychology and neurological impairment. These findings verify the fact that psychological process is a function of neurological process. The classic studies of the effects of commisurectomy (Sperry, 1985 and Gazzaniga, 1985), which cuts off most of the communication between the two hemispheres of the brain, demonstrate that dramatic alterations occur in the ways we perceive and organize sensory information as a result of that operation. The lobotomy operation, which interrupts communication between the cortex of the prefrontal lobes of the brain and the core brain (the neurological ego), tragically alters the relationship of the person to his or her emotional process as well as to other psychological integrating processes.

Within another realm, the premenstrual hormonal levels of estrogen in women have profound effects on (1) mood changes—for example, depression, paranoid feelings, irritability, and anxiety; (2) associated behavioral disturbances, such as increased alcohol and drug use and suicidal behavior; and (3) illnesses related to mood changes, including migraine headaches, gastrointestinal disturbances, and schizophrenic episodes (cf. Kaplan, 1974).

The studies of Heath (1964) show that orgasm is associated with electrical discharges in the septal region of the limbic system. Olds and

Milner (1954) demonstrated that stimulation of similar areas in the rat brain produce behaviors that look like pleasure seeking. Furthermore, it is common knowledge that fantasies trigger orgasm. This is evidence that personality process has the capacity to trigger core brain operations. Heilman's (1976) brief survey of frontal lobe dysfunction reports research findings consistent with my hypothesis that the prefrontal lobes are a major residence of the person.

Sacks's (1987, 1990) clinical observations about the relationship of personality to brain process are especially relevant to this theory. He consistently points to the need to recognize the effects of brain damage on personality and the need to know about personality variables in order to understand the behavioral and experiential effects of brain damage. His observations about the importance of the self in relationship to brain damage are particularly congruent to my theory. This will be a major theme throughout the rest of this text.

My second reason for disagreeing with Robinson is philosophical. He espouses an idealistic solution to the mind/body problem. He postulates an unspecified spiritual relationship between the mind and the body. He stands in the Cartesian tradition of great neurologists like Sherrington, Eccles, and Penfield who leave the scientific tradition in their explanation of the apparent duality of the mind and the brain (cf. Sacks, 1990, for a broader discussion of this issue). They look to spirituality as the bridge that relates the body to its mind. I believe that they depart from science because they were unable to comprehend the information-processing characteristics of Robinson's "gray figure," consciousness.

Third, I do not agree with his assertion that "triangles, gravity, relativity" are "facts." The dictionary definition of the word fact is a thing or event that has an objective reality that exists independently in the external environment.

In fact, his "facts" are not facts at all. Gravity is not a thing that exists independently in the external environment. Gravity is an *explanation* about the physical relationship that exists between two objects with unequal masses. As an explanation, gravity is a cognition, not a fact. The same argument holds true of relativity, which is, in any sense, a cognitive construction about physical reality. It is a description of relationship; it is not a "thing."

The "facts" to which Robinson refers are linear and nonlinear cognitions about phenomena. Cognitions about things and relations between things are different from the things themselves. Robinson's assertion that gravity is fact is an example of cognitive transformation. The cognitive classification of gravity as an explanation is transformed into a delusional classification that gravity is a thing.

When I formulated the ideas that the mind emerges into awareness from (1) the neurological operations of the brain and (2) the formatting of cognition, I understood why we have thought about the mind and the brain as being two different "things."

Formatting and Cognition

It is obvious that the mind and the body are not experienced in the same way. The differences are based upon the ways in which they are perceived, cognized, and displayed in our awareness. The mind is experienced differently from the way our arms and legs look and feel when they move. In other words, there is a qualitative difference in the kind of experiencing that occurs in the display of sensory information from that which occurs in the display of nonsensory information. The experience of vision is qualitatively different from the experience of feeling or thinking. Furthermore, the experiences of linear and nonlinear information are also qualitatively different. The experience of stillness is qualitatively different from the experience of movement. Furthermore, formatting affects the ways that phenomena are classified (cognized).

We are in the habit of thinking that, when we have two different kinds of experience, they emerge from two different objects. We see sunrises and know that they are not milk bottles. There are, however, obvious exceptions to this type of perception. It is possible for two different kinds of information to arise from the same object. For example, the sound that an idling engine of a parked car makes is different from our visual experience of it. In this case, we have no difficulty cognitively integrating different sensory experiences. The visual image of a stationary object (a car) with the auditory image of its moving engine is readily recognized to be an auto with an idling engine. As long as the different experiences remain within the linear sensory format, they are readily cognized as different parts of the same object.

There is a striking similarity between the mind-body problem and the wave-particle problem in physics. Both are thought to be *dichotomous* paradoxical phenomena that exist in the external environment. The particle is a unitary thing—that is, a linear concept. A wave is movement—a nonlinear concept. It is possible that the *dichotomous* paradox of the mind-body and the wave-particle split arises only from the ways in which we organize information in our brain and is not a property of the external world. Since we format information in doubly dichotomous ways, we classify and experience different precepts of the same phenomenon as being fundamentally different things.

We often have difficulty cognitively integrating linear, sensory information with nonlinear, nonsensory information. It is hard for us to think of the brain—an object—and feelings or thoughts—nonlinear, nonsensory processes—as being different aspects of the same thing. This is particularly true of nonsensory, nonlinear processes that are frequently transformed into religious beliefs. Remember my ghost, as well as Jaynes's (1976) description of the Greek gods as the Trojan warriors' explanations of their motivations. If the experience of information is organized within two different formats, it will most readily be classified (cognized) as two separate and distinct phenomena.

The brain as a physical object is thought of as a thing, and so it is. The mind that emerges from it does not have sensory substantiality and, therefore, it is not generally considered a "thing." It consequently is classified into a different category. The brain and the mind are experienced in separate ways and, as such, are classified as separate kinds of phenomena.

In fact, they *are* separate phenomena. The brain is an organ of the body, and one of the operations of the brain is to display in awareness information that it cannot automatically process. The mind is the experiential display of some of the brain's autoregulatory operations. The person is an aspect of the mind devoted to the regulation of the hypothalamic limbic system—the neurological ego.

The Presence of the Person

Up to this point, I have used the word *person* as it is commonly used, without defining it. Having laid the conceptual groundwork for this word, I will briefly define it here, in order to continue my discussion on the role of the self in the classifications of the mind and the body. I will discuss the person more fully in the rest of the text.

The person is a system of cognitive formulations about the neurological ego, its disturbance, and its relationships with the external environment. These emerge into awareness as (1) self phenomena, (2) feelings, and (3) "reality." Previously, I stated that feelings and emotions are different phenomena. This definition of the person enables me to more specifically differentiate feelings from emotions. In the following discussion, I will be primarily concerned with the self in its relationships to both emotion and feelings.

Emotion is the disturbance of the neurological ego associated with an experience of self or "I." Feelings are the explanatory component of emotional experience. Feelings and emotion are usually experientially blended, which gives them a unitary quality. Theoretically, however, feelings and emotions are separate phenomena. Emotions are experiences of physiological processes associated with an experience of self. Feelings are explanations of these experiences.

Until now, I have presented experiencing and formatting as explanations of why we have had difficulty seeing the relationship between the body and its mind. One other variable plays a role in this conflict. As I mentioned above, the experiential presence of the self is the third span of the theoretical bridge relating the mind to the brain.

The Functional Significance of the "I"

The self, in the form of the "I," has a different relationship to the experience of physical objects than it has to psychological process. For example, the experience of a kettle can quite comfortably occur without its being intimately connected with the experiencer's "I." I can go into the kitchen, put water in the kettle, put it on the stove, and turn it on without experiencing myself as an intimate part of the kettle. The kettle is not a part of me, but it *is* mine.

This is not true of cognitions or feelings—that is, of mental process. One may experience a feeling without also tying that experience to a consciousness of self in the form of an "I." One can become so deeply involved in the pleasure of a symphony, an art work, or a play that the "I" is not experienced. However, once a feeling or emotion is not automatically being processed, self-consciousness occurs. Then, an "I" is involved in experiencing a feeling. If I have a thought or feeling, it is mine. I invariably think that it comes from *me*. If you will remember Descartes' famous statement, "*I* think, therefore, *I* am." My thinking or feeling is mine. The kettle is also mine. But we have two different kinds of "mine." Alice's Duchess would be delighted. These "mines" are also different, in the sense that, with feelings, "mine" identifies the feeling as arising from the essence of "me." The kettle that I own is "mine" in the sense that I have possession of a physical object not experienced as an expression of my self.

Crossing the Bridge

We can now cross the conceptual bridge that connects bodily process with psychological phenomena. The bridge relating the mind to the body takes four steps to cross.

First, nonsensory, nonlinear information about brain process is formatted.

Second, the cognitive systems either find an existing category or create a category for that information.

Third, cognitive classification is displayed in awareness.

Fourth, the classification is related to the self of the person.

When this happens, the individual has an experience of psychological process. In the case of the body, information is usually organized within a linear, sensory format; it is cognized and displayed in awareness as something that is distinct and separate from the mind. The experience of the mind is organized within nonlinear, nonsensory formats and is displayed in awareness differently from information that is organized in linear, sensory formats. Also, the body and the mind are experienced as having different relationships to the person. Ergo, the brain and its mind are thought about as being fundamentally different phenomena.

The conceptual bridge linking neurological process to psychological phenomena is completed. This is not a reductionistic explanation of the mind-body relationship. The mind is not reduced to neural operations without describing its experiential relationship to them. I have presented a neuropsychological explanation of how psychological process can *emerge* from neural process. It is incomplete because it does not attempt to describe the information-processing structures of the brain or how they interact with one another to give rise to the experience of the mind.

Despite its shortcomings, this bridge enables me to develop a theory of personality that conceptually integrates bodily and psychological phenomena. Instead of thinking about these phenomena as parallel functions that either mirror or reflect one another, psychological operations are regarded as equilibratory processes that constantly stabilize living biological systems.

This hypothesis is applicable to all psychological phenomena, and within it, I am able to construct theories of emotion and motivation that are free of phenotypic definitions existing in commonsense-based theories. Furthermore, the hypothesis of biological equilibration enables the theories of emotion and motivation to explain the intimate relationship that exists between them. I have included preliminary definitions and descriptions of the person, emotion, and feelings in this chapter because they illustrate how the conceptual bridge connecting the brain to the mind operates.

Summary and Conclusion

This chapter began with a description of the emergence of neurological operations into consciousness, which gives rise to the experience of psychological process, including the mind. Cognitions are classificatory operations that arise from brain process and are displayed in awareness as ideas, thoughts, and feelings. Cognitive transformations are modifications of ideas, thoughts, and feelings that stabilize disequilibrated neural structures.

As part of this theoretical foundation, I explained why we experience the brain and the mind differently. This experiential difference creates the mind-body duality. The explanation bridged the mind-body chasm by demonstrating that the display of linear, sensory information has experiential qualities that are different from the display of nonlinear, nonsensory information. The brain is cognitively classified within linear, sensory formats. The mind, which is the system of operations that emerge from brain process, is organized within doubly dichotomous formats. The experiential differences that arise from these formats give rise to the varied experiences of the brain and the mind. I also described the experiential relationships of the self to the body and its mind. These differences lead to the belief that they are two different things. In fact, the brain and its mind are comparable to a car and its own movements.

Having crossed the bridge that relates the body to its mind, I will describe the person and its component systems in the concluding chapters of the text.

CHAPTER VIII

The Unseen Dance

Throughout this text, I have consistently referred to the *movement* of psychological process. The task of this chapter is to define it further in order to provide a background for the description of the person and its parts.

Movement represents the activity of motivation and being. Motivation is the process within us that leads to goal-directed behavior and experience. Being is the vigilant stillness that exists in us when we are not involved in goal-directed activities. It is the incessant process of our mentation. The antique psychological term "conation" denotes this condition. It is the movement that arises from the affect hunger of the brain. Movement is the dance of life, and the dynamics of the body and its person are partners in this dance.

Three traditions of explanation endeavor to describe movement. They are spirituality, a machine model, and homeostatic equilibration. These explanations are usually structured within the linear, sensory format (common sense). It is easier to think in commonsense terms about psychological phenomena for several reasons. First, we are much more skilled in processing sensory information than we are in processing the nonsensory information of cerebral (neurological) processes. The data base of common sense is sensory information, and its explanatory classifications are about phenomena in the external environment.

Second, an external orientation saves us from the pain and confusion of having to look inward for information about our internal (personal) process. Looking inward makes us confront not only the confusion and pain of unskilled emotionality, it also forces us to face our ignorance about it. Historically, explanatory systems about psychological process have been based on hypothetical external mechanisms. Jaynes's (1976) hypothesis that the ancient Greeks explained their motivations and actions as a result of direction by the gods is an example of how we look to the outside world for explanations for our internal dynamics.

And, third, it is easier to think in commonsense terms about psychological phenomena because the vocabulary of sensory language is richer and more descriptive than that of nonsensory, nonlinear process and experience. Often when I encourage clients to experience feelings that lie hidden within anxiety, they will angrily turn on me and bitterly complain that I am making them feel stupid. It is much more comforting to look at a machine and understand the relationships that exist between its parts. This kind of examination gives us the validation of "knowing" something and having a sense of mastery. Confrontations with unskilled emotionality, a realm that lies largely outside intentional control, creates anxiety and abhorrence. Similarly, Pagels (1988) described St. Augustine's anguish concerning his inability to comprehend or control his sexual lust as a part of the "origins of sin" in Catholic doctrine.

Medieval philosophers found it more acceptable to describe the dynamics of psychological movement as the operation of a newly developing machine. This was the beginning of a long-standing tradition in Western thinking. As we grew more sophisticated, the machine model became a psychohydraulic system, then a telephonic one, and finally we are in the midst of the computer metaphor. When we employ the machine paradigm to explain our psychological process, we can either ignore our emotionality and our persons or deny their meaningfulness. I have yet to run across a consideration of the person as a significant part of our understanding of the mind/body problem (cf. Fodor, 1991). Unfortunately, machines as metaphors of psychological process are awkward conceptual tools.

Yet, most theories of personality are based upon the Cartesian assumption that we are machines. The clumsiness of this assumption lies in the fact that it confronts the theorist with two issues that have not been satisfactorily explained. First, the theorist must account for what activates the machine. Second, implicit in the machine model is an assumption that the human being is an inert object, without an inherent movement of its own.

Blackmore (1977) in discussing Descartes' dualism—a belief that the mind and the body were two distinctly different phenomena—says:

> Not the least of Descartes' achievements was his introduction of the automatic "reflex" as an extension of Aristotelian and Medieval ideas of a hydraulic system of spirit (p. 23).

This mechanistic assumption has influenced our thinking about the nature of the movement of human process from before the seventeenth century to present-day beliefs in "libido," "energies," and "tension reduction," which are presumed to serve as activators of the "machine." None of these concepts has been experimentally validated, nor are they conceptually sound (cf. Holt, 1989 and Weiner, 1991).

Classically, psychological machines are thought to be inert, nonorganic structures reluctantly activated by an external stimulus, spirit, or circumstance. Descartes described "nerves" as a system of tubes through which "animal spirits" flowed to activate our being. In other words, spirituality is invoked to jump-start the inertness of the machine body.

When I began writing about this theory of personality, I found myself walking the line that separates heaven from earth and spirituality from functionalism. Ideas about the functional relationships between psychological processes have provided me with a simpler and more scientifically testable way of understanding human nature.

The idea of functionalism compels me to think about the interactions of things that are either doing something or having something done to them. However, my conclusion at the end of the last five chapters was that psychological phenomena are simply displays of neurological operations and that, as such, they have no direct operational effects. If this is true, where does psychological functionalism reside? If the experience of psychological process is nothing more than a hologramlike display of neurological operations, then it is obvious that, in and of itself, it does nothing.

Personality does not *do* anything either. It is just a scintillating display of equilibratory neurological process. It is Fourth of July in the sky, but the fireworks remain unseen in the darkness of unexperienced neurological process. The darkness of this unseen process is too much for our biological need for explanation, which causes our automatic cognitive systems to invent explanations about how psychological processes activate experiences and behaviors, and then to find experiences that will validate these explanations.

This realization helped me understand the appeal of spirituality, which puts agency, operationalism, or functionalism into the sky above—heaven. Many believe that something must be keeping the system alive and moving. If it cannot be identified as an operating system here on earth, then with our insatiable need to explain, we assume that there must be some extraterrestrial agency responsible for it. However, this kind of explanation is not meaningful for scientific theory construction.

I finally realized that I did not have to make a choice between simplistic functionalism and spirituality. A third course is more direct. The equilibratory purposiveness of neural interactions, which I described in the last chapter, is the source of the agency or functionalism of personality. I will be using the word *functionalism* only to denote Granit's (1977) purposiveness as biological adaptation (cf. Edelman, 1989, for a more extended discussion of functionalism).

This hypothesis does not mean that psychological interventions are meaningless. Despite the fact that psychological process does not activate behavior or experience, inferences from it can provide meaningful clues about the structure of the motivational process of the individual. These clues can guide the therapist, or any other motivating person, to provide or create information that activates an interpersonal engagement. The effectiveness of the engagement, which is expressed in movement, is a function of how accurately the participants are able to read the clues that psychological information provides.

In this theory, movement emerges from the equilibratory arrangements among (1) the affect hunger of neurological systems, (2) disequilibrating information from the external environment and (3) the equilibratory interactions of the information processing systems in the person/neurological ego transaction. The homeostatic interactions of each of these processes emerge into awareness as either the process of the person or its motivation. They are cognitively and experientially blended with the self and are experienced as the desires, drives, needs and/or will of the person.

This hypothesis about the source of movement (the dynamics) of personality is so unfamiliar that I had to constantly guard against the misdirection of commonsense explanations. When I overlearned this way of thinking, common sense no longer misguided me. I wish that I had been more tolerant of B.F. Skinner, for if I had been, it would have been easier for me to rid myself of the idea that linear intentionality activated behavior. I now see personality as the ideational stage upon which our neurological demons learn to dance with one another.

The belief about the human being as an inert machine activated by spirits, energies, or the need to reduce tension held sway with Freud's teachers, Brucke and Meynert. Following their teaching, Freud conceptualized the nervous system as a passive stimulus-aversive system. This idea was the cornerstone of his theory of motivation, and it is the theoretical underpinning of the Pleasure Principle. The quiescence and pleasure of satisfaction was interpreted as the nervous system's reaction to relief from stimulation (cf. Bowlby, 1969 and Holt, 1989).

Freud's model had the characteristics of a psychohydraulic system. As I have noted, our technologies have become more sophisticated, and other mechanistic models of the mind and our psychologies have followed. Telephonic or computer systems are now used as models to explain the "mechanisms" of psychological process. All of these models are similar in that they assume that the machine does not move until it is prodded by some external stimulus. The stimulus-response model of behavioral arousal, which was popular in my academic youth, also contains the implicit mechanistic assumption that arousal is caused by a stimulus. There was the further implication that, without stimulation, there would be no arousal.

The idea of arousal carries within it an implicit assumption that before arousal there was stillness—the stillness of the turned-off machine. When we think about a living system, arousal takes on a different meaning. Here, arousal does not mean being turned on or off, but rather becomes a modification of ongoing equilibratory process.

When the steady-state condition of the person/neurological ego system is disequilibrated, equilibratory experience and behavior are activated to restore the individual to her/his steady-state condition. This describes the essence of both arousal and change in this theory.

Disequilibration, interruption, and *deautomatization* are words describing essentially the same structural process within the nervous system. When a neural system is unable to automatically process information, it can be described by one of these terms. System-incompatible information disequilibrates the system, interrupting its steady-state process, and deautomates it, creating an opportunity for change and growth. These are the conditions that are essential for personality changes, whether they occur in normal development or in psychotherapy.

In this explanation of arousal and change, external stimulation may be a trigger for the former as an accommodative or assimilative process. Arousal is, in this sense, an interruption of the ongoing automatic flow of equilibratory process occurring within the individual. For example, being robbed is an external event that disrupts the usual flow of process, and the disruption initiates an emotional reaction. There is an obvious validity to this explanation, but it tells us little about the nature of a specific individual's emotional reaction. A description of the robbery alone cannot illuminate how a particular individual will react. My emotional reaction to robbery would certainly be different from anyone else's reaction.

Furthermore, explanations of emotionality that focus on external events are limited only to the contemporary situation as the "cause" of the emotional reaction; the historical and cultural structuring of the individual's emotional system are not considered. A simple acknowledgment that an individual had a family history in a particular culture does not tell us very much about how that person will react.

If you throw a rock into a stream, you will, of course, see the water splash as the rock hits and the see resulting ripples on the stream's surface. However, the surface phenomena are all that will be experienced. You will not see the rock's effect on the dynamics of the flow of water in the stream. Similarly, thinking of emotion as a response to a stimulus, the "splash" of emotionality in the individual's emotional expression can be seen, but the equilibratory movement that flows through the structure of the person and produces his or her idiosyncratic behaviors and interpretations is invisible.

The analogy of the stream is limited and inaccurate, because the equilibratory responses of emotionality are not simply reactions to internal and external sources of disequilibria. Physical objects are affected by events that act upon them. Living process, however, is homeorhetic (cf. Piaget, 1985) or autopoietic (cf. Mahoney, 1991). That is, living process is self-regulating. It not only adjusts to events, it reaches out and grapples with them in an attempt to shape them to its structure, while also creatively changing its own information-processing structures. Both assimilation and accommodation occur simultaneously.

Personality movement is the interaction between internal and external processes. External circumstances affect the operations of ongoing internal systems. Internal processes, such as the affect hungers of the neurological systems of the person, the homeorhetic process of the neurological ego, and the structural incongruities that develop within and between these systems, are the ongoing processes that interact with external stimulation. The arousal of experience and behavior does not emerge from a stimulus-response mechanism. The assumption that we are inert machines reluctantly activated by external stimulation flies in the face of our undeniable awareness of the dreams, fantasies, ideas,, and desires that flow through us in the total absence of external stimulation.

In order to overcome this dilemma, medieval philosophers combined the machine model and spirituality within a commonsense frame of reference. Spirituality is invoked to explain the flowing, nonlinear process of psychology ignored in the mechanistic interpretations of our humanity. Psyche activates the machine. The poetry of spirituality is more descriptive of human movement than is mechanics, but it lies outside the scientific tradition of this theory. Instead of spirituality, my theory rests on the model of equilibration.

Homeostatic Equilibration

Homeostatic theories and/or theories of equilibration have the capacity to describe the flow of human process, but they are usually cast within a commonsense format, which limits their ability to take into account the transformations of emotionality. The following description of psychological movement is based on a homeostatic personality equilibration.

Cannon's (1939) definition of *homeostasis* has been criticized as being a static, closed-system balancing process. This is a common misinterpretation. He actually called it a dynamic, "open," autoregulatory system. Ideas about the stabilization of living structures have become more complex and detailed. They now include information about an active self-regulatory process.

Piaget (1970) defined *psychological structures* as "self-perpetuating wholenesses," referring to Waddington's (1957) concept of *homeorhesis* as a kinetic equilibrium in embryological development, where structural regulations and regenerations compensate for deviations from necessary paths of growth. In other words, there is within living systems an active, ongoing organizational process maintaining the integrity of these systems. Mahoney (1991) discusses Maturana and Varela's concept of *autopoiesis* as the self-organization of living systems. All of these ideas are descriptions of the entropy-resistant characteristics of living process. The work of Prigogine (1980) and the growing body of work in Chaos theory are reformulating the second law of thermodynamics, where even the movement of inorganic, nonliving systems has properties that tend toward organization and resistance to entropy. All these lines of thought provide theoretical support for the long-recognized holism of personality.

Homeostasis, paradoxically, requires both stability and change at the same moment. Change and stability are characteristics of personality, whose primary function is to regulate the stable-state condition of the neurological ego. The experience of the movement of personality is the cognitive/experiential emergence into awareness of the homeostatic relationship that exists between the neurological ego and the person.

At the phenomenal level of description, personality is frequently seen as the interplay of change and stability. As with other paradoxical phenomena, they are tricks of the formatting process of the mind. Change is classified in a nonlinear category, and stability is a linear classification. In the last chapter, we saw that the mind and the body are classified in different formats and are, therefore, thought to be different phenomena. So it is with change and stability. They can lead to the assumption of a false dichotomy that conceals the self regulating wholeness of living process (cf. Mahoney, 1991 for an extended philosophical discussion of this issue).

Ancient Chinese philosophers recognized the movement of life as having the same dualistic, oppositional characteristics that exist in our classifications of change and stability. They described this movement as the *yin* and the *yang* of human existence. They had the wisdom to see that these were two parts of the same thing. Dancing together, these elements were thought to be a dynamic, growing whole, the *Tao*. The *Tao*, or the self-perpetuating wholeness of living systems, is the central process that underlies this theory of personality. In my theory, the *yin* can be seen as the nonlinear movement of relationships that permits us to grow and create. The *yang* is the linear whetstone of information-processing that sharpens our experiential and behavioral skills, helping us to grow and change within the framework of the stable personality systems that keep us alive.

Homeostasis or *autopoiesis* are words that denote the essential movement of our personalities, which maintains the integrity or wholeness of structures or systems. Herein lies the appearance of paradox. Integrity has the phenomenal appearance of stability or stillness. However, this kind of stability is not the stillness of a stone; it is a quivering moment of vigilance. The equilibratory moment can be instantly transformed into the process of homeostatic regulation. On closer inspection, stable living systems are growing, changing, moving systems. They must be so to accommodate and/or assimilate increasing amounts of information. We grow or we die (Ainsworth-Land, 1986).

The experienced movement of psychological process represents the display of the operations of neurological systems. Movement can be classified as occurring in three different, intimately related ways. The process of the development (maturation) of neurological structures, their equilibration (maintenance), and their growth (changes) all produce movement. Growth is an equilibratory operation, in the sense that it modifies structures to fulfill their homeostatic mission more effectively. Equilibration is dependent on the way that structures are formed and how they are related to one another.

These ideas enable this theory to describe the arousal of both behavior and experience. They act as the linch-pin that connects this theory of personality to the practice of psychotherapy. One of the major goals of intensive psychotherapy is to modify the operations of personality formations that were developed in the infancy and/or childhood of the help-seeking person.

The Formation of the Person

The systems of the person mature and change throughout the course of an individual's life. They grow and interact, modifying one another and participating in the creation of new structures. The drama and creativity of the human being emerges from this movement. The development of personal systems throughout the course of an individual's life rely upon interactions similar to those involved in the development of psychomotor skills. Repetition, rehearsal, and experiential feedback stabilize and change the ways in which they equilibrate the neurological ego.

When I began thinking about the structural aspects of personality, my mind returned to the learning theories that I studied in undergraduate and graduate psychology. I received my doctorate in the early 1950s, the heyday of reinforcement theory. It is a simple, straightforward model exemplified in Pavlov's conditioning of dogs. When a stimulus of some kind, such as the ringing of a bell, is associated with a reward, such as a morsel of food, the dog will learn to respond to the stimulus in ways somewhat similar to its response to the unconditioned stimulus of food—that is, the ringing of the bell will trigger salivation. At UCLA, this was the premier theory that entranced most of my professors. However, the idea of feeding the appetitive needs of laboratory rats to reinforce learning was very boring to me.

It was difficult for me to see the relationship between feeding appetitive hunger on a reinforcement schedule and the transformations of emotionality. Nonetheless, along with my new understanding of affect hunger, the idea of reinforcement took on additional meaning. I now believe that feeding affect hunger does reinforce existing structures and/or facilitate the creation of new ones.

Having accepted this belief, I found myself once again at B. F. Skinner's side. The research literature on learning reports that positive personal validation and meaningfulness facilitate learning, the development of skill, and the creation of attachments. These findings provoked me to raise the following question: Could bonding be created by feeding the affect hunger of the neurological structures of the person and the neurological ego? I believe that it does. Bonding or attachment of systems occurs when their interaction repeatedly feeds the affect hunger of at least one of the personal systems. This repetition is similar to that which functions in reinforcement schedules of behavior modification programs.

Feeding affect hunger and *validation*, in my theory, are synonymous terms. However, there are two important differences between traditional reinforcement and validation. First, validation has to do with stabilizing the neural structures of the person and the neurological ego. These ideas are anathema to most classical reinforcement theorists, who believe that concepts about the mind, the person, or emotionality are unscientific and irrelevant. Second, traditional reinforcement has to do with feeding appetitive needs, whereas validation feeds the affect hunger of neurological structures that underlie the emergence of the person and the neurological ego. When the neural structures of the person are validated, they become stable and, over time, operationally habituated.

Reinforcement is not the only condition that produces learning. Association (contiguity) and intensity (vividness of stimulation) contribute to the creation of the durable and reliable neuropsychological structures of cognition that the person comprises. After much practice, these structures become highly reliable and change resistant. This is particularly true of systems laid down in childhood. Learning from repeated interactions with the external environment and the genetic endowments of the neurological ego are essential parts of the maturational process of the individual.

Nature and Nurture

As the cortical structures of cognition mature, they interact with the genetically based structures of the neurological ego. When these structures acquire firm and reliable neuronal connections with one another, a person emerges. At birth, the infant does not have a self. Stern's (1985, 1990) descriptions of the infant's developing experiential and behavioral structures are a welcome departure from the anthropomorphizing descriptions of infantile experience that characterized psychoanalytic theorizing. These, in turn, interact with the family and culture within which the individual is raised.

Not much is known about the specifics of the genetic contribution to the creation of the person. However, anyone who has spent time in the delivery room of a hospital has observed that at birth, infants' personalities differ from one another. There must be some genetic process that accounts for these variations.

The recent twin studies performed by Bouchard and his colleagues (1990) show that genetic endowment significantly influences the formation of intelligence and personality in the individual. In these studies, Bouchard compared groups of identical twins reared apart and together and found that there was a .50 correlation on eleven multidimensional personality questionnaire schedules for twins reared apart and a .49 correlation for twins reared together. He found: "For almost every behavioral trait so far investigated, from reaction time to religiosity, an important fraction of the variation among people turns out to be associated with genetic variation."

Genetic studies of schizophrenia (Rosenthal, 1970) and Jerome Kagan's (1989) work on the neurological foundations of temperament also evince the theory that the formation of personality is influenced by the genetic endowments of the neurological structures of the individual. There can be no doubt that genetic variables contribute to personality development.

I do not believe that specific personality characteristics are transmitted genetically. Neither kindness, nor a belief in God (Bouchard notwithstanding), nor membership in the Republican Party is transmitted in this fashion. Rather, it seems to me that broad structural capacities—such as abilities to respond to intense stimulation, ego strength, or information-processing characteristics—are inheritable. The stability and flexibility of information-processing relationships between neuro-logical systems are most likely to be the stuff of genetic inheritance.

The image of different kinds of clay comes to mind when I think about the nature of the genetic contribution to personality structures. The malleability, strength, and tempering qualities of this property are metaphorically similar to the capacity for integrating intensity, the ego strength, and the information-processing skills of the person.

Before clay is molded into art by the hands of the sculptor, or before the birth of a child, neither physical clay nor the psychological clay of personality have specific form or cognitive content. From the moment the sculptor begins to manipulate the clay, it takes shape. Also true, from the moment of birth, through the hands of physicians, nurses, and mothers (Brody, 1956) the personalities of children begin to take shape.

The specific personality structures that emerge in infants are prod-ucts of genetic endowment and interpersonal engagement. Kagan's (1989) work illustrates how nature and nurture combine to create per-sonality. His findings demonstrate the interaction of genetically trans-mitted capacities with the environment. This interaction affects the temperamental orientation that people have toward others and the world at large. He presents convincing evidence that timid and adven-turous orientations of children are a function of the genetically given underlying information-processing strengths and capacities of the neu-rological ego. He does not refer to a neurological ego, but he does show that these orientations are related to the amygdala, a part of the hypo-thalamic limbic system, which is synonymous with neurological ego.

He goes on to show that these initial orientations toward the world and others set divergent paths of personality development. These orien-tations can be modified or stabilized, depending on the kind of nurtur-ing environment within which the infant is raised. A timorous initial orientation can be modified in a child who is raised in a consistent, sup-portive, and encouraging family system. An adventurous initial orienta-tion can be discouraged in a repressive, punitive system. The kinds of structures resulting from the interaction of genetically determined capacities of the personal systems and from social molding determine what kind of person emerges.

Maturation

Maturation arises from the interaction of genetic endowment and learning. In recent years, studies of maturation have changed their focus from observing physical growth as a reliably predictable maturational product, to elegant studies describing the interactions of genetically given neurological systems interacting with environmental stimulation. These newer studies also are consistent with, and support, my hypothesis of the neurological ego.

There are two lines of investigation that use the idea of maturation as a function of genetically endowed structures interacting with environmental stimulation. The first has been described as *prepared learning*. The second investigates the maturation of neural systems.

Waber (1982) describes prepared learning in the following quote:

> The concept of prepared learning has enormous applicability for developmental research. For example, naïve Peking ducklings, who have had no previous exposure to the parent, will, in the vicinity of several birds, selectively follow the bird that is emitting the call of its own species.
>
> At first glance this appears to an example of 'instinct' à la Lorenz. Gottlieb (1975a, b, c) showed experimentally, however, that in order for this following to occur, the duckling auditory system had to be primed by the sound of its own voice during hatching. Devocalized ducklings did not show the following response at twenty-four hours of age. Gottlieb was able to restore the following response in the devocalized duck by exposing it during hatching to a recording of a sibling call in the same auditory range as the call of its parent. In yet another experiment Gottlieb found that if he waited to test until the birds were forty-eight hours old, the unprimed devocalized ducklings showed the following response with the same strength as controls. *Maturational processes appeared to compensate, but experience had accelerated the appearance of the response.* By sixty-five hours, however, the unprimed devocalized ducks had begun to show deterioration of the response, suggesting that early experience during hatching is required to maintain the maturational effect that appears without experience forty-eight hours later.

Not only is learning prepared here, . . . but learning is intimately tied to the maturational state of the animal. *Moreover, the maintenance of the mature response depends on an experiential event earlier in life* (pp. 13-14) (Italics inserted by author).

The contribution of genetic endowment and the kinds of stability and nurturance that exist for the infant determine the nature of the individual's eventual character structure and her/his ego strength. Character structure is stability and durability of overlearned personality structures, and ego strength is the ability to maintain normative consciousness, integrities of cognitive capacities, and behavioral action programs in the face of stress. In other words, ego strength is the ability to remain aware, think, and delay action under intense pressure.

I have observed that people who have suffered abuse or emotional and/or physical deprivation during infancy have the most difficult time modifying their character structures. In the early years of my work as a therapist, I found that I was able, with relatively little difficulty, to assist some of my psychotic clients to return to a normative state of consciousness—that is, to help them step out of the psychotic dream within which they were enshrouded. However, we were then confronted with characterological structures that were excruciatingly difficult to modify.

Personal structures are formed during infancy. These structures, which are repetitively rehearsed from childhood to adulthood become extremely durable. They are the most stable systems of personality; they become character structure. The specifics of this structure are displayed in the self phenomena, emotionality, and the personal reality of the individual. In the following discussion, I will differentiate between personal and objective sensory reality. Personal reality will be more extensively discussed in chapter X. It is an aspect of personality very different from sensory reality, with which it shares experiential qualities.

Maturation involves the construction of complex neural structures that result in personality formation. Rose (in Caplan, 1982) describes the maturational aspects of neurological development:

Does the brain get bigger and better in some general fashion, or do differential rates of development in various structures result in a brain that reaches maturity through successive addition of separable components? The answer appears to be, . . . that the brain matures as a collection of organs, each of which matures at its own rate. Consequently, at any point during the development of the whole brain, individual components or organs may be in quite different stages of development with respect to one another, and some components obviously reach maturity before others (p. 28).

Rose's description of neurological development is consistent with observations about personality systems, which also develop at different stages, and some reach maturity before others. Despite the continuity of development, some systems are more stable and change-resistant than others.

Clinically, I have observed that people who have suffered either emotional deprivation or abuse during infancy find it extremely difficult to modify their character structures in psychotherapy. The earlier the suffering, the greater the difficulty in escaping the traps of their attachments and fixations.

Miriam's Hunger

A conversation with Miriam, one of my clients, illustrates the concept theorized above. Miriam began her session by smiling joyfully at me. Since she had been seeing me, her life was in much better shape than she had ever hoped it would be, and her depression had significantly improved. She had lost twenty-five of the excess fifty pounds that she had wanted to lose. Her social life was improving, and she was becoming successful with her own work as a psychotherapist. She had been in psychoanalytic therapy with various therapists for the past thirty years, with moderate degrees of satisfaction. At the time of the interview, she was fifty-three years old.

She experienced her work with me as a dramatic relief from depression and its accompanying hopelessness. She was even beginning to be optimistic about developing a loving relationship with a man. She had lived in a lonely and isolated marriage for about ten years, and then the subsequent ten years were also lonely and did not provide much in the way of male contact.

I responded to her warm smile with a delighted observation about how attractive she was. She laughed, turned her head away in embarrassment, and complained that I was relentless. "I haven't even sat down and you start right off." She was referring to the anxiety and discomfort she experienced whenever her warm and affectionate feelings for me or mine for her became the focus of attention. For years she had hidden her painful shyness behind the patrician aloofness of a dowager queen.

After a moment of silence, she said she wanted to confess that during the Christmas holiday she had gone off her diet. However, after two days of transgression, she had embarked on a fast in order to lose weight. I said that I understood the temptations surrounding the holidays, but that it might be wise not to deprive herself too severely; otherwise, she might totally abandon dieting altogether.

My cautionary words were quite unnecessary; she knew more about dieting than I will ever know. However, I sensed that she was expecting me to ally myself with her self-criticism. If I had done that, she could have escaped from the discomfort of her closeness with me, and I did not want that to happen. After I encouraged her, I waited for her reaction.

Miriam responded by telling me about making a whipped cream horseradish sauce for a roast beef dinner she had been preparing. She went on and on about other minor deviations from the fast. As she spoke, I noticed that the "glaze" had passed over her eyes and that she was speaking in a monotone. Her response was only tangentially related to my comment to her. When she came to a pause in her monologue, I commented that, whenever she wished to resume talking to me, I would be available.

She again burst into embarrassed laughter, complaining and complimenting me on my sensitivity. She acknowledged that I had caught her doing something she frequently did when she was uncomfortable with the person with whom she was talking. I innocently wondered what I had done to discomfit her. She told me that she hated my mock innocence and wanted to discuss a new appointment schedule. I suggested that we wait until the end of the session to discuss this issue. She fell into an uneasy silence, and then asked me to start a conversation. I remained silent. After a few moment's pause, she said that she had frequently thought about volunteering at the UCLA School of Medicine's Pediatric Ward to care for the infants there.

Then she began to weep. Finally, she said that there were no words for the feelings that she was experiencing, as she believed that they were similar to those she had had as an infant. She felt that the painful experiences of her infancy caused her to avoid the loving feelings she was having with me at the beginning of the session.

In earlier sessions, she had described her early childhood as one with little or no physical contact with her mother, who had always been kind, but formal. Most of the physical care she received in her childhood was provided by maids or nannies. She was raised during a period when the most authoritative pediatric advice prescribed little physical comforting, no rocking or cuddling, and rigidly scheduled feeding of infants (cf. Montagu, 1971). I strongly suspect that her parents were cognizant of the conventional pediatric wisdom of the time and raised Miriam accordingly. This practice was also consistent with the constrained emotional tradition of the family as a whole. Unfortunately, the structures of emotional deprivation and unfamiliarity with loving physical contact continued to operate in her adult life.

She had become habituated to the experience of infantile isolation. Her regression to emotionally deprived infancy was congruent with the sense of emptiness that existed in her relationships with men. Her marriage, cordial though it may have been, was bereft of vivid emotional expression. Her husband was so uncomfortable with his sexual experience that he ejaculated at the moment of penetration. Isolation was much more familiar to her than the experience of pleasure that occurred when she was with me, the first man for whom she had had an intensely warm and affectionate feeling laced with her sexuality.

Miriam exemplifies the dilemma that many people experience in a loving relationship. On the one hand, there is an intense desire to love and be loved to assuage the aching loneliness that exists for most people who do not have an ongoing relationship with another individual. On the other hand, the loving experience can force the individual to confront emotions and feelings with which he or she may have had little or no training. The inability to experience feelings in an intimate relationship sets into operation childhood personal structures—that is, it activates regressive emotional experiences. These are frequently accompanied by pain. I have found that this type of regression occurs most often in individuals who were abused in infancy and childhood. The earlier in the history of the individual that the abuse occurred, the more painful the loving experience is likely to be.

All neurological systems are self-perpetuating. This includes personality systems. Those that are laid down early in the life of the individual are the most practiced, rehearsed, and reinforced, so they are the most stable and skilled information-processing personal systems. For all of these reasons, they are the most durable systems of the personality, and they have a profound effect on the way that individuals live their lives.

Habituated and Fixated Personal Structures

Personal structures are created in two ways, which are not mutually exclusive and that emerge from different social conditions, interacting in the development of personality. The first occurs in maturational growth, where genetic structures interact repetitively until a mature system has become skilled, self-perpetuating, and habituated. Personal systems become accustomed to various kinds of interpersonal emotional conditions and develop different types of information-processing skills. These differences are expressed in the three personal systems as variations of self-phenomena, emotional skills, and "realities."

Miriam's unfortunate discomfort with intimate loving experiences is an example of an habituated personal structure. She developed personal structures designed to cope with the absence of contact. Using them, she became habituated to her isolation.

Second, structures formed under conditions of unusual intensities become fixated. Fixated systems are created when an infant or very young child is subjected to either physical and psychological intensities or both. Painful physical and sexual abuse, frequently experienced pleasurably, create fixated personal structures. In addition to these abuses, one of the major causes of fixated personality structures is humiliation, a particularly painful and destructive psychological affliction.

Fixated systems are rigidly structured, requiring very specific kinds of validational response to feed their affect hunger. Without this feedback the individual is likely to experience either acute anxiety or pain. These systems are constantly reinforced outside awareness. Constancy of repetition adds to their rigidity and resistance to change. Clinically, I have found that habituated childhood structures are more readily modified than are fixated ones.

Earlier descriptions of Karen, Raymond, my friend in San Francisco, and Naomi exemplify the formation of enduring childhood structures based upon fixation. They all had intensely painful infancies and found it extremely difficult to experience vivid emotional loving experiences *as adults*. Even though they could experience sexuality, they all became extremely anxious in the face of an adult, autonomous, loving experience. They suffered from anxiety when they were loved simply for the beautiful and independent people they were.

Separateness during infancy is a devastatingly painful condition.

The most dramatic experimental evidence of this is the tragic research of Renee Spitz (1946), in which adequately fed, untouched infants suffered weight loss and depression, while equally nourished, heavily cuddled infants flourished. Obviously, the affect hunger of the brain's developing neural systems requires stimulation. The nourishing stimulation of loving, physical contact during feeding, bathing, and play are as essential to the growth and development of the person as is oxygen and food. Aloneness for adults can be a revitalizing and liberating condition; for infants, it is a painful form of starvation.

During emotional isolation, the affect hunger of childhood personality structures is not being fed, providing them with an opportunity to become reorganized. The reinforcing input of feeding personality structures with invariant information stabilizes them and maintains their integrity.

The Maintenance of Personal Systems

By *maintenance*, I simply mean mindless homeostatic regulation. We maintain the tonus of our muscular systems with physical exercise, and we maintain the steady-state condition of our nervous systems by engaging in activities that feed their affect hunger. Most of the beauty and tragedy of human nature resides in the domain of maintenance. The attachments that are essential parts of the loving experiences emerge from maintenance operations. Hellmuth Kaiser's (1965) concept of the fusion delusion is an explanation of the interpersonal dynamic that saves those of us who suffer during aloneness from despair. Living in the delusional belief that we are one with another enables us to elicit invariant feedback from the fusional other. The comfort and familiarity that are a part of daily routines arise from the satisfaction of validating exercises. Obsessions, compulsions, and addictions are all maintenance operations.

Established personal systems are automatic processes whose only purpose is homeostatic regulation. They are activated only by the equilibratory requirement of living process. *There are no motives contained in them.* They have no emotional or teleological needs. They are not driven by pleasure or life-or-death instincts. And they certainly do not have a mentality that provides a rational course to their operations. There are no homunculi hidden in their operations to determine the nature of their process. From their equilibratory imperative flow the drama and the esthetic of human nature.

Once a personal system has been formed, it becomes a self-perpetuating wholeness. Like any other biological system, it pursues its own entropy-resistant path. It requires appetitive nutrients, oxygen, temperature control, and waste elimination, as does any other physiological system. Also, its affect hunger causes it to automatically operate in ways that are likely to produce validating feedback.

The development of a system requires that it has built-in relationships with other systems to provide it with validational feedback. These systems import external (sensory) and internal (nonsensory) information. This is the operational foundation of bimodal equilibration. The duality of our mind arises from cerebral specializations that have grown from the need to process these two sources of information.

Sensory systems import validating information from the external environment. The neurological ego and the cognitive systems are stabilized by sensory information, and they also require internally generated information to satisfy their affect hunger. The affect hunger-satisfying operations of the personal systems will be described in the next two chapters.

Any system that endures increases its skill at importing information. Along with this increased skill, it becomes more stable and reliable. It operates automatically as long as it receives invariant information—that is, information that matches the receiving structure, permitting it to automatically process it. This is the "exercise" to which I have previously referred.

When a skilled system develops a stable relationship to a source of validating information, an attachment to it is formed that is indiscriminate. Systems become attached to anything that validates them—that is, they satisfy their affect hunger. When the person is consistently validated, he/she will become attached to the validator and experience a loving relationship.

Information-processing systems that are most intimately related to the sensory systems are more skilled than internal systems. For example, visual systems are more stable, more reliable, and process information more rapidly, than do emotional systems. We respond to visual inputs more accurately, rapidly and with a greater sense of certainty than we respond to feelings. Such phrases as "seeing is believing" are expressions of the stability and reliability of sensory information processing. (I will discuss this in greater detail shortly.)

Systems honed on the stable and invariant input of information about objects in the external environment are among the most change resistant of all mental systems. Since the personal reality of the individual is largely based on the sensory experience of the external environment, it is the most stable of the three personal systems. Clinically, I have observed that personal reality is used to stabilize and maintain the integrity of both the self and the feeling systems. In the next chapter, I will describe how personal reality is used to rationalize and organize the experience and behavior of the individual.

Early in my career, I found that people who suffered from borderline character disorders or who were subject to psychotic breaks had almost impenetrable realities. For example, I never tried to talk Roger out of his paranoid delusions. To attempt to convince him that there were no listening devices planted in his home would have been fruitless. Yet, when I was able to help him express angry feelings and stabilize his self system and neurological ego emotionally, he lost interest in his paranoid preoccupation. Paranoia is an example of the stabilizing characteristics of cognitive transformations, which are constant equilibratory operations.

Before I entered private practice, I worked at a number of hospitals caring for people suffering from psychotic disorders. During those years, I increasingly had the impression that the psychotic patients I saw were not disorganized. Instead, they appeared to be *over*-organized. They were preoccupied with highly condensed emotional issues.

I recall attending a staff meeting where a psychiatrist was discussing a patient who complained of hearing "voices." He told the doctor that he heard the voice clearly saying something to him. The psychiatrist asked him what the voice was saying, but the patient refused to answer him. After a few moments of discussion with the staff, the psychiatrist went on to describe the patient's attachment to his mother and her devotion to him. Upon hearing this, I suggested that the voice was calling the patient a "motherfucker." At that time, I thought that I had made a wild but educated guess. A few days later, the psychiatrist told me that my guess was correct. I now have a way of explaining that guess. The "motherfucking" voice was a cognitive transformation of the patient's complex emotional conflict about his mother.

Transformations of Personal Systems

Transformation from one cognitive system to another is one of the major maintenance operations of the person. Anger can emerge to avoid sadness. Sexuality can replace confusion. Anxiety falls in the center of attention when the person is unable to experience some other feeling. A childhood personal structure appears when an adult one cannot process stressful information.

Transformations are not confined to emotional process, though. Rather, they occur in all the personal systems. My friend in San Francisco became a little boy when she could not contain the delight she was experiencing as a young adult woman, an operation of the self system. Roger's paranoia was a transformation of his personal reality.

There is nothing intentional or "driven" in anything I have described. Transformations of self, feelings, or realities are automatic. Structures operate as equilibratory systems. When a system is unable to automatically process information, a related and more stable (skilled) system will be activated to manage the disequilibrating information. Even though structures are not driven by instincts or energies, they do have needs. These structures need to have their affect and physical hungers fed.

When a system is unable to operate automatically, either because incoming information mismatches its structure or because its affect hunger is not being fed, it will emit error signals, homeostatically activating related and more stable personal systems. Error signals can either be feedback or feedforward signals seeking equilibratory input (cf. Powers, 1973). Generally, the more stable system is the one that has existed within the personality for a longer period of time. This is an explanation of regression. In all the clinical relationships that I have described, my clients have at one point or other regressed to an earlier stage of their personality development when they were unable to cope with an ongoing situation.

Intrapersonal conflict comes into play when an infantile personal system creates interpersonal or social malfunctions. What may serve the stabilizing needs of the neurological ego may also create havoc in family relationships. For example, my client Irene's father learned to use anger and contempt as a way of avoiding the pain of loving. I believe that his rage, which stabilized him and drove his daughter crazy, was an early childhood formation.

In other words, for him rage was a regressive expression. He is a dear and caring person who deeply loves his wife and daughters. His eldest daughter was born with a birth defect that killed her. When she was born, he and his wife knew that she would die young. The other two daughters lived for years in the shadow of their sister's impending death. During these years, he would fly into chaotic rages whenever he perceived his wife and daughters to be in any kind of jeopardy. His youngest daughter began experiencing, as an adult, mild aphasias, which were later diagnosed as resulting from a minor brain hemorrhage. Upon hearing this, he flew into one of his rages, triggering his daughter to retreat into an infantile panic at the sight of her father's agony.

Both the father and the daughter automatically retreated into regressed personal structures. That these structures were interpersonally inappropriate and destructive was irrelevant. Inappropriateness has nothing to do with the automatic equilibratory response of a more skilled personal system becoming operative. When less skilled and more recently formed (adult) systems could not manage heart-rending information, the stability of childhood rage was activated. The invalidation of adult, loving personal systems was so intense that only the more skilled infantile personal systems could serve to stabilize their neurological egos. Unfortunately, this was at the expense of providing one another with the support and care that they both needed.

As is the case with other cognitive systems, early personality systems serve an ongoing equilibratory function. In a sense, they are back-up systems, automatically called into action when a less-skilled system is unable to process disequilibrating information. They continue to exist over long periods of time, and their repetition provides them with stability and skill, which is a primary equilibratory characteristic of personal systems.

The Concept of Skill

Stability and skill are essential operational characteristics of a system. Skilled systems can be delightful, aesthetic personal processes, and they can also be loathsome gargoyles. Whatever their form, they tend to be the oldest systems in the personality. Consequently, they are more practiced and validated than personal structures developed later in life.

The concept of skill is one of the most important components of this theory. I will be describing the information-processing skills of neurological structures by describing (1) the stability of neurological structures, and (2) the creation of new structures and their modification (change).

Skill is the word that denotes the capacity of a system to process information rapidly, automatically, and with complexity. A skilled system is able to maintain its integrity in the face of novelty. It also has the ability to change without disintegration in order to accommodate increasing amounts or varieties of information. The degree of skill that a system possesses is measured by its ability to transmit information reliably and automatically to cognitive and behavior systems that serve the equilibratory requirements of the person/neurological ego relationship. Skill is achieved through repetitive practice that provides invariant validating feedback to affect-hungry or disequilibrated neural structures.

Invariant feedback stabilizes affect-hungry structures and those that cannot automatically process incoming information. We are all familiar with the calming effects induced by providing a hungry child with food or a lonely child with attention. These are examples of the equilibration of feeding nutrient or affect-hungry systems.

One of the most dramatic examples I found of the equilibratory effects of providing invariant feedback to a disturbed person occurred when I was in graduate school. At the end of a testing session with a patient suffering from general paresis, I escorted her back to her ward. As we stood at the door of the ward, she became agitated, indicating that she did not want to go in. Since I was a young graduate student, unaccustomed to mollifying agitated people, I became agitated, too.

At first, I tried to reason with her. However, our communication was limited and ineffective. As I was about to physically restrain her, I remembered that whenever she experienced difficulty with me or with the tests, she happily told me that she was enjoying the loveliness of day.

I turned around and looked at the hospital gardens that lay behind us. The sun was setting, illuminating the gardens in golden autumnal light. I pointed out this beauty to her, and she calmed down, her face and body becoming more and more relaxed. By the time I unlocked the door of the ward, she turned to me, smiled, and told me that she had had a delightful time with me. I had unwittingly introduced the invariance of a set of values about beauty and gentle behavior. I had also reinforced images of affection and respect. She had been well trained, and, as a result, I was very relieved and better skilled.

Reinforcement is most effective when structures are able to use invariant sensory information that matches structures within the personal systems or the neurological ego. The feedback that sensory systems receive from the external environment is more stable and consistent (invariant) than the nonsensory feedback that physiological systems provide one another, that is, feelings are much more variable than the sight of wooden boxes. For this reason, visual information processing is much more highly skilled than emotional information processing. The dining room table looks the same morning, noon, and night. Use of stable information enables the system to become skilled—that is, to process information reliably under varying circumstances. Our anger, love, anxiety or any other emotion feels different from moment to moment and shifts with the slightest change in the social situation to which we are emotionally reacting. It is obvious that we are much less confused by sensory information than we are by emotional information. Becker (1932) elegantly described the birth of eighteenth-century philosophical empiricism as a negative reaction to the unreliability of emotional information processing and as a positive reaction to the security of sensory information.

The skill of visual information processing is greater than that of any of the other sensory systems. When any system becomes highly skilled, it operates automatically and outside awareness. When driving a car, one does not often think about the need to stay to the right of the white line in the middle of the road; one just automatically does it. On the other hand, emotional information processing is so unskilled that we can be disturbed without having a feeling. In that moment, we are upset, confused, and anxious, but we do not have a feeling. After a bit, we may begin to feel something, but often it is a guess or an approximation. Then, we frequently mistake anxiety for fear, jealousy for envy, or unhappiness for depression, or we do not know that we are furious until the next day.

We maintain skill with continuous practice. Without practice, skill levels deteriorate. Recall the debilitating effects of sensory deprivation that I described in chapter V. Skilled artists, dancers, athletes, performers of all sorts, and psychotherapists need constant practice to maintain their ability to perform at high levels of skill. Within the language of this theory, the affect hunger of the neurological underpinnings of a skilled system requires validation provided by the repeated invariant use of the system to maintain its optimal level of functioning.

All systems have information-processing skills in one degree or another. As I have indicated above, visual information processing is more highly skilled than emotional information processing. Different kinds of information formatting also have varying skill levels. Linear, sensory (commonsense) formatting is much more highly skilled than nonsensory, nonlinear formatting. Personal systems such as self concepts, feelings, and personal reality also have different skill levels.

The stabilities that skill produces underlie a variety of personality phenomena, which range from spontaneity to habituation and fixation. *Habituation* or *fixation* are terms that can also describe attachments of various kinds.

In the following chapters, I will be describing behaviors and experiences that are called by many different names, but which are different kinds of explanations of the effects of skilled systems. *Addictions* are skilled systems that allay anxiety generated by the disequilibrium the neurological ego/person system. *Obsessions* are skilled, repetitive operations that feed the affect hunger of personal systems. *Regression* is the use of a more skilled childhood structure, when mature systems are either not available or unable to automatically process information that is disturbing the individual. Multiple personality phenomena are relatively complete personal systems that have been fixated in early childhood. They reside in the background of awareness within the personality of the individual. When the normative adult person is unable to automatically process information, an earlier, more skilled childhood personal structure is activated to manage the emotionality of the situation. In other words, multiple personality phenomena are forms of regression.

Spontaneity requires a foundation of skill, from which creativity springs. The durability and automaticity of personality and neurological structures are products of the habituation or fixation of structures. The behavioral manifestations of habituation or fixation occur in almost everything that we do. Attachment, the structural foundation of love, is another manifestation of habituation and/or fixation. All of the loves that we experience are "explanations" of the attachments that we have to people, institutions, belief systems, habitats, or anything on which we become dependent to feed the affect hunger of either our personal systems or our neurological ego. Feeding the affect hunger of these systems stabilizes them and facilitates the maintenance of their structural integrity.

The homeostatic stability of all neuropsychological systems is reflected in their wholeness or integrity. The wholeness of a system arises from the stability that overlearning provides. Overlearned systems have continuing sources of validational feedback. They maintain their integrity by automatically providing themselves with validation to satisfy the affect hunger of the neurological systems of which they are composed. Resistance to change, repetition compulsion, and habits are different terms describing the same structural process. These aspects of skill will be discussed in the next chapter. The following description of change is also a brief description of the nature of psychotherapy as I practice it.

The Concept of Change

I have described only half of the structural dynamics of personality, for stability alone cannot account for the dramatic variety and variability of personality operations. Once established, personal systems operate in conditions that have changed from those that existed when the systems were first developed. From the instant of birth, infants are involved in constantly changing socializing processes. These processes operate to facilitate the individuation and separation of the child, who must cope with more and more information throughout the course of life. Changes in maturity, social position, and knowledge require corresponding changes in personalities. The freedom of adulthood requires the abandonment of the attachment (dependency) structures of childhood.

One of the most dramatic changes required of people is to learn that *the loving experience they have as adults is interpersonally the opposite of the loving experience of early childhood.* During infancy, bonding is needed and encouraged. The developing neural structures of the person require constant validational feedback in order to develop mature stability. When this occurs under ideal conditions, the child develops loving (habituated) attachments to parents. During adulthood, separateness and autonomy are essential. This change is the source of exquisite confusion for many people. In early childhood, loving attachments are essentially fusional. In adulthood, fusional relationships stifle growth.

Fusion occurs when experiential boundaries do not exist between the child and the parent (cf. Silverman, et al., 1982). When individuals with habituated or fixated attachments to their parents fall in love as adults, they are confronted with the need to differentiate between child-hood feelings and attachments and adult feelings. Yet the breaking of the fusion delusions of the fixated personality structure can be a source of unendurable pain. Throughout the course of life, we are constantly faced with having to alter varieties of attachments to ideas, feeling, explanations, things, and people. All these alterations require personality changes.

The following ideas about personality change provide a theoretical foundation for the practice of psychotherapy. These concepts describe the everyday operations of childhood personality structures. This orientation enables the therapist to observe the maintenance processes of the client's personality in the "here and now" movement of the therapeutic relationship.

Freud, in his recognition of the therapeutic benefits of interpretation, realized that cognitive input contributed to personality modification. He observed that interpretations about the relationship of the past to the present did ameliorate suffering and enabled his patients to understand the nature of their emotional pain. However, this understanding was cast within the framework of explanations or discoveries about forgotten, and later remembered, emotional relationships in the patient's childhood. Consequently, most of the analyst's interventions were limited to explanations of how infantile and childhood relationships continue to operate in the adult life of the patient.

The emotionality of the therapeutic relationship was confined to explanations based on the misconception that the patient simply transferred emotional reactions of past relationships onto the blank screen of the therapist. Transference interpretations are essentially explanations about how relationships with parents or others created expectations or expressive patterns that continue to operate in the patient's relationship with the analyst. However, no one can be a blank screen in any form of psychotherapy.

I discussed this issue earlier, in chapters II and IV, where I concluded that transference interpretations are limited, when they are accurate, because they fail to account for the effects of the therapist's personality in the relationship. They are also misleading, because they blind both the client and the therapist to the emotionality of their own relationship. Their engagement is an intensely emotional one, in which it is impossible for the therapist's person to be invisible. That being the case, he/she is also responsible for what is occurring in the therapeutic hour. Failure to accept this responsibility creates an atmosphere of unfairness that disrupts the free flow of validating information on the baseline of the dyadic triangle. When this occurs, the depth and meaningfulness of the therapeutic process are limited.

Much of psychoanalysis is bound up with explanations about how the person developed patterns of expectations, desires, and/or realities about who the person is, and about the kind of world in which he or she lives. The blank screen model of the psychoanalytic relationship limits the work of psychoanalysis to an examination of the ways that the person was formed.

Transference and dynamic explanations may be helpful in the alleviation of suffering and confusion, but they only help the client to "understand" her/his problem. Most of these understandings are linearly formatted explanations, long recognized in psychoanalysis as having limited value.

A sad joke about a stutterer illustrates both the satisfaction and limitations of linear understanding in psychotherapy. After fruitlessly searching for help, this stutterer heard about a wonderful therapist in Europe. He went there with high hopes and diligently worked with the therapist for five years. At the end of the treatment, he returned home. His friends greeted him at the airport and heard him respond to them with the same old speech impediment. Despite the stutter, he told his puzzled friends that he was deeply gratified by his work with the therapist. When they asked him to explain, he replied, "Yea yea yea yes, I I I still stut- stut- stutter, but now I know the reason why!" Unfortunately, this is not a rare case.

Knowing "why" presents two problems. First, it creates a sense of relief that misleads the individual into thinking that a structural change has occurred in his/her person, when it has not. Second, this relief encourages the client to stop looking for information about ongoing personal process. If a ready explanation is presented, the person feels that he/she has control through understanding. Unfortunately, intentional control over personal process is illusory.

I know of many people who proclaim that they earnestly and honestly want to change some aspect of their behavior and yet are much more interested in finding an explanation that will preoccupy them in order *not* to change. During a group therapy session, I had an interesting experience while observing three people do exactly the same thing with different personal processes. They all provided themselves with explanations about relationships that they wanted to change without having to alter anything within themselves.

Irene, already mentioned in chapter V, was getting married. She was also compulsively binging and becoming obese. Her family was delighted about her impending marriage and her father wanted to stage a beautiful wedding. Though her mother looked forward to buying Irene a lovely wedding gown, they could not find one that would fit. In the group session, Irene was obsessed about how to lose weight, even though she already knew how to do so. She had been involved with every weight-loss program in the city. However, she was much more interested in giving herself the appearance of controlling her weight by engaging in a weight-loss program than in experiencing the pain that lay beneath her binging behaviors.

Across the room, Harry worried about her and tried to help her with her problem, until I suggested that he knew exactly how she felt because he lived in the same morass that she occupied. He was puzzled. He acknowledged that he was a little overweight, but he was not concerned about losing it. I agreed that he was not worried about weight, but I sympathized with his desire to escape from his successful hot dog stand.

Harry was a top-notch businessman. From nothing, he had built a business in three years that provided him with an excellent living, but it no longer challenged him. He could sell the hot dog stand at a profit, or he could keep it and supervise its operations while he explored other business opportunities. His wife, who worked with him, was in many ways a better staff supervisor than he. She could keep the restaurant functioning smoothly while he pursued a more profitable and pleasurable business life elsewhere. But Harry could not go outside the business. He felt safe, secure, and bored there. Although he declared that he wanted to escape from the restaurant with the same sincerity that Irene said she wished to lose weight, he did not believe that he could leave it to explore other ventures any more easily than Irene could stop binging.

Ryeland appreciated their dilemma. He wanted to have a sense of clarity that would enable him to pursue his career and marriage more successfully. Yet he clung to his confusion because it provided him with an excellent explanation about how miserably his wife treated him. Complaining about his wife enabled him to remain attached to childhood structures, which obscured an experience of himself as a separate adult because this experience would force him to confront his essential, painful loneliness.

All three of these people were clear about *wanting* to change an aspect of their behavior and experience. After I complimented them on the honesty and sincerity of their desires, I observed that, despite their honorable protestations, they seemed committed to staying where they were, and that they used their protestations to camouflage their attachment to the status quo.

Irene wanted yet another diet program that she could violate. When I urged her to try to experience standing in front of the wedding altar before her parents as a radiant beauty, she became nauseated. Harry talked about how much control he felt when he was at the restaurant and how unsafe he felt when he left it for any substantial period of time. When I pressed Ryeland to try to experience any feelings that might be lurking in his confusion, he spent all his time describing his wife's passionate denunciations of him. Each of them had an explanatory system (an understanding) that rationalized their unwillingness to change the wretchedness about which they so earnestly complained.

Their complaints enabled them to avoid experiencing feelings existing in younger parts of their personality structures. Irene could not bear to be a beautiful bride, as long as she and her parents were still mourning the death of her sister who had died fifteen years before. Irene, the youngest of three sisters, spent her first three years in hospitals where her tragically ill sister was being treated. Early childhood formations, laced with guilt about, and anger at a dying sister, in combination with her father's rage, fixated her to a childlike position in life.

Harry's father had never been able to stand his son's brilliance. The only times that he cared for his son were when he was in trouble. At these times, his father would heroically rescue him and then complain about him to anyone who came within earshot about having to do so. His father demanded almost total dependence from everyone in the family, and any deviation from prescribed family norms invited humiliation. Harry was not yet ready to leave his father's home and risk humiliation, even though his father had been dead for two years.

Ryeland, too, had been raised in a fusional family constellation that did not foster a respectful and loving appreciation of his competence. He was a successful accountant, and his wife was an extraordinarily powerful businesswoman. One of his reasons for marrying her was the childhood fantasy that he had wherein she would rescue him from his sense of inadequacy. He believed that her success and renown would somehow rub off on him, and he would no longer feel inadequate. Of course, this did not occur. Ryeland still felt inadequate, and he was furious with his wife because she did not meet his expectations. His confusion also shielded him from the embarrassment of his own duplicity.

Ryeland understood the reasons for his discontent in the marriage. He even understood his wife's dissatisfaction with him. His rational, linear explanations about his unhappiness created no personality change, so he continued to infuriate his wife. In other words, rational understanding does not change character structure. Many explanatory systems can match some aspect of personality process and relieve anxiety without changing the process.

During my youth, I envied the tranquillity of people who held powerful belief systems. The "born-again Christian," the communist ideologue, the rational empiricist philosopher, the devout Hasid all experienced a joyous certitude that escaped me. I gradually came to realize that they all had one thing in common. They tranquilized their anxieties in their various devotions. These devotions, however, did little to alleviate the underlying tumult of their character structures.

Psychoanalysts dealt with the problem of intellectualization with the concept of "working through." They recognized the need for repetition and rehearsal of the information of insights. Unfortunately, the concept is so poorly defined that analysts are unable to determine whether a "worked-through" insight has modified a character structure or whether it has become a psychoanalytic devotion, something that provides the tranquillity of a good explanation.

The work of therapy results in greater understanding, but it is based more on discovery than on insight or deduction. Discoveries about emotional process arise from the engagements that deautomate ongoing systems. Recall Miriam's recovery of memories about her infancy, triggered by my refusal to collude with her preoccupation with holiday overeating. Naomi's anguish about the physical abuse of her late infancy occurred when I was not distracted by her seductive overtures. Raymond discovered the painfulness of love, when I refused to be alienated by his hostility.

Discovery is most likely to occur when an automated system is being invalidated. The invalidation of overlearned systems is a primary operation in the psychotherapy of engagement. Others have discussed essentially the same process, using other terms. Deikman (1975) describes the benefits of meditation as arising from the deautomatization of ongoing systems. Mahoney (1991), too, regards interruption as essential to change processes. Mandler (1984) discusses interruption as an opportunity to restructure ongoing systems. He describes interruption and change in the following passage:

> Most cognitive change involves some kind of interruption. These are essentially of two types: first, the new event that is not "expected"—that does not fit into the ongoing interpretation of the environment—and, second, the "expected" event that does not happen. While distinguishable, these two types have the same kind of interruptive structural consequences; the new event is disruptive because it occurs instead of the "expected" event, and the absence of the "expected" event implies the presence of something else that is "unexpected." In either case the ongoing cognitive activity is interrupted. At this point, coping, problem solving, and "learning" activities take place. It is apparently also at this point that the focus of consciousness is on the interruption (p. 188).

This description of interruption is similar to Inhelder et al.'s (1966) discussion of disequilibrium as an essential ingredient in cognitive development. Inhelder makes the point that cognitive disequilibrium provides the optimal condition for cognitive development or reorganization. Piaget (1985) describes the role of disequilibrilation in the following terms:

> Disequilibrium and conflict [are assigned] the same role in development. In both cases they motivate searching; without them knowledge would remain static. But in both cases also, disequilibria play only a triggering role. Their fecundity is measured in terms of the possibility of overcoming or escaping from them. It is obvious, therefore, that the real source of progress is reequilibration. . . . Progress is produced by reequilibration that leads to new forms that are better than previous ones (p. 11).

This statement describes the goal of the psychotherapy of engagement.

Deautomatization, interruption, or disequilibrium all reflect the optimal condition for personality change in psychotherapy. The current popularity of paradoxical interventions, the use of metaphors, and the increasing use of the interpersonal process in psychotherapy are exercises in deautomating cognitive/emotional systems. However, deautomatization is not enough. Active participation by the self is a necessary part of any kind of change process, including psychotherapy.

Richard Held's (1968) work on learning dramatically illustrates the importance of self-guided activity as crucial in the learning process. His experimental work shows that the individual (animal or human) learns a route or a maze more effectively when it actively moves itself through the maze. One learns a complicated route to a destination more effectively if one is in the driver's seat than if he/she is riding in the passenger's seat. When one is driving an unfamiliar route, one's attention is not only focused on the road, but one is also acutely self-conscious. In psychotherapy, clients learn more about the intricacies of their emotional structure if they are actively engaged in experiencing the process than if they are simply told about the complexities of their emotional process.

These three aspects of the psychotherapeutic process—interruption, skill formation in all three sectors of the person, and discovery—are fundamental to psychological growth and change in both the normative life of the person and in psychotherapy. The effectiveness of the dramatic interpretations of Melanie Klein (1975) and John Rosen were due more to the disruptive contact that they made by these interpretations than by the accuracy or meaningfulness of their content. Their interpretations interrupted, disequilibrated, and deautomated automatic personality structures. The interruptions created a focus of attention on self and a cognitive restructuring that facilitated emotional change.

Central to the effectiveness of interpretation is contact, which in chapter V, I described as emotional congruence between two people on the baseline of the dyadic triangle. This congruence not only facilitates meaningful informational exchange between the members of the pair, it also feeds their affect hunger. In the case of psychotherapy, the therapist is trained not to require personally validating feedback from the client. However, it is essential that the client receive a form of validational feedback from the therapist, or the client cannot use the therapist's information constructively or tolerate the invalidations of therapeutic interruptions. Baseline validation that occurs in psychotherapy feeds the affect hunger of very lonely people.

The therapeutic relationship relieves the anxiety of aloneness from which clients suffer. In the first and second chapters, I described the significance of the emotional relationship that existed between Anna O. and Dr. Breuer. It is the relationship between the therapist and the analysand that is the motor of psychotherapy. In this type of interaction, the client has an opportunity to both deautomate conflicting personality structures and to learn new personal skills. The client can best do this when the therapist requires little or nothing in the way of validational feedback. The therapist's affect hunger is best met in the excitement of the work itself. As in any other art form, the validational needs of the therapist occur in the practice of the art.

When a personality structure develops skill, it processes information automatically. Skill emerges in experience or behavior as a part of the self, feelings, or personal reality. One of the major tasks of psychotherapy is the modification of information-processing skills in the client's personality and the creation of new ones. This happens when the client, with the help of the therapist, is able to interrupt the automaticity of a skilled personality structure. This is the psychotherapeutic stage upon which I play.

When the automaticity of a structure is interrupted, the structure is displayed in awareness. The conscious display of information is intimately related to cognitive reclassification. One of the functions of experiencing is to display information until the cognitive systems can either find a classification for it or create one that will accommodate it. Information displayed in awareness will be reclassified or reorganized if it cannot be automatically processed by an existing structure. The new structure is displayed in awareness as growth or change. Mahoney (1991) describes this reclassification as the autopoietic process. I finally was able to understand the role of consciousness in psychotherapy, which confused me in the beginning of my practice, for consciousness facilitates homeorhetic reclassification.

As with insight, reclassification is not enough. New information processing structures must, as in all new learning, be practiced before they can acquire stability and skill. The reclassification of a structure underlies what I have been referring to as cognitive transformation. New structures take on new meanings and are associated with different behavioral programs.

If this is the case, then psychotherapy is not simply an explanatory enterprise. It involves repetition, interruption, feedback, and validation. Psychotherapy is more about learning to develop complex skills on the order of any other art form than it is about solving a mystery. Too often people enter therapy in order to understand why they are behaving or experiencing themselves in disturbing ways. They have been taught to believe that if they understand *why* they can solve their problem. Too often, this is simply not the case

Psychotherapy, as I know it, provides an interpersonal environment within which the client has an opportunity to interrupt the operations of automated systems, especially the childhood personality systems. The interruption and modification of automated systems enable the individual to learn new personality skills. Psychotherapy is an open environment, allowing the client to try a variety of different solutions. It also allows the client time to practice and rehearse (repetition, feedback, and validation) these new solutions until they become stable enough to operate outside the therapeutic relationship.

Summary

In this chapter, I described the movement, the being, and motivation of the person as emerging from the equilibratory relationships between (1) the affect hunger of neurological systems, (2) information entering the person/neurological ego from the external environment, (3) the skill or degree of overlearning of the person/neurological ego relationship, and (4) their cognitive transformations. The interactions of these variables are cognitively blended with the self and emerge in awareness as the person's desires, needs, and/or will.

Having described the movement of the person, I can now describe the nature of the person and its component systems. The same structural dynamics and motivational processes operate in each of the three processes of the person.

CHAPTER IX

The Person as a Whole

Adventures in Psychological Theory

Having described the conceptual and philosophical underpinnings of this theory, I can now describe the person, for as a clinician, I am better acquainted with this subject than I am with the hypothalamic limbic system. My initial superficial belief that I understood the person led me into thinking I knew more about it than I actually did. In order to theorize about it, I needed to have a definition of what it was, and I did not have one. This deficiency impelled me into theoretical adventures, which I faced with trepidation and reluctance. I much preferred to remain in the clinical domain of knowing than to venture forth into less familiar philosophical, theoretical, and general psychological areas.

The commonsense data of personal experience can be organized in ways that create inappropriate and incomplete beliefs. In ancient times, the immediate experience of our senses led us to believe the earth was flat and that it was the center of the universe. The superficial experience of our residence on earth enabled us to create explanations that became axiomatic beliefs. Beliefs such as these can be so dearly held that we are willing to kill to preserve them.

When we cannot explain our behavior, an emptiness occurs within us that can provoke such anxiety and dread that it can cause us to lose our humanity. History is tragically marred with examples such as the Crusades, the Holocaust, and even the Cold War. Aside from the socioeconomic reasons for these tragedies, social systems employ explanations about what a person is or is supposed to be to motivate the citizenry to commit atrocities and rationalize their murderous irrationality (cf. Milgram, 1974).

Explanations and beliefs are essential to our existence. We need them almost as much as we need food. When we believed that the earth was flat, we knew so little about its oceans that we "populated" them with sea monsters to explain the anxiety generated by our ignorance of their nature. The repetitious use of explanations tends to transform them into beliefs. Beliefs are embedded in our conceptions about the world and our relations with it. When they are fully engraved in our understanding, we react to them as though they were as literally real and as immutable as the stones that lace the Rocky Mountains. When our sense of certainty is attached to an explanation, it results more from repetition and its ability to stabilize our fragile psychological equilibrium than it does from truth or being in touch with what we casually call reality. Frequently, we do not differentiate between sensory and personal realities. We are devoted to explanations that provide us with a sense of certainty.

Fortunately, discrepancies in our commonsense experience of the planet created knowledge that forced us to change our understanding of its shape and its relationship to other celestial bodies. These discrepancies interrupted habituated cognitions, which created modifications in cognitive organization. We do the same with our understanding of the person. Interruptions of personal understanding activate cognitive restructuring.

I did not want to think about the lack of integration in psychological theory, but I could not progress with the theory until I could describe the functional relationships that exist between psychological processes. Even though the relationships that I have described in the preceding chapters are not worked out in detail, they have sufficient form to enable me to continue with my portrait of the person. I have described the relationships between the mind and the neurological ego. I have also described relationships among cognition, consciousness and perception—in other words, the classification, display, and import of information.

In the following section, I will describe some of the problems I encountered in my attempts to define the person. Then I will discuss a solution to the problem of psychological isolationism. Finally, I will describe the person as a total holistic cognitive construction, which involves the description of the relationships among self phenomena, emotionality, and personal reality. In the next chapter, I will describe the processes of the person and their relationship with one another in greater detail.

Problems with Defining the Person

During my early attempts to define the person, I found myself in a strange quandary. The experiences of "mind" and "person" were familiar. I knew that I had a mind. As I wrote, I could experience my *self* thinking with my *mind*. I dealt with and saw persons every day. I even knew that I was a person. Yet my inability to define what a person was confused and embarrassed me. I was a Ph.D. in clinical psychology, who had practiced psychotherapy for more than twenty years, and yet I could not define the phenomena with which I dealt every day of my life.

When I recalled that Gordon Allport (1937), a wise classical psychologist, had called attention to the fact that "person" is used in fifty different ways, my embarrassment faded. His discussion about the multiplicity of meanings of the word "person" reminded me that the same situation holds true for other psychological terms. Hampden-Turner (1981) describes sixty definitions of the mind. Natsoulas (1974) describes eleven uses of the word *consciousness* listed in the Oxford International Dictionary. In 1943, Allport described eight different uses of the term *ego*. The same problem of definition holds true of *cognition, perception, emotion,* and many other words used to denote psychological process.

Almost all the texts I have read about emotion begin with an apology about the lack of clear or consensually agreed-upon definitions of it. In the following quote, Mandler (1984) describes the continuing vagueness of definition of emotion. I now know that what he says of emotion holds true of other psychological phenomena as well. In answer to the same question that William James (1890) asked a hundred years ago, "What is Emotion?", Mandler wrote:

> Is there a cohesive psychology of emotion? And if there is, what is "its" history? I pursued these questions in volumes of histories, symposia and textbooks. It may be symptomatic that the best summary was provided by Madison Bentley. He knew in 1928 what too many psychologists still fail to accept today, that there is no commonly, even superficially, accepted definition of what a psychology of emotion is about. Not even our positivistic friends have been able to construct an operational definition. Bentley lists all of the various things that psy-

chologists do when they claim to be studying "emotion." And he concludes: "Whether emotion is today more than the heading of a chapter, I am still doubtful. Whether the term stands—in the regard of most of us—for a psychological entity upon which we are all researching I do not know. Whether it is the common subject of our investigations I am not sure enough to be dogmatic" (p. 16).

As early as 1890, William James had the same realization about the definition of consciousness. He said that we all knew what it meant "so long as no one asks us to define it." I was comforted by the knowledge that I was not alone in my epistemological confusion. Comfort notwithstanding, I was faced with the question: "Why are psychological terms so difficult to define?"

I knew that psychological terms are labels we apply to things and processes displayed in awareness. We experience ourselves engaging in a variety of psychological operations, which we label "thinking," "understanding," "learning," "dreaming," "remembering," "feeling," "knowing," "experiencing," and so on. We also experience something that we label as our "self." It occurred to me that we label psychological processes in the same way we label boxes, knives, and shoe strings—as static objects that are perceived visually.

This is the reason why psychological terms are so poorly defined. As I have said before, defining nonlinear, nonsensory process in the same way that we define linear, sensory things causes us to classify them inappropriately.

For the most part, personality phenomena are organized within linear, sensory cognitive formats and labeled as though they were things. These cognitions are then cognitively related to the self. Rarely do we experience a psychological process without also associating it with an "I," presumed to be the operator of that process. There is always an experienced "I" associated with the operation of a psychological process. "I" think, see, feel, remember, dream, and on and on. The creation of a relationship between a classification and the self gives rise to an experience of meaning, delusional though it may at times be. With this experience, we have the sense of "knowing" that William James described—that is, we can "know" without being able to define.

It is simpler to label physical objects, because their meaning is relatively independent of the validational needs of the self. All psychological processes are intimately related to the steady-state condition of the person/neurological ego, so their essential characteristics are based on their homeostatic competency rather than their phenomenal appearance. Consequently, labels attached to experiential display are irrelevant for processes organized in nonlinear, nonsensory formats.

Experienced personality processes are cognitively classified in misleading ways. We shall see that many processes that have traditionally been thought of as being different are essentially (functionally) the same. For example, I will describe how feeling and explanation are functionally equivalent. On the other hand, I will also argue that processes that have the appearance of unity are in linear reality experiential blends of two or more different processes—that is, what we ordinarily call perception is an experiential blend of the import of information, its classification (cognition), and its display in awareness.

So it is with the words of psychology. They look the same as the words that label the things of the world existing outside our skins, but psychologically they are not the same. Personal reality and sensory reality are both products of the mind. However, the mind formats them differently. When we reach into the meaning of words that describe psychological phenomena or processes, instead of hitting a hard understanding based on a solid definition, our hand disappears into a cloud of conflicting meanings.

When I first became aware of the difference between words that defined objects we visually or tactilely experience and words that define the movement of our feelings, our selves, or our personal realities, I empathically understood Alice's Wonderland.

When Alice fell into the hole running after the White Rabbit, physical dimensions lost their reliability. She could be tall or tiny in an instant. Time lost its regularity. Creatures transformed themselves from cuddly, soft pleasantnesses into enigmatic, quasi-menacing images that refused to communicate and who would appear and disappear without a by-your-leave. So it is with the meanings of personality process, especially feelings.

The Isolationism of Personality Theory

It was not until I was well into the task of writing this book that I became aware of how incomplete and scattered the underlying theory of psychology is. The metatheory of psychology is a disjointed array of concepts with little or no relationship to one another. (cf. Staats (1991) Consistent with my theoretical position, I believe that the major reason for this disunity exists as a result of the paradigmatic stance of traditional psychology. Psychology is, largely, stuck at the phenotypic level of description. We are dependent upon commonsense observations about our experience of psychological phenomena.

For the most part, our knowledge of personality is limited by our ability to experience it. We know that we have feelings, because we experience them. However, since we have no adequate theory of consciousness, we are unable to see the illusional nature of the mind. Our classifications of brain processes are limited by the way that we display them in awareness.

As we saw in chapter VI, the presentation of psychological process in awareness is a partial display of complex neurological stabilizing systems. Using only the information that is displayed in what we variously call experience, awareness, or consciousness, we labeled the processes as "perception," "sensation," "cognition," "feeling," "consciousness," "personality," "learning," "memory," etc. All these terms are vaguely and imprecisely defined. Without getting involved with the complexities of the relationships that exist between naming, classification, and explanation, I use the term *labeling* to denote the naming of an object, process, or phenomenon. Definition is a form of explanatory classification.

In addition to the absence of precision in our definitions of them, psychological processes themselves are not theoretically related to one another. Words designating psychological systems—the "person," "emotion," "self," "perception," "consciousness," "character," "learning," "defenses," "needs," and so on—are randomly strewn across the landscape of psychological literature. They lie in the ground with little or no theoretical relationship to one another.

These processes are also frequently cognitively fused because two or more processes emerge into awareness as a unity with consistency and regularity. When we see or hear something, we call that "perceiving" something. We know that we are perceiving because we label our awareness of the import of sensory information as "perception." In the first few sentences of this paragraph, I have used three different words designating three different psychological processes that are related to one another. However, we do not have a way of describing how "perceiving," "awareness," and "knowing" are related.

While it is true that under many circumstances perceiving, awareness, and knowing occur together in some psychological contexts, they also happen separately. We frequently perceive without either experiencing or knowing. One has but to recall one's unconscious ability to drive over familiar routes to know that visual information was used—that is, perceived—without having been experienced.

When any area of knowledge is dependent only upon its surface appearance, our knowledge of it is limited. As we develop concepts about the structural relationships existing within and between processes, we are liberated from the limits of phenotypic description. In this theory, experiencing, perceiving, knowing, and the person have functional relationships to one another. Each does not occur in isolation.

The phenomenal appearance of perception and learning leads us to think of them as separate processes. Instead, I propose that our experience of them is a limited display of underlying neurological information-processing operations. When we have sufficient knowledge about neurological information processing, it is speculatively possible that the import (perception), storage and retrieval (learning) of information will be thought of in entirely different terms from those that are presently used.

What is true of general psychological processes is also true of personality operations. Self, feelings, and personal reality are aspects of a single inextricably interwoven process. Having described the limitations of conventional definition and the absence of conceptual relationships between psychological processes, I will now proceed with the functional definition of the person.

A Functional Definition of the Person

The position that I will be taking as part of this definition is a variation of Descartes' often-quoted proof of existence: "I think, therefore I am." He took the experience of thinking as evidence that his person/self existed. Rather than dealing with the question of whether or not "I" exist, let us read his statement much more literally. If we do, then his statement says that our ability to think is the reason for the existence of the person, because the experience of the person is a display of a kind of thinking. In other words, automatic, undirected, nonlinear, nonsensory thinking about the neurological ego creates cognitive systems that are experienced as a person.

This idea turns traditional personality theory upside down. The person is usually thought to be the captain of the ship of individual existence. "I am the master of my fate." It is generally assumed that the intentionality of the person's "I" is the motor and rudder of behavior and experience. However, none of these thoughts or beliefs is true.

The platonic assumption that the body serves the mind is the foundation upon which most theories of personality are built. Unlike Plato's, my definition of the person is based upon its functional relationship to the brain. Cognition is an equilibratory function, stabilizing the neurological systems of the brain. The person is a system of cognitions. Ergo, the person is an equilibratory system of the brain. It has a biological function that operates in the existence of the individual. The prime directive of all living systems is to resist entropy—that is, to stay alive. This is certainly true of the neurological ego. It keeps itself alive by regulating all the physiological systems that reside below it in the hierarchy of homeostatic regulation of the body.

The biological purpose of the person is to stabilize or equilibrate the neurological structures of the brain, of which it is a part. Equilibration is, you will recall, the restoration of a biological system to its steady-state condition. However, this condition is not defined as some immobile ideal state. Rather, the steady-state condition of a biological system is a vibrant stillness in vital communication with its surroundings. The steady-state condition of the brain facilitates the continuation of its growth and change.

If what I am saying is true, our conventional understanding about the nature and meaning of psychological phenomena must be altered. Although we (our persons) are not hostage to a mindless neurological process, it is important to know how the mind is related to the body. This knowledge releases us from the prison of automaticity. The results of successful psychotherapy attest to the fact that the person can liberate itself from habituated patterns of information processing in the body.

It is irrelevant whether its processes manifest themselves either hideously or beautifully in experience or behavior. Neither goodness, beauty, nor pleasure is a significant purpose of personality operations.

The primary purpose of the person is the equilibration of the neurological ego. Its secondary purpose is the stabilization of its own personal systems.

Initially, I thought of the *person* in two different ways, without recognizing the difference between them. First, I classified it as the psychological phenomena we experience as the integrated psychological organization of the self, feelings, and personal reality of each individual. Second, I perceived it as the neurological underpinnings of the psychological organization that is experienced as the person. The first conception of the person is about the experiential display of an operating neurological system. The second is about the operating system itself.

Until I became clear about this differentiation, I confused myself by looking at these two ways of thinking about the person as though they referred to the same thing. I thought about the psychology of the person while I was intending to understand its neurological characteristics, and vice versa. I resolved this confusion by using the phrase "personal systems" to designate the neurological systems that underlie the experience of the person. The doubly dichotomous equilibratory capacities of the personal systems enable them to internally equilibrate the neurological ego, as do other homeostatic systems, *and* to engage the external environment for adaptive purposes.

A central hypothesis of this theory is that *the person is a system of cognitions about the neurological ego and its relationships to the external environment.* I have described these systems of cognition as classifications about (1) the neurological ego, which emerges into awareness as self phenomena, (2) the disturbance of the neurological ego, which emerges as emotionality and (3) the relationship of the neurological ego to the external environment, which emerges as personal reality. I will describe each of these systems in much greater detail in the next chapter.

The person of this theory is not the robust creature that it is usually thought to be. In some respects, the experiential display of the person is like a hologram, a visual representation emerging from the interactions of physical processes on a photographic plate. Unlike the visual experience that one has of an individual, involving a concrete physical body, there is no physical substance existing within the experience of the hologram. I can pass my hand through the hologram of an individual, but I cannot pass my hand through the body of that individual when we stand next to one another.

The experience of the person is the "hologram" of the personal systems. (I am using the idea of the "hologram" metaphorically.) I empathize with Pribram's (1977) interest in the hologram as a model that might be used to facilitate our understanding of brain process. Not only do the information retrieval characteristics of the hologram resemble (in some respects) remembering, but the display characteristics of the hologram may also inform us about consciousness. The interference patterns of a split laser beam produce a hologram. I am tempted to wonder if the "interference patterns" of linear and nonlinear information-processing systems of the brain could emerge as the conscious display of cerebral information. This is one of the many places in this theory that I stand at the edge of my ignorance.

Regardless of the merits of the hologram metaphor, the person is the cognitive container of our humanity: our self, our feelings, with all of their magical transformations; and our beautiful, troublesome, and confusing personal reality are blended together within it.

This tripartite classification is reminiscent of, but different from, Freud's Ego, Id, and Superego formulation. His Ego has a superficial resemblance to my definition of the person. However, even though it mediates the relationship of the neurological ego to its environment, it is not a rational executive. The Id is more like what I have classified as the neurological ego, but it is not activated by libido. It simply lives on in its entropy-resistant way until it dies. And the Superego is, within my system, the personal reality system of the person. However, it is not a harsh repressor of the Id. It stabilizes the neurological ego with whatever cognitions, values, and beliefs it has acquired in its development.

I found this way of classifying the person to be meaningful, because the three subsystems encompass the totality of the behavior and experience of the person. They are involved in all the motivations and engagements that occupy the individual. The self lies at the center of all experience and behavior. Feelings accompany practically everything that moves the person, and personal reality programs the individual's relationship with the external environment. The cognitive, behavioral, and experiential regulatory processes that I have described are aspects of the dynamics of the person. When looked at in this way, the person takes on a surprisingly neat appearance.

The Person as a 2 x 2 Matrix

The person can be diagrammed as a 2 by 2 matrix, in which the cognitive classifications about the neurological ego are organized within the linear, nonlinear and sensory, nonsensory formatting systems. In this section I will describe the holistic nature of the person, the effects of formatting on its operations, and the effects of fixation and habituation on personality process. It is the holistic nature of the three different kinds of cognitive classification that led me to see it as a single unitary system.

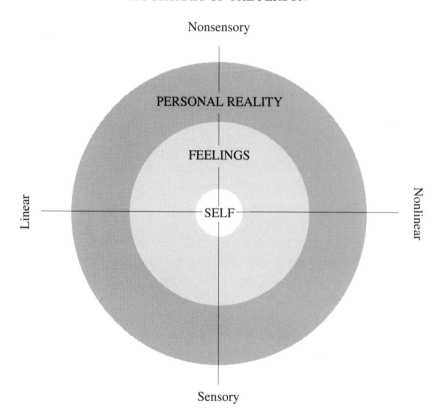

A PORTRAIT OF THE PERSON

FIGURE 5.
THE PERSON: A 2X2 MATRIX

When we think of three different parts of a machine, each part has a separate unitary integrity. For example, a gear within a machine has essentially the same structure when it is in its place in an engine as it does when it is taken out of the engine. It has the same number of teeth inside or outside the engine, and its diameter remains the same, as does its metallurgic composition. This is not true of the subsystems of the person. They are organically interdependent and do not exist as separate, extractable systems.

In the performance of everyday tasks or relationships with others, the threeness of the person is irrelevant. In the hurly-burly world of interaction, we observe a single unitary equilibrating process that encompasses three different aspects of the same stabilizing system. Escher, Cézanne, and Picasso were entranced by the experience of the unity of multiplicity. Each in his own way was fascinated by the relationship between figure and ground and the dimensionality of figures, and each tried to encompass the unity of these relationships.

The Holism of the Person/Neurological Ego

The person is a self-regulating wholeness. All three aspects of the person move together as a coordinated whole. In some respects, this idea about the person resembles a complex computer database program. For example, I have a bookkeeping program on my computer. When I write a check to the gardener, the amount is subtracted from the balance in my checking account. But that is not the end of it. The debit is also reflected in the program that tells me my net worth, and it is also added to the budget of my overall household expenses. More specifically, it is also added to the budget that tells me how much I am spending on landscaping.

So it is with the person. Modifications or inputs into any one of its three cognitive systems automatically affect and create adjustments in the other two.

It is in this wholeness that the unity of the person is experienced. The personal systems and their emergent person are related to the neurological ego as a unitary system. The integrity of the wholeness of the individual resides in the capacity of the person/neurological ego interaction to maintain the steady-state condition of their relationship with one another. When the wholeness of the person/neurological ego relationship is in its stable-state condition, experiences of control, well-being, mental health, and happiness occur.

In the following discussion, I will describe the relationships that exist between the structural dynamics of the person and the contents of the person's subsystems. That is, I will describe how holistic, formatting, and skill functions affect the operations of self process, feelings, and personal reality.

The holistic processes of the person do not only involve the wholeness of the three subsystems of the person; they also encompass the equilibratory function of the person in its relationship to the neurological ego. In this discussion, I will return to the theme of cognitive transformations and describe them more specifically in relation to self, feelings, and personal reality. The discussion of formatting will describe processes that create paradox and absurdity in personality. And finally, the discussion of skill will describe the effects of fixation, habituation, regression, repression, and alternations of personality process.

The person is a paradoxical phenomenon. On the one hand, it is experienced as a highly integrated unity, and on the other, we also experience fragmented persons within us that can be embarrassing and act as sources of dismay and confusion. The wholeness or integrity or sense of unity that we experience within ourselves arises when the neurological ego and the person are operating within their normative parameters. When the neurological ego becomes severely disturbed, the individual frequently has experiences of "falling apart" or "flying into a million pieces." The wholeness of the person that we experience does not arise from the presence of a singular "object" or system that exists within us, but from the "wholeness" of the interactions of the neurological ego and its person. This is the foundation upon which the well-being of the individual rests.

The tripartite classification of the person is not incompatible with the idea of personal holistic integrity. The equilibratory dynamics of the self, feelings, and personal reality are the same. The invalidation of any of the three systems produces the same kinds of emotional reaction. Whenever there are changes in any one of the systems, the others alter to retain the wholeness of the person. When a self-concept is modified, the individual's emotional repertoire is altered to fit these changes, and so is her/his personal reality.

Personal classifications may or may not be displayed in awareness. When they operate outside awareness, they become part of what is commonly called *the unconscious.* Even though they are not displayed in awareness, they continue to operate and affect the steady-state condition of the whole person/neurological ego system. In the last chapter, we saw how systems that were created in childhood continue to function outside awareness, becoming sources of both confusion and creativity.

One of the major tasks of psychotherapy is the illumination of the operations of childhood systems. The psychotherapy of engagement is not only concerned with developmentally created dynamics; it is also actively involved in restructuring the content and format of more mature personal classifications. Restructuring or reorganization of a personal system occurs when its automatic operation is interrupted. The experiential display of the automatic operation of any one of the systems of the person interrupts the automaticity of their operations and provides the individual with an opportunity for change.

Different cognitive structures about the neurological ego give rise to the varying experiences of the person. A self-concept and a belief about the value of birth control (personal reality) are experienced separately, and both of these are experienced differently from feelings.

However, structurally they are more similar than their content would lead us to believe. Each of them has the same equilibratory characteristics. When any one of them is invalidated, the person will experience discomfort and/or anxiety. If people are told by others that they are is bad or awful, are in error with respect to their religious beliefs, or are having feelings that they are not having, they will be hurt and offended. The same is true when the person has thoughts that violate internally structured standards about any one of the three systems of the person.

The contents of the three systems, while referring to different aspects of the person, are congruent with one another. This is another characteristic of the wholeness of the person. Self, feelings, and personal reality display different facets of the person's equilibratory process, yet the contents of these displays, under most circumstances, do not invalidate one another.

Take Jack and Henrietta, for example. They will react very differently when insulted. He has a foul mouth, claims that he is a tough guy, and knows that if you show any weakness, "they will get you." Henrietta, on the other hand, is very ladylike, believes that there are kind people "out there" who are willing to help if you are nice and are in need, and she never gets angry. Jack is skilled with the expression of anger; Henrietta is not. Jack's self-concept is shaped to permit angry expressions;

Henrietta's is designed to exclude the expression of anger. Jack's personal reality requires that he be able to express anger, while the expression of anger on Henrietta's part would violate her self-concept and surpass her emotional skills in that area of her emotionality.

These systems are congruent with one another, within a given context. Jack would never talk to his mother the way that he addresses his buddies at a bar. Henrietta could say things to her lover in the bedroom that she would never say in "polite company." The three systems of the person move with one another to shape themselves to fit the context within which the person is engaged. The "fit" is a function of the person's capacity to arrange itself to maximize validating response and minimize invalidating feedback.

People change depending on the context within which they are operating. Regardless of the changes that are made within the person to accommodate the new context, the congruency, the "wholeness," of the person is maintained.

For example, if a young man is questioned in church about his sexuality, his self-concept, feelings about sex, and social values (personal reality) with respect to this issue will be highly consistent with one another. On the other hand, if he is questioned in his fraternity house, his responses to questions about sexuality could be quite different from those he gave in church. In some respects, he will be a different person in the two different contexts. Yet the same consistency will exist among his self-concept, feelings, and social values regardless of whether he is in church or at the fraternity.

Despite the modifiability of the social adaptations of the person, there is an underlying integrity within. The momentary adaptations that a person may make do not alter the basic makeup. This integrity exists in the deeply ingrained emotional structures between the neurological ego and the emotional personal system. These systems are developed from birth onward. They are embedded in their equilibratory relationship with the neurological ego.

When, for any reason, the emotional person system is unable to fulfill this task, it will display some form of emotionality that reflects the disequilibrium of both the neurological ego and the person. The disturbance within the person affects all three of its systems. The self, feelings, and some explanation about the external situation will occur. In addition, they harmonize with one another when an individual is occupied by only one person.

People with multiple personalities switch identities in order to adapt to an interpersonal situation, when their normative person is unable to meet the emotional requirements of the moment. The ability to maintain congruity between their personal systems and the neurological ego varies for different persons. Recall the descriptions of my relationships with Naomi and the young woman in San Francisco.

The Equilibratory Operations of the Personal Systems

The essence of personality exists in its cognitive and behavioral equilibratory operations. Cognition, which formats and classifies information, serves both internal and external equilibratory functions. Formatting organizes information within the double dichotomy of sensory, nonsensory and linear, nonlinear dichotomies. Classification of information emerges in awareness as different kinds of explanation, which enables the personal systems to either accommodate or assimilate disequilibrating information. You will recall that explanation in this theory is not a simple cause-and-effect description. Feelings are a form of nonlinear, nonsensory explanation. Explanations are intimately related to "action programs."

Externally, the person initiates "action programs," which activate behavior. Theoretically, action programs are the same as the "plans" that underlie the structure of behavior and which have been described by Miller, Galanter, and Pribram (1960). Once information is cognitively organized, it activates purposive behavior.

In short, cognized information of the person provides the neurological ego with stabilizing, validating feedback. The purposive behavior, which it activates, elicits validating responses from the external environment and interrupts or modifies invalidating feedback from the external environment.

The personal systems provide validational feedback internally by triggering cognitive processes that emerge into awareness as fantasy, daydreams, internal dialogue, stream of consciousness, and self-concepts. Externally, the personal systems search for sources of validational feedback and trigger action programs enabling the individual to work, play, and engage the world. These action programs range in complexity from automatically displaying simple, affection-seeking personal presentations or complex, lifelong devotions to enterprises that are emotionally meaningful to the individual. In the pursuit of validation, we plunge into work, religion, patriotism, or just complexly playful activities, to name a few. Work, play and interpersonal engagement are the situations that provide external sources of validational feedback. Each person searches for this type of response in the two ways that I described the theory of the dyad, found in chapter III.

In terms of the dyadic triangle, validational feedback is sought through the apex of the triangle in task-oriented behaviors. The growth that occurs in productive, task-oriented behaviors provide external validation for both the person and the neurological ego. Validation is also sought on the baseline of the triangle. Self-presentations are signal systems advertising the kinds of responses that will validate both the emotional structures of the neurological ego and the cortical structures of the person. In a sense, personal presentation is a behavioral signal system organized to elicit validating feedback for both the structures of the personal systems and the neurological ego.

In addition to the search for validating feedback, personal systems activate simple or complex processes to equilibrate the effects of negative feedback. The definition of *negative* is dependent on the structure of the personal systems and their relationship to the neurological ego. Negative information invalidates the organization of a structure. The effects of invalidation are most vividly displayed when information violates the position of the "I" of the person.

Affection most vividly exemplifies this concept. For most people, it is a source of validating feedback, but I have known severely depressed individuals who experience affection with pain because their person/neurological ego systems are invalidated by love. Recall the pain and anguish that tormented Raymond when he expressed his love for me.

The equilibration of negative information can be both external and internal. Internally, these regulatory operations involve cognitive transformations, including regression, and/or modifications of experiential process, such as repression, glazing, and/or other figure-ground alterations. Externally, action programs, which underlie behavior, are used to modify or eliminate the effects of negative information.

The disequilibrated neurological ego activates the experiential display of cognitions about its relationship (1) to the disturbing situation, (2) to itself in the disturbing situation, *and* (3) to its own disturbance. These are experienced as (1) the person's *personal reality* of the situation—that is, the meaning that the situation has for the individual, (2) some self-experience such as an "I" or a "me," which orients the individual to the situation within which she/he is functioning, and (3) a feeling, which explains the relationship of the individual to the disturbance with instructions for action. These three sets of cognitions merge into the experience of an integrated person reacting meaningfully to a situation.

For example, in an anger-provoking situation, I will experience a self, a set of ideas about the meaning of the situation to which I am reacting with the emotionality of anger. Sometimes these experiences of the person are blended into simple expressions such as "I hate your guts!" The "I," which is an aspect of self phenomena, will *feel* angry and will have an impulse to do something, which is an aspect of feelings. The "I" will also have a sense of "knowing" that "I am *right and justified*," which is an internal validation. The expression of this feeling of anger is an aspect of *personal reality*. The angry experience of emotionality is the experiential display of the neurological ego's disequilibrium and its bimodal autoregulatory process. The action programs that lie behind the impulse to *do something* and the expression of the angry feelings are external equilibratory activities designed to alter the external situation. The experience of the feeling and the righteousness are internal equilibratory processes.

The experience of "I" serves as a "locator"—that is, it locates the person in relationship to the disturbing situation. When any information is not being automatically processed by either the neurological ego or its person, an "I" will be displayed in awareness. The "I" is not the display of a stable "thing"; rather, it displays the neurological ego's relationships to disequilibrating information. The "I" is always displayed in relationship to something else. That something may be anything in the environment, or some internal process, which is not being automatically classified. By internal process, I mean feelings, thoughts, or bodily movement such as stomachaches.

Feelings will be described as "explanations" and as instructions for behavior about the nature of the neurological ego's disturbance. As I have stated above, feelings are both internally and externally equilibratory. Internally, feelings are a form of explanation that provide the neurological ego with validating feedback about itself. An explanation is usually associated with a set of "instructions" for action. These take the form of emotional expression and behavioral programs designed to alter or eliminate external sources of disequilibrating feedback.

These three aspects of the person are conceptually and experientially blended, producing a sense of an integrated and unified person. This blend gives rise to the "understanding" that it is the person who is in charge and is the entity that has felt, experienced, and acted upon the information of any given situation.

Whenever the automatic operations of any personal system are interrupted, a self with a set of feelings and explanations about personal reality will be displayed in awareness. Interruptions of processing are caused by both internal and external sources of negative information. Internal incongruities within and between the linear and nonlinear formatting systems and the adult-versus-childhood formations of the person are the primary internal sources of personal disequilibrium. Any unusual movement in the external environment is an external source disequilibrium.

Repression and cognitive transformation are primary stabilizing processes that maintain the internal integrity (stable state condition) of the person. Inhibition and facilitation are the neurological counterparts of repression and cognitive transformation. I will describe cognitive transformation as a stabilizing process in the next section.

Cognitive Transformations

Anomalous information that cannot be automatically dropped into an existing category will usually be reclassified or transformed. Whales were initially classified as fish—a sensory, linear classification based on visual similarities. Later, incongruous information about the suckling behavior of infant whales violated the classification of whales as fish. They were reclassified as mammals—a sensory, nonlinear classification with a different content.

Using the same logic, personal systems can be transformed and reformatted. When people are unable to explain their anxiety, it is transformed and reclassified as fear. If there are no "lions" or "wolves" in the immediate environment to explain the "fear," as we have seen above, we can invent and project "creatures" into the environment to explain it. Ghosts, spirits, poltergeists, and heavenly projections are sensory linear reclassifications of nonsensory, nonlinear phenomena. They explain mysterious movement within us that is not perceived with our senses.

Sensory, linear classification of nonlinear nonsensory processes can have disastrous effects on the development of the person. The most tragic example of this is the reclassification of sexuality from a simple physical and complex emotional act into a mortal sin. This has led to insulting and insanity-producing interpretations of one of the great beauties of human existence.

Cognitive transformation is part of the complex equilibratory relationship that exists between the person and the neurological ego. The person/neurological ego, as a brain system, is in constant need of equilibratory regulation. Transformation is a neurological/cognitive process, whose primary biological purpose is to stabilize the person/neurological ego. The equilibratory relationships of this system are at the center of our humanity and are the source of the distinctiveness of our personalities and motivations.

The person is a changing, problematic phenomenon. Changes are displayed in awareness as moods, daydreams, night dreams, untoward feelings, and unusual and/or embarrassing thoughts. Even different persons can stream across the landscape of our everyday life without much apparent rhyme or reason. These are all moments of equilibration, stabilizing the movement of the person/neurological ego dance. They are cognitive transformations maintaining the steady-state integrity of the person/neurological ego.

Transformational process occurs in either cognitive classifications or dynamics. The information in a classification is found in the nonlinear, nonsensory explanations of our person that we use to orient ourselves in our lives. The explanations to which I am referring are the three systems of the person. Self concepts, feelings, and personal realities are explanatory phenomena. For example, if an individual becomes sexually aroused by another individual in a socially inappropriate situation (a clash between linear and nonlinear personal realities), the arousal frequently becomes transformed into an experience of anger and disgust—that is, these are explanations that rationalize an avoidance of an embarrassing self-disclosure. Structural dynamics to which I am referring are (1) alternations between figure-ground process, (2) linear and nonlinear formatting, or (3) states of consciousness.

When the neurological ego of the individual is disequilibrated (the individual is emotionally aroused), it will (automatically) search for matching cognitive structures. When found, these structures emerge as ideas and/or courses of action used to elicit validating feedback or to avoid or modify invalidating (disequilibrating) information. Experiences of hunger or thirst cause thoughts of food or water to emerge in the stream of consciousness. Or if someone treats us disrespectfully, we can either avoid them or express anger to get them to stop mistreating us.

Everything that emerges as personal process is shaped by the context within which the individual is living and the structural characteristics of the individual's personal system. Therefore, when an individual is in a situation that evokes a reaction inconsistent with his or her person or with structures of the neurological ego, he/she will attempt to find alternate cognitive structures within the person that appear to fit the equilibratory requirements of the disequilibrating situation. This is another way of describing the social constructionist view of psychological process (cf. Scarr, 1985; Gergen, 1984; and Mahoney, 1990).

Individuals are frequently puzzled by the fact that they experience themselves as the same persons, yet find themselves reacting in strikingly different ways in a variety of contexts and in varying states of consciousness. When individuals are drunk or "stoned," they will frequently find themselves behaving in very uncharacteristic ways. These persons might say, "*I* don't do things like that! It just wasn't like *me!*" Most frequently when this occurs, individuals are escaping from the excessively constricting confines of their linearly formatted personal systems. This common understanding is expressed in the psychoanalytic aphorism, "Alcohol is the solvent of the superego."

The person that emerges from drunkenness is an example of a transformation of the person as a whole. Usually, however, most of the transformations of the person occur in the emotional subsystem. Here, feelings are primary equilibrators. Conventional meanings of feelings are frequently laid aside at the service of managing or restoring a steady-state condition. When this happens, the other subsystems of the person can become disequilibrated.

I have described the transformational process of the person as changing or modifying the contents of cognitive classifications and/or the structural dynamics of the person. The next chapter will describe the contents of the person subsystems in greater detail. In the discussion that immediately follows, I will cover the formatting dynamics of the person.

Formatting the Person

Paradoxes and illusions occur when the mind is confronted with information that is formatted in two or more different ways. Usually these phenomena are thought about as philosophical dilemmas or visual illusions, but they are common occurrences in personal process as well as in philosophic discussion or visual perception.

Paradox occurs when an individual is forced by a set of formal (linear) "rules" to conceptualize a (nonlinear) *relationship* that does not and cannot conform to a linear set of rules. For example, in Zeno's paradox, the formal rule is that the tortoise moves half the distance to its destination from one position to the next. The nature of the rule creates the paradoxical conclusion that the tortoise could never get to its destination. The linear rule excludes the nonlinear spatial relationship of the tortoise and its destination, which, in sensory reality, makes the "half-the-distance rule" irrelevant.

When individuals are set to experience something within a linear format, but are forced by the nature of the information to process it nonlinearly, they experience paradox. Being set to think within a linear frame of reference, individuals have difficulty shifting to a nonlinear way of organizing information.

The figure-ground illusion has similar characteristics. When an individual experientially alternates between figure and ground, the experience of the illusion occurs as the figure experienced becomes the ground, and vice versa. When an object is visually experienced within the linear format, it is at the center of attention. While the background affects the ways that we experience and cognize the central figure, the features and psychological effects of the background operate outside focal awareness. That is, the features of the background are not "seen"; they are not experienced in the ways that objects in focal awareness are displayed. The central object is seen as a separate, static thing, even though it may be moving. The experiential and cognitive processing of a background is the processing of *the relationship* between the central figure and the surrounding within which it is set. The experience of background is a visual, nonlinear process, which has experiential characteristics that are different from focal (linear) experiencing. In other words, the experience of attention (focal awareness) has different experiential and cognitive consequences than does the experience of ground (nonlinear) process.

Our relationships with one another in the dyad involve the figure-ground process. In every engagement we have with another person, we figurally attend to the content of what she/he is saying and at the same time we are affected by the ways we are validated on the baseline of the dyadic triangle. Throughout most conversations, we guide one another nonverbally with our smiles, nods, shakes, frowns, and grimaces. All this occurs on the baseline, in the background of our awareness.

The formatting of psychological information is not limited to visual or philosophical information, though. All psychological information is organized within the four formats that I have previously described. We are much more skilled and familiar with the experiencing of linear process than we are with nonlinear process. Consequently, information that is organized within the linear formatting system is more likely to be used for equilibratory purposes than information that is nonlinearly formatted. This is true of any cognitive construction.

The differences between linear and nonlinear personal processes cause confusion and are major sources of agony and alienation in loving relationships. A man or woman may be dedicated to the idea (a linear conception) that he or she is a "good, decent, and loving" person, devoted to the well-being of his or her mate. This linear idea requires behaviors that are based upon "rules" of what "goodness" or "lovingness" should be, regardless of who the other person is or what is actually happening in the relationship. These rules are, within the framework of this theory, expressions of the individual's personal reality.

The loving relationship is frequently confounded by the dichotomous formatting and experiential operations of the mind, as well as by the usual dynamics of personality. Dynamics are the transformational movements of the classifications of the three subsystems of the person that are learned as the fetus matures from infancy through childhood. The confounding dynamics to which I am referring are the classifications that have become either habituated or fixated during childhood. Our interactions with mothers, fathers, siblings, families, schools, and the culture at large are integrated into explanatory systems that describe who we are, what the disturbance of the neurological ego means, and what our relationship "is" to the external environment. In using quotation marks around "is," I am indicating that the definition of the relationship to the world is a function of the personal reality of the individual. Personal dynamics are, therefore, the equilibratory operations of formatted classifications of the person.

When any of the three personal systems is either invalidated or violated, the person experiences injury, pain, and anger. Insulting a person or incorrectly telling a person what she/he is feeling or thinking are examples of personal invalidation. When this type of behavior happens, the other person's unique individuality is ignored or not seen.

Depending upon the emotional skills and repertoire of the invalidated person, she/he will experience some variants of insult, humiliation, or anger at the linear other. The pain of invalidation is the experience of emotionality of the neurological ego interacting with the person. When the relationship is undervalued and injury results from it, the invalidating person is frequently nonplussed and angered by the accusation of being a "bad" person. That injuring party's personal reality becomes violated, and he or she is disequilibrated. How could the other person feel upset, when everything that is being done supposedly comes from the "goodness" of "my" intentions? In some respects, the injuring party is in the position of kicking the other in the shins and then becoming offended when the kicked person grimaces with pain and becomes angry at the mistreatment.

Let me put this set of ideas more concretely. I love my youngest son dearly, and I am a good father. For his sake, I want him to be fit and healthy. Therefore, I believe that he should go to bed every night at 9:30. Even though I am aware that he is a rock musician, I know that it is more important that he get a good night's sleep than that he stay up all night and carouse with his friends, who, in my opinion, are worthless. Everything that I do in relationship to him is for his own happiness. It is very important to me to be a good father, because I had a bad father, and I do not want to make the same mistakes that he made with me. Furthermore, my son's health and well-being are most important at this developmental stage of his life.

Despite my caring, he is angry with me, which greatly hurts me. He calls me terrible names and accuses me unjustly of being a bad father. He is totally wrong about me. He must not love me as much as I do him. What did I do to raise such a bad son? If he were a good son, he would clearly see how important he is to me and how much I want to be good to him and want him to be happy. He is terribly mean to me, and when I try to show him how mean he is, he becomes furious with me. I do not know why he insults me so much!

In my linear concern with being a "good" father, "I" and my personal reality are at the center of my attention (figural experiencing). I am blind to the existence of my son's person and to his relationship with me. My single-minded focus on his physical fitness is at the service of (1) my conception of myself as a good father (this reflects the operations of both my self system and personal reality), (2) my fusional possessiveness of him (a dependency-based love in the feeling system), and (3) my preoccupation with my struggle with my own father (a childhood formation) that continues to destabilize me in my present-day life.

This linear focus on my own personal process prevents me from seeing my son's striving to achieve both excellence and autonomy as a part of his relationship with me. When I treat him the way I do, I insult and hurt him, and I deprive him of the emotional support and validation that are more important for a maturing adolescent than a good night's sleep. I further heap insult on injury when I become offended and punish him with guilt for expressing his pain and anger about my blind, restrictive attempts to confine him.

When one individual conceives of his or her *self* and his or her relationships with others only within a linear format and is blind to the relationship and the integrity of the other person, emotional pain results. In terms of the theory of the dyadic triangle, an exclusive focus on apical issues and a dismissal of baseline process creates interpersonal injury. This is one of the most common and painful sources of conflict between two people. It not unusual to see both of them unwittingly humiliate the other. In the language of this theory, my experienced "I" (an aspect of self phenomena) is linearly formatted with a linearly formatted personal reality that I am a good father. When my son invalidates that personal reality and tells me that I am bad father, I feel (the feeling aspect of the person) as hurt and humiliated as he is, for the same reasons.

The following account of a psychotherapy session with a client will further illustrate how the formatting of linear and nonlinear personal systems and their experiential displays as figure and ground operate within the individual. In this case, my client's dependency upon his linear personal systems contributes to his alienation and affect hunger.

Sam's Dilemma

Sam began the session by pulling out a "do-it-yourself" paperback on time management. He felt that the book had great merit but that there was something wrong with him that prevented him from using it effectively. He believed that his problem was that he could not decide what his priorities were. The key to using the book's wisdom lay in his ability to rank the importance of his weekly activities. He complained that he was bored most of the time and that nothing was important.

He then turned to me and demanded that I help him solve his difficulty with determining priorities so that he could organize his time effectively, which would allow him more time for pleasurable activities and thereby end his boredom. In the previous two sessions he had expressed dissatisfaction with me and my work with him, complaining that he wanted to see some "practical" results come from the work that we had been doing. All that "stuff about feelings" might have been a bit helpful, but it made him uncomfortable, and he did not understand it too well.

I laughed and teased him about trying to seduce me into leaving my therapeutic task and becoming his counselor. Then, with mock reluctance, I said that I would forsake honor and do his bidding. After answering a series of questions, he was able to consider reducing his work schedule to thirty hours a week. But then it struck him that this would not be possible because Helen, his girlfriend and employee, had to work forty hours a week. He could not go out and play while she stayed in the office and worked!

He went on to complain that he felt burdened by his relationship with her. He was not as excited as he had been when he was first infatuated with her, which brought on feelings of guilt and resentment. His frustration and unhappiness were compounded by feelings of obligation, which prevented him from seeking sexual relations with other women.

I noticed that during this part of the discussion, he had become more animated and interested in the issues about which we were talking. Observing his emotionality on the baseline of our triangle, I applauded him for his ability to show me the nature of his highest priority. He looked puzzled and asked me to tell him what I had seen. I said that more than anything else, he wished to spend his time complaining and making some woman responsible for the wretchedness of his existence. He protested that he did not understand me. I reminded him of what he had told me about his ex-wife, Marjorie. He then realized that he held both women, who incidentally were the only women with whom he had had an intimate relationship, responsible for the boredom in his life.

Instead of being grateful to me for being so obedient and helpful to him, he told me that he was "pissed off" at me. He acknowledged the relevance and accuracy of my observation, but that only fueled the fire of his resentment toward me. His ingratitude did not deter my sympathy. I told him I was sorry that I had angered him, and asked him to tell me as specifically as he could what I had done to offend him.

He said that I had now made him face a problem that was much worse than the one he had originally wanted to solve. He complained that the problem of how to "prioritize" his time was much more palpable. He could do "things" about that, and there were issues within that kind of problem about which he could "think" (linear cognitive processing). But the observation that he was using women as scapegoats left him confused and ashamed of himself. This was an unthinkable problem.

I understood and agreed with his understanding. Thinking, as a linear enterprise, would not be very productive at this stage of his work, because he did not have enough information. He looked puzzled. I went on to say that he did not have enough information about his emotion and feelings. I told him that I realized that complaining and boredom were extremely familiar emotional positions for him. However, I suggested that if he were willing to risk unfamiliarity, he might become conscious of other feelings about himself and women. At this point he looked very unhappy, and tears welled up in his eyes.

He lamented that I was taking the light of reason away from him and was asking him to go into a dark place that filled him with dread and anxiety. As long as he believed that reason would help him, even in the midst of his boredom, he had hope that someday he would find "the" answer: a comforting solution to the feeling of emptiness that served as his constant companion.

I commiserated with his dilemma and told him that I felt guilty about the discomfort I had caused. I suggested that perhaps I could compensate for the pain by telling him a story. Knowing that he could not take me literally, he suspiciously agreed to listen to my tale.

I told him the story of a drunk who, late one night, was discovered by a policeman searching around the base of a streetlight. The policeman inquired if he could be of assistance. The drunk looked up at the policeman with gratitude and in a slurred voice asked for help in finding a watch he had lost. After looking for a few minutes, the policeman asked if the man knew exactly where he had lost the watch. The drunk pointed down a dark alley that ran behind the lamppost. The policeman irritably asked, "Then why the hell are we looking here?" The drunk, incredulous at the policeman's stupidity, replied, " 'Cause it's so much lighter here!"

Sam's desire to solve his problems with the light of sweet reason by identifying his emotional difficulty as a time management problem is a rational (linear) orientation toward personal problem solving. This kind of thinking is very effective in the solution of physical problems, and it is inevitable and necessary that we use this form of thinking in our everyday lives. It is so useful that its familiarity breeds hope and comfort and causes us to use it as our first cognitive tool whenever we are confronted with a problem, even an emotional one.

We love our linear systems. It becomes much "lighter" when we can think logically. On the other hand, our intuitive processes are much "darker." They are shrouded in mystery and confusion. At times they even seem to arise from extraterrestrial sources, to which some of us react with awe, dread, or anxiety.

Before I continue with the discussion of personal skills, I wish to comment briefly on my work with Sam. Sam's poor emotional skills and his emotional isolation were the sources of the relative lack of feedback in his life. This caused his affect hunger (loneliness and boredom). My playfulness with Sam was designed to help him shift from his linear set. Shifting to the nonlinear format, I interrupted his linear preoccupation, which enabled him to move into a nonlinear frame of reference where he could understand the difference between logic and feelings. This difference provided him with information that enabled him to develop emotional skills that would "satisfy" his affect hunger and escape from the trap of his boredom. These skills also, incidentally, helped him to better understand his dilemma. Had I taken a logical stance with him, he would have logically (linearly) seen what I was talking about, but he would not have been able to experience his anxiety about bringing feelings of love, loneliness, and the barrenness of his emotional relationships into awareness.

Personal Skills

Up to this point, I have delved into the three doubly dichotomized cognitive subsystems of the person. I have also described the nature of these systems and the cognitive transformations that enable them to maintain their holistic integrity.

The skill of a cognitive system plays a decisive role in the transformational process that equilibrates the person/neurological ego. Various cognitive structures that are developed from birth onward exist within the personal categories from which the person evolves. Older operating structures receive more exercise and become more practiced in processing the information for which they have become specialized. The oldest personal structures in personality are those that were formed in childhood. They are the most stable and have the greatest equilibratory value. Although they ordinarily operate in the background of awareness, they are available to reequilibrate the person/neurological ego when more adult systems are ineffective. These old structures are automatically brought into play when a more recently developed structure is unable to process either emerging or incoming information. Practice alone is not enough to develop skilled personal systems, which are parts of ego strength.

The strength of the neurological ego is a crucial factor in the creation of durable and effective personal systems. Ego strength is defined by stability and integrity of the autopoietic (self-regulating) skills of the neurological ego and is a function of genetic endowment interacting with a rich, secure, infantile experience. When a genetically well-endowed infant is provided with a stimulating, secure environment within which she/he can exercise self-regulatory systems, a strong neurological ego emerges and endures. A highly skilled neurological ego is better able to develop stable adult personal structures than is a less skilled ego. Regression to childhood formations is less likely when stable adult personal structures are developed.

In the next chapter, I will be describing the three subsystems of the person in greater detail. The dynamic underpinning of these systems is their affect hunger and their transformational skills.

CHAPTER X

The Tripartite Person

It is obvious that self, feelings, and personal reality—the systems of the person—are experientially dissimilar. However, they are not only experienced differently, each also has varied meanings in our interpretation of personal existence. Yet, as I discussed in the last chapter, the dynamics of their movement in relationship to one another led me to see that each is a display of different aspects of a single system. The observation of their equilibratory activity reveals a unity of process. Each of them has the same equilibratory function. Psychologically, each has essentially the same explanatory function. One system cannot alter its activity without the others congruently shifting their positions; each marches in lock step with the other.

The self systems contain an explanatory code that inaccurately describes them as the initiators of behavior. The myths of intentionality and free will are examples of this system of explanation about the self. Feelings and personal reality, as cognitions about different aspects of the neurological ego's process, are related to different action programs and different kinds of explanation. Feelings are explanatory systems about the disequilibrium of the neurological ego that contain prescriptions for action that equilibrate emotionality. Personal reality contains classifications and explanations about social conduct. In the following discussion, I will describe each of these systems in greater detail.

The Doubly Dichotomous Self

The self is displayed and explained in ways prescribed by the manner in which it is formatted. This is a reason why *self* has so many different meanings, definitions, and explanations. The self, the ego, the spirit, and the soul are labels of the self that reflect differences in formatting. The self is experientially and cognitively blended and formatted with the other two subsystems of the person. These combinations create different kinds of self phenomena. When they are displayed in awareness, they become Allport's (1937) hyphenated selves. These selves are labels of self-experiences operating in different contexts. In the index of his book, Allport lists *self* hyphenated with *assurance, consciousness, deception, determination, distrust, esteem, judgment, justification, objectification, rating, recognition, regard, seeking, study,* and *validation.* These terms denote different blends of self with emotionality and personal reality in different settings.

Self-concept is usually a linear description of self in a social setting. *Self-presentation* is the external behavioral and emotional display of self in an interpersonal or social situation. *Roles* are socially defined patterns of behavior and experience in which the self is at the center of the display. *Self-perceptions* and *self-images* are perceptions and fantasies about self-phenomena. Nonlinear, nonsensory self process is usually experienced as different forms of spirituality, as in the case of my "ghost." The varieties of self phenomena are too numerous to be described in this overview of the person, so I will confine myself to the description of *self* as a system of cognitions about the neurological ego as it operates normatively in everyday life. I will be defining the self and describing it in relationship to the other personal systems.

The self is both the most constantly experienced part of our psychological process and the most neglected in attempting to understand its crucial relationship to every engagement of the individual. Its role in learning, meaning, and motivation is either ignored or misunderstood. Even its relationship to the individual is confused.

In ordinary conversation, we use the words "I" or "me" to designate who or what part of the individual is in control of conduct or thought. "I think," "I did," "I intend," are sentences that describe a presumed controller of thought, action, and intention. However, it is not always clear, when one is experiencing one's "I," whether it is the self or the individual as a whole that is being labeled.

In the following discussion, I will use "I" or "me" to designate the totality of the individual. Contrary to the tradition recommended by Strunk and White (1972), I have, throughout this book, constantly referred to myself. In this usage, I have been referring to myself as a part of a process. I have not used my "I" to describe it as an operator. I used the "I" simply as it designates my person as a whole in relationship to a situation.

In previous chapters, I have argued that since the person is a cognition about the neurological ego, it cannot be the activator of either behavior or psychological process, which arise from regulatory systems of the brain equilibrating the neurological ego. The individual emerges from the interaction of the body, the neurological ego, and its equilibratory systems—the person. There is no single system or entity within the individual that is totally responsible for conduct or experience.

The self is not the intentional executive of free will that it is usually thought to be. Instead, I propose that the self is a nonintentional, automatic system that has the following properties: (1) It is a "cursor" that orients the individual in relationship to sources of the neurological ego's disequilibration, (2) it is experienced as being the center of the individual, (3) it is thought to be the activator of action programs, and (4) its validation is a primary source of reinforcement for itself and other systems.

The Self as a Cursor

Self is a system of cognitions identifying the relationship between the neurological ego and the sources of information that are disequilibrating it. This is the reason that the experience of self is so ubiquitous in our thinking and feeling. The self is the orientor or the locator of the position of the neurological ego with reference to the sources of its disturbance.

Both self-process and consciousness are activated when the neurological ego is disequilibrated. When this happens, we experience ourselves as being in focal awareness. The interaction of consciousness and self process create focal awareness that facilitates cognitive reequilibration. The marriage of self with consciousness in the equilibratory process led James (1950/1890) to describe the self as knower, doer, and observer. The experiences of knowing, intention, and awareness all have an experience of self as an essential part of these psychological functions. Knowing is always the knowing of the "I." The same is true of intention. Any intention, desire, or need is the condition of the "I." Sensory perception is also affixed to the "I." Ordinarily, this intimate relationship presumes that it is the "I" who is the source of the function. "I do . . . I think . . . I see . . ." are all statements encompassing the presumption that it is the "I" who is initiating the function.

This is an erroneous explanation. The intimacy of the "I" with other psychological processes occurs because it is an orientational process, identifying the position of the neurological ego's relationship to a disequilibrating situation. Self either exists in focal awareness or it resides in the background of awareness, ready to take center stage whenever automaticity is interrupted.

In order to describe this movement, I will briefly reiterate the paradigmatic shift in the meaning of self that exists in this theory. The self, being a product of the mind, has the same kind of relationship to action that the mind has. Because it is so constantly associated with action, the self, as a part of the mind, has a more intimate, but not exclusive, relationship with action than with memory, perception, or language.

When an appropriate classification of disorganizing information is made, it is matched with action programs designed to restore the neurological ego or the systems of the person to their steady-state conditions. There is no need for intention or instruction to activate an action program. All that is necessary is a matching of categories. Within the theoretical framework of this theory, intention is a displayed (conscious) cognition about a reorganization. It is an ex post facto signal of a new solution having been found. It is not the source of action.

Intentions are fragile constructions that exist between reorganized cognitions and action programs. They are most robust with linear, sensory cognitions about objects. If I intend to pick up a glass of water, this intention is tightly attached to an action program—that is, it has a high probability of occurring. However, reorganized cognitions about emotional or personal process are extremely unreliable. The intentions of alcoholics and other addicts are relatively powerless in the activation of behaviors designed to liberate the individual from the addiction.

The self, being a psychological process, is no more an activator of behavior than is the mind. The belief that the person is an *operator* reflects the erroneous assumption that either the person, or its "I," is *doing* the thinking. The person is a system of cognitions; therefore, it cannot be a governor of conduct or cognition. The person is a product of cognition. Within the logic of this theory, it is simply an explanation—that is, an idea. Ideas are classifiers or explainers; therefore, in and of themselves, they are incapable of operating a system. The neurological ego/person interaction, not the self, activates behavior, cognition, and experience. There is no homunculus in this theory directing experience or behavior.

The Self as the Center

The self of this theory is a complex system of sensory/nonsensory and linear/nonlinear "ideas" about the neurological ego. One of the major phenomenal features of the self is that it is experienced as being at the center of the person. There are four reasons for this.

First, it is the cognitive system that creates ideas about the neurological ego, which *is* the center of our existence. Second, in modern times, the popularity of Freudian theory, following the platonic tradition, led us to think of it as the "executive" in charge of managing the internal and external complexities of our existence. Such expressions as "I am the master of my fate" or "It is my choice" express the sense of mastery and control that is attributed to the self in the form of its "I." Third, the self is experienced as being at the centerof all of our mentation and conduct. "I think, therefore . . . ," "I see . . . ," and "I know . . . " are statements describing the centrality of the "I" in psychological process. This centrality and the ubiquity of self-experiencing contributed to the mistaken belief that it is the control center of our existence. From Sallust in 41 B.C. to Nehru in 1958, at least, there are many who subscribe to Henley's (1980) attestation that:

I am the master of my fate:
I am the captain of my soul.

Fourth, the self is at the center of both internal homeostatic regulation and external environmental or interpersonal engagement. Its centrality is functionally based on its orientational operation. The classificatory process of the cognitive systems uses the self as the reference point where the individual is located in any situation within which the individual is involved.

There are structures within the hypothalamic-limbic system that have to do with temperature regulation, digestion, sexuality, and other metabolic processes. It is therefore reasonable to believe that there are structures that serve an orientational process. Without being able to locate them anatomically, I would guess that there are structures within the hypothalamic-limbic/prefrontal cortex systems that are specialized to process information about the orientation of the individual in both spatial and interpersonal relationships.

The imprinting phenomenon in ducklings that Lorenz (1969) and

Rose (1982) describe could be a rudimentary self structure. The fixated attachment of imprinting is an example of the self-orientational process in its primitive form. This is the system that creates bonding to the mother. It is reasonable to speculate that there are analogous structures in our brain that are cognitively elaborated in our neocortex, giving rise to an experience of self. Since ducks do not possess our massive neocortex, it is unlikely that they experience a self.

As I stated in the last chapter, awareness of the source of disequilibrating information and the display of self facilitates cognition to reequilibrate the person/neurological ego. Metaphorically, the first question that is programmatically asked at the moment of interrupted automaticity is, "What does this mean to me?" The second question raised is, "Is there anything that I should do about the disturbance?" Once these questions are answered, other cognitive search activities and action programs are set into motion, leading to behavior that restores equilibrium.

The Self as a Reinforcing System

In addition to its orientational operations, the self is a primary validational process. Validation occurs when any kind of matching occurs, but the validation that involves the self is usually more effective than repetitive matching without self-experience. This is demonstrated in traditional learning studies where intentional learning is far superior to accidental learning.

Most validation occurs when the self is associated with the matching of a category about disequilibrating information with an action program and an equilibrating outcome. Earlier, I described this process as the feeding of affect hunger. Matching occurs in everything we do from problem solving to simple exercise. In both circumstances, neurological systems are reinforced by the restoration of equilibrium. Neural systems that restore either the person and/or the neurological ego to their steady-state conditions are reinforced.

Consistent reinforcement or validation of a relationship between systems creates an "attached" or "bonded" relationship. These systems can be anything from mothers to ideas. If they consistently validate the person/neurological ego complex, they become bonded to it. Bonding and attachment are synonymous.

In this theory, attachment is an emotional process because attachments stabilize personal structures and their associated systems in the neurological ego. When emotional explanations (feelings) are associated with an attachment, they are experienced as loving feelings. Loving emotionality is powerfully significant to the individual, because it is a primary source of validation that reinforces the steady-state condition of the person/neurological ego complex.

The relationship between sex and love begins during infancy when the physical contact of nursing, bathing, and cuddling creates an indelible bond between caretakers and the emerging self of the baby. Infant care is therefore a generalized erotic experience. Erotic contact is a powerful source of bonding (cf. Duyckaerts, 1970; Masters and Johnson, 1974). This issue deserves a book in and of itself. However, since I am only drawing the rough contours of the continental masses of a personality theory, the following sketch will have to do.

The infant's emerging self is bonded to the primary caretakers of the infant. The bonding contact of physical care, affection, and nutrient feeding is accompanied by generalized erotic experiences. As the infant develops, she or he cognitively elaborates on this bonding and its emotional experiences into feelings of love. The kinds of loving experience that eventually become parts of the adult personality are functions of the cultural, familial, and personal cognitive elaborations that grow within the individual.

The automaticity of these three processes, self, attachment, and erotic arousal, creates an experiential fusion between attachment and sexuality, or bonding. In its adult forms, this bonding of sexuality and attachment is experienced as infatuation. Infatuation is a delightful fusion delusion of "true love," and will be discussed in a later section on emotionality.

The Experiential Properties of the Self

A common erroneous assumption about the nature of the person is that it lies outside emotion and reacts to it in much the same way that a person perceives and reacts to sensory information. Regarding emotionality as a troublesome intrusion on the serenity of rational thought organizes emotional information into a linear, sensory format and construes it to be an objective thing. As I described before, the relationship between the "I" and objects is experientially different from the relationship of the "I" to the psychological process of the individual.

The experience of sensory information has an "I–It" quality (cf.

Buber, 1970). The experience of the external object and the self or "I" is one of separateness. The "I" and the "It" are displayed in experience as separate, discrete phenomena. On the other hand, we rarely experience emotions without feeling as if they arise *from* the self. Within the experience of emotionality, "I" am angry, jealous, hurt, miserable, happy, and so on. The feelings are descriptions of "my" emotional condition. As I have pointed out before, this is very different from the experience of the relationship of possession that we have with objects.

As I previously said, *the relationship of self phenomena to emotionality is centrally important to an understanding of emotionality.* The intimacy of self and emotionality led me to the hypothesis that both self and feelings are equilibratory subsystems of the person. When one "sees" that feelings are a part of the person, an integrated theory of self, emotionality, and personal reality can be constructed.

With the restoration of the steady-state condition of the person/neurological ego, the display of self recedes into the background of awareness. Self-experience is an omnipresent companion to everything we do or experience. It is an integral part of both emotionality and personal reality. Consequently, there are varieties of self phenomena that are blends or integrations of self, emotionality and personal reality.

Feelings and Emotion

Reiterating what I have said before, emotion is the disequilibrium of the neurological ego associated with an experience of self. Feelings are cognitions about nonsensory inputs from the disequilibrated neurological ego, which are organized within either linear or nonlinear formats. Emotion is experienced movement of the disequilibrated neurological ego when it is displayed with the self. In the following discussion, I use the term *emotionality* to denote the blend of both feelings and emotion. This formulation is another expression of the way that my theory addresses the mind-body problem.

Two aspects of that problem require clarification. First, the experience of emotionality has a unitary quality, while, like William James (1950/1890), I am proposing a dual theory of emotion. My theory proposes that the experience of emotion is the experiential *display of a physiological process,* and the experience of feeling is the *display of cognition.* However, they are experientially blended, giving them the unitary quality that we ordinarily experience. Therefore, it is difficult to think of them as two different phenomena. In the following discussion, I will describe the nature of the difference, as well as some of the epistemological issues that made perceiving them as different phenomena difficult.

The second aspect has to do with the fast-fading assumption that it is possible to construct a psychology of emotion without regard to the underlying neural substrata from which emotionality emerges. Even though the doctrine of psychophysical parallelism is theoretically being disavowed, it continues in theories that do not have a way of conceptualizing the emergence of psychological process from neurological operations. I regard any theoretical formulation about the relationship between the mind and the body stating that they "mirror" or "reflect" one another or that the difference between them is only a semantic difference, as a form of psychophysical parallelism. This assumption still exists in the major theories of emotionality that are in today's marketplace.

When the differences between bodily and psychological processes are not clearly differentiated, the relationship between them cannot be understood. In order to have a sense of understanding about an emotional experience, we tend to conceptually fuse bodily process with emotionality; that is, we "psychologize" bodily process. This overlaying experience of feeling causes us to interpret *the experience of emotion* as though it were a *feeling*.

Anxiety and depression are common examples of this process. They are frequently experienced and explained as being fear or unhappiness, which are feelings. In other words, the experience of physiological process and the experience of a cognition about that process are not understood as being displays of different phenomena.

Izard (1977), citing his own and the work of others, says:

"Ten fundamental emotions have been identified and defined (Darwin, 1872; Ekman, Friesen, & Ellsworth, 1972; Izard, 1971; and Tomkins; 1962)" (p. 83).

Without attempting to present a detailed theory of emotion, I suspect that Izard's "fundamental emotions" are, within my frame of reference, experiences of the disequilibria of the neurological ego blended with an experienced "I." In my theory, anxiety, depression, rage, hunger (affect and physical), panic/fear, attachment, pain, and arousal/interest/orientation are emotions.

We classify them as psychological phenomena, because a self and a set of explanations are attached to the emotional experience. For example, an experience of anxiety is commonly referred to as fear. When I suggested to a client who had difficulty experiencing anger that she was angry with me, she denied my suggestion and told me that I frightened her. Being unable to experience her anger, she experienced it as anxiety and then labeled her anxiety "fear." Since I was the only "tiger" in the room, she "explained" her "fear" by saying that it was I who frightened her. This was psychologically reasonable and is an example of cognitive emotional transformation. I had triggered the anxiety by confronting her with her anger, a feeling from which she was alienated.

In short, I believe that it is important to distinguish between the experience of a physiological occurrence—that is, increased heart rate, hyperventilation, the "rush" of adrenalin through our breasts, dryness of our mouths, orgasm, and so on as emotions and feelings that are experientially displayed as labels and explanations.

Emotional Arousal

The nature of emotional arousal illustrates my theory's conception of the mind-body relationship. Most psychological theories about the activation of emotion encompass at least one of three assumptions: that (1) emotionality is a response to a stimulus; (2) a conception of psychophysical parallelism can account for the relationship between the mind and the brain, and (3) perception and experiencing are the same process. Ordinarily, these assumptions occur in combination with one another.

Conventional theorists assume that an emotion is a response to a stimulus of some kind. The stimulus is usually some external event to which the individual is presumed to be responding. In the modern period of theorizing about emotionality, beginning with James (1950/1890), emotion was thought to be a reaction to "something." James proposed that emotion was a reaction to the "perception" of a bodily movement that was stimulated by an "exciting object."

It is here that my theory differs from James's understanding of emotionality. Conventional theory regards emotion as primarily an intrapsychic phenomenon. However, in this theory, emotionality is largely, but not solely, an interpersonal process. On this issue, James wrote:

The reaction called emotionality terminates in the subject's own body, and [does not] enter into practical relations with the exciting object (p. 331).

Emotionality in this theory is the food and drink that nourishes the affect hunger of individuals in their commerce with one another. The external part of the cognitive dichotomy of emotionality actively engages the external environment. Emotions are either the affect hunger needs of the individual or responses to disequilibrating inputs from the external environment and other persons who inhabit that environment. The expression of emotionality in relationship with others is either a search for validating feedback, or it is an expression designed to alter the other person's behavior.

The equilibratory assumption of my theory describes emotionality as a constant, ongoing condition of the living individual. Therefore, emotionality is *not* stimulated by either internal or external events. Emotionality does not operate on the principles of the stimulus-response mechanics of the machine model. It is a continuous movement arising from the inherent instability of living systems, which respond to external events *and* to the complexities of internal autoregulatory systems. This formulation enables us to explain both the internal and external sources of disequilibrium that give rise to emotion and feeling.

The interaction between internal and external processes is the most common condition for the arousal of emotionality. External sources of arousal are the intrusions of information that cannot be automatically processed on the person and the neurological ego. The internal sources of disequilibrium are the affect hungers of the various systems of the person, the neurological ego, and the structural incongruities that are developed within and between these systems. In chapter VIII, I described the equilibratory movement of homeorhesis or autopoiesis. This is a more complex formulation than the simple stimulus-response explanation.

In addition to the stimulus-response assumption, some current theories of emotion reflect an assumption that a kind of psychophysical parallelism must exist in order to accommodate both physiological and psychological components of emotionality. These explanations are attempts to cope with the absence of an understanding of what Reiser (1984) calls the "interface" between the mind and its body by simply stating that they operate in parallel and that they are essentially the same phenomena, described in different ways.

Pribram and Melges (1969) describe a sophisticated form of parallelism that resembles Kohler's (1959) discredited concept of psychoneural isomorphism, which proposed that psychological process is isomorphic with neurological structures. Pribram and Melges describe their position in the following terms:

> It is our view that these communicative signals (. . . affects, the "feelings" and emotional expressions) are, as it were, optical isomers, mirror images . . . of the ongoing neural mechanisms, and that both processes are organized to function-in-view-of-the-same-ends . . . . Different universes of discourse are used to describe the mirror-images—which may therefore display different characteristics in the two contexts—but the events described are identical. More concretely, according to this view description of a given neural excitatory pattern does not produce what we call anxiety; *rather the two reflect one another* (pp. 316-317) (Italics inserted by author).

I am in agreement with Pribram-Melges's assertion that emotionality arises from neurological underpinnings. However, their concept of "reflection" as a means of tying psychological and neurological process together omits and ignores the equilibratory nature of psychological process. Furthermore, they ignore experiencing or awareness as a part of emotionality. These omissions deprive the theory of conceptual ingredients necessary for a full description of the operations of both personality and emotionality. Without an understanding of the equilibratory role of cognition, the variety and variability of emotional process cannot be understood. Without a theory of experiencing in emotional process, the theory is unable to adequately describe the development of emotional skills.

Finally, the fusion of perception and experiencing caused me to initially misunderstand James's (1950/1890) theory of emotion and delayed my understanding of emotionality. As I clarified my thinking about emotionality, I became aware of the genius of James's thinking, which is relevant today, when in 1890 he wrote:

> Our natural way of thinking about these *coarser* emotions is that the mental perception of some fact excites the mental affection called emotion, and that this latter state of mind gives rise

to the bodily expression. My theory . . . is that *the bodily changes follow directly the perception of the exciting fact, and that our feeling of the same changes as they occur is the emotion.* Commonsense says, we lose our fortune, are sorry and weep; we meet a bear, are frightened and run; we are insulted by a rival, are angry and strike. The hypothesis here to be defended says that the order of sequence is incorrect, that the one mental state is not immediately induced by the other, that the bodily manifestations must first be interposed between, and that the more rational statement is that we feel sorry because we cry, strike, or tremble, as the case may be. Without the bodily states following on the perception, the latter would be purely cognitive in form, pale and colorless, destitute of emotional warmth. We might see the bear, and judge it best to run, receive the insult and deem it right to strike, but we should actually *feel* afraid or angry (pp. 449-450).

James's brilliance resides in his ability to see that emotionality is a relationship between bodily and psychological process, and that emotionality arose from bodily process. My difficulty in understanding James's hypothesis was caused by my inability to recognize the different meanings in the word *perception*. I now realize that perception can mean (1) the import of sensory information, (2) an understanding and/or an experiencing of a psychological process. For example, I can "perceive" a lamp in the den—that is, sensory perception. I can also, "perceive" what James meant in the italicized statement I quoted above—that is, perception as understanding. Additionally, I can "perceive" a feeling that I am having—that is, there is the experiential display of a cognition about an emotion.

In the first instance, the perception refers to a sensory *experience* of the lamp; in the second example, perception refers to an *experience* of an understanding—that is, the *experiencing* of a cognitive process; in the third example, the perception refers to the *experiencing* of emotionality, a nonsensory process.

Experiencing becomes so fused with other psychological processes that we have difficulty understanding that experiencing and cognition and the import of information (perception) are three different psychological operations. With this in mind, the word *perception* in James's statement that "bodily changes follow directly the *perception* of the exciting fact," can be read to mean "the *experience* of the exciting fact . . . *is* the emotion." If James meant that perception is the experiential display of an "exciting fact" rather than the importation of information, which I have defined as perception, then I understand and am in agreement with this part of James's theory of emotion. Within the definitional framework of my theory, *perception is the import of information, and experiencing is the display of information.* These are two very different psychological operations.

My theory is structurally the same as the one that James (1950/1890) proposed. It is a dual theory. *Emotions,* as I have defined them, are his "coarser emotions," and what I call *feelings* are his other "emotions" or "feelings." He did not differentiate between the terms *feelings* and *emotion.* He did, however, recognize that there were two different emotional processes. It is interesting that he did differentiate between the "coarser" emotions and the feelings that existed without them. He saw that feelings without emotion were "pale and colorless, destitute of human warmth." Unfortunately, he confused things a bit by using *feelings* and *experiencing* synonymously.

From the perspective of today's cognitive psychology, it is not too great a leap of understanding to see the parallel between the "coarser emotions" as emotion; the disequilibrium of the hypothalamic-limbic system and the "pale and colorless" emotion as feelings—cognitions about emotion without an associated experience of bodily process. My theory, like James's, proposes that bodily process is the source of emotionality. He thought of bodily process within the empiricist tradition of his time.

That empirical tradition limited scientific meaning to linear cognition about the data of sensory perception. Therefore, James used the metaphor of visually seeing the body move as the trigger of emotionality. Despite the inaccuracy of the metaphor, it did contain the essential theoretical ingredient. Bodily process is the source of emotionality, rather than the other way around.

Both feelings and emotion have an additional component that differentiates emotionality from physical discomfort or pain. Within the experience of emotionality, there is also an experience of "I," as I described above. The difference between the emotionality of nausea and nausea as a reaction to the ingestion of a toxin is the relationship of the "I" to that experience. In the nausea of emotionality, it is the "I" that is nauseated. However, when I have a reaction to food poisoning, it is my stomach that is nauseated. All emotional experiences, outside of intense emotionality, such as panic, contain an associated experience of self with them.

In the case of intense emotionality, where the neurological ego becomes violently disequilibrated, cognitive processes are suspended. This suspension includes both the ability to think and to experience self, which is a nonlinear, nonsensory form of thinking. In rage or panic, we react automatically with the action programs of the neurological ego. Another example, in the opposite direction, is sexuality. When the individual is unable to be released from a focused (linear) experience of self, erotic expression and involvement are inhibited.

Feelings, as do the other personal systems, have the doubly dichotomous property that I described when I discussed the formatting systems of the mind. Internally, they have the equilibratory function of explanations. Externally, they are manipulations to influence others in the interpersonal process.

This internal/external property of emotionality is reflected in the formatting of feelings. I found that my clients in the course of my practice and friends outside my practice would be confused about various pairs of feelings. They confused jealousy with envy, fear with anxiety, guilt with shame, unhappiness with depression, joy with euphoria. These pairs are confused because they share the same experiential quality, although they are formatted differently and have different equilibratory functions.

Each of the pairs represents the internal/external dichotomy. In the case of jealousy, the individual fears the loss of an external coveted person or object, whereas envy explains that another person has something that the envious individual internally desires. As I mentioned above, fear is a reaction to an external danger, and anxiety is an internal inability to experience a feeling. Feelings of unhappiness occur when the individual is faced with externally difficult circumstances; depression is a reaction to the internal repression of the experience of feelings.

Emotional Skill

People have different emotional skills, and cultures differ in the kinds of emotional expression they regard as normative. For example, there are obvious differences among British, Italian, Japanese and American traditions and patterns of emotional expression. The labels and meanings of feelings in these different cultures vary widely. At the same time, the experience and expression of emotion across cultures are the same (Izard, 1977). This finding is consistent with my theory's differentiation between feeling and emotion. Emotion is the display of the neurological ego's disequilibrium in relation to the self. All humans have the same neurological ego. Feelings are systems of cognition about that disequilibrium. Cognitions are learned within families embedded in cultures that differ. Hence, people differ in their experience of, and meanings about, feelings and are essentially the same in their experience and meanings about emotion. People raised in emotional isolation are not taught how to label or experience their feelings as skillfully as those raised in environments rich with emotional expression, nor are as respectful of the integrity of the children whom they teach.

I know a very successful computer engineer with a girlfriend who consistently insulted and cheated on him. He related this to me in an emotionless and matter-of-fact manner. I, on the other hand, found myself identifying with him and felt angry with her. I was curious about his lack of feeling. I asked him how he felt about his girlfriend when she treated him so badly. He said that he thought that she did not mean it, and that she promised she would not do it again. I pointed out that he was telling me what he *thought* and was not telling me how he *felt*. After some fruitless prodding, I told him that when I was listening to him tell me about this part of his relationship with her, I had felt angry. He said, "Of course, I had that feeling." I asked him why he had not told me that when I asked him in the first place. He said, "I don't know. But when you said it, I remembered how I felt." I then chided him about his emotional ignorance, hoping to elicit a feeling toward me. I was partially successful. He became defensive and protested that he had feelings, but he could not describe them. However, when I told him about a feeling, he could then recognize what it was. This is an example of a very emotionally unskilled man.

In the course of my practice I have found the following four-part classification of emotional skill useful in helping people understand where they stand with regard to their emotionality.

LEVELS OF EMOTIONAL SKILL

Level I	Experiencing emotion without labels or meanings. Usually the experience occurs in a form of confusion, anxiety, pain, or depression, with an experience of self figurally. "Something is happening to me."
Level II	Experiencing an emotion, with a label—that is, anger, affection, envy, etc., and experienced with an "I." I am angry . . . I like. . . I envy, etc.
Level III	Experiencing a feeling (a label and an explanation) with an associated "I"—that is, commonly experienced feelings, with an ability to think about and evaluate the meaningfulness of the feeling.
Level IV	Experiencing intense emotion, while at the same time retaining the ability to think and evaluate the meaningfulness of the emotional situation.

Information-processing skill exists in all three of the person subsystems. The skill of a cognitive system contributes to the stability and flexibility of its equilibratory function. I will describe below the nature and contribution of skill to personality dynamics.

Emotional Transformations

In previous discussions, I have described cognitive transformations. Emotional transformations are the same, except that in this category I am referring to the emotional content of transformational process. In earlier chapters, I described Raymond's rage or anxiety about homosexuality as a transformation to equilibrate childhood personal structures that became disturbed when confronted with loving feelings. In psychotherapy, the client frequently uses sexual feelings to equilibrate his/her confusion about the loving experience that emerges when contact is made in a helping relationship. Anger is perhaps the most common emotional transformation used in this culture. It is much easier to experience and express anger than it is to experience love, sexuality, or tenderness. This is more true of men than it is of women. It is not unusual for women to use sexuality as an emotional transformation in a situation in which they feel powerless.

The selection of alternate feelings to replace disequilibrating emotionality is based on (1) the skill of the replacing emotionality—that is, its stability and equilibratory power, and (2) the compatibility of replacing emotionality with abiding structures in the personality. As I wrote in the last chapter, skill is a function of the age of the structure and its information-processing abilities in the face of stress. In addition to skill, a feeling must be congruent with the operating self systems and the personal reality of the person. It is unlikely that a woman who was trained to be a "sweet young girl" would use anger as an alternate emotion in her transformational repertoire: charm or the appearance of ineptitude would more likely be her automatic selections.

Emotional transformations are intimately related to those classifications of personal reality that are culturally learned. The skill and, therefore, the stability of personal reality classifications form the basis of most emotional transformations.

On the Nature of Personal Reality

Personal reality is the way that I designate the cognitive constructions that people create about their relationships with the external environment. In some respects, my concept of personal reality is similar to Mahoney's (1991). He writes that personal reality is based on "our tacit theories of self and world [which] lie at the heart of all of our experience" (p. 177). I would add with personal reality that self and emotionality (in other words, *the person*) are essential processes that also lie at the heart of all of our experiences.

I decided to call this system *personal reality* because its experiential quality is similar to that of sensory reality. It is experienced as existing "out there," in the external environment. Historically, in the Western philosophical tradition, personal reality and sensory reality have not been clearly differentiated. However, with the import of Eastern and the recognition of Native American mystical traditions, there has been a growing awareness of the difference between sensory and personal process.

The operational dynamics of personal reality as an equilibratory system are threefold: (1) personal reality, as a cognitive system, organizes information about the neurological ego's relationships with anything, including classifications about its own operations, (2) it provides stabilizing feedback to the neurological ego, and (3) as a psychological system with a neural substrate, it too requires validational feedback from the external environment to maintain its own integrity.

As I have previously described, the relationship of the experience of self to sensory reality is different from the experience of self *in* personal reality. The experienced "I" is separate from objects displayed in sensory perception, whereas the "I" is an integral part of personal reality.

I know of no adequate word in English to adequately label the psychological systems of the person that cognitively organize his or her relationship to the external environment. While the German word *weltanshauung* approximates my meaning for personal reality, it contains connotations of intellectuality that are so far removed from the profound emotional operations within it that I have chosen to use *personal reality* as the descriptive term for this equilibratory system.

Personal reality is primarily organized within linear formats. As a result, it has a stability and an experiential quality so similar to sensory experiencing that it is experienced as though it were, literally, a perception of the external environment.

My concept of personal reality is, also, similar to the psychoanalytic "reality principle." Psychoanalytic theory describes the "reality principle" as the ego incorporating "objects" from the external environment in order to guide the person's conduct. Similarly, I assume that personal reality systems are developed from the interaction of information from the external environment and the structure of the neurological ego. At this point, however, my theory and psychoanalytic theory part company.

The first difference is that the interaction of the neurological ego and cognitive constructions about it have an equilibratory purpose rather than having a homunculus within it deciding what is most reasonable. The second difference is that psychoanalytic theory proposes that an "Ego" exercises a reality principle to modulate the Id's impulsive drive for the gratification of the pleasure principle. In my theory, there is no pleasure principle. Instead, the person, including personal reality, regulates the neurological ego rather than an "Ego" regulating the person.

For heuristic purposes, I have classified the different aspects of the personal reality system as (1) cosmological reality, (2) epistomological reality, (3) social/moral reality, and (4) psychological reality. These categories are not operational systems. The classification is simply a description of the contextual contents of the personal reality system's classifications of different categories of relationships. The dynamics of stabilization or destabilization are essentially the same for each of the categories.

Cosmological reality refers to the understandings and assumptions that the person has about his or her relationship to the world at large within which he or she is living. Within this category are ideas about the source of orderliness that exists in the world, whether or not it is based upon the existence of a deity or on a scientific faith system. Galileo's tragic confrontation with the Catholic Church is an example of the reactions that can arise when cosmological belief systems are violated.

Epistemological reality is the category that describes the characteristic ways in which the person thinks about him- or herself, about the nature of the world, and her or his relationships with it. Kuhn's (1970) "paradigms" are examples of what I mean by epistemological reality. Another example can be seen in the "commonsense" assumptions that underlie some theories of personality. These assumptions form the grounds on which logical positivism, which is based on the idea that sensory information is the only reliable data for scientific investigation, is built.

Social/moral reality concerns the ways in which the person is organized with respect to her or his self systems and feelings in relationship to the social world within which she or he lives. During the course of the person's development, she or he may become fixated within a particular reality, which gets overlaid by other realities during the aging process. These overlaid realities most frequently function in the ground process of the person's everyday experiencing. Within this reality are the sexual and social mores that attempt to explain and govern relationships between men and women, parents and children, and individuals and social authority. Western religions, for the most part, are institutions that create and disseminate this reality. Social/moral reality classifications become so automated that the person is unaware of them as belief systems and experiences them as having the same objective reality as static physical objects in the external world.

Social/moral reality provides the neurological ego with validational feedback and action programs for social conduct and the maintenance of stability in emotionally disorganizing social situations. It is the warehouse of the rules of conduct and appropriateness. Frequently, this system is associated with cosmological reality when it is used in religious explanation. This association provides the person with a more secure sense of certainty about the ways in which the person "should" or "should not" conduct him- or herself. The operations of this reality are most vividly seen in the crippling sexual mores of Western Civilization that contribute to the anguish of human love.

The social/moral reality is also the background upon which the conventionalized social roles, including personal presentations, emotional expressions of the person, and the understanding of the person's relationship to the social environment are figurally displayed. The individual is trained in the processes of this "reality" by the conventions of families and cultures within which the individual is raised. This reality is the system that rationalizes man's inhumanity to man.

Personal reality, feelings, and self are essential for the maintenance of the person's normative state of consciousness. Severe invalidations of the person can cause the neurological ego, depending upon its strength, to alternate between the normative and psychotic states of consciousness.

The information that is part of any reality defines the parameters of the neurological ego's stable-state condition. Feedback to the neurological ego validates and reinforces its labile structures. *It is here that the "need for meaning" resides.* Here, too, the "I" or self of the person is an essential part of the process.

The matching of cognitions about the "I" with cognitions about external events creates the experience of *meaning*. Personal reality cognitively structures the neurological ego's relationships to its own person, significant others, and society in general.

Psychological reality is the dwelling place of the personal themes around which the repertoire of our emotional skills is organized. In this reality there is a self-concept that has a menu of feelings and expressions appropriate for the stability of that concept. For example, I know a man who has defined himself as a "nice guy." Within his definition of "nice guy," it was inappropriate for him to be angry, aggressive, or self-serving. In addition to his presentation of being sweet and helpful, he had a lifelong theme, which stated that one could only be loved if one did not offend. Other themes have premises that have imperatives to be safe, brilliant, impregnable, brave, just, and on and on.

Themes are powerful personal structures that define boundaries of behavior. Only under great duress will individuals violate the prescriptions of their personal themes. For example, if individuals have an idea that they must be good and moral people, and that a good and moral person should only have sex after marriage, then engaging in premarital sex becomes extremely difficult. Themes about being "safe," "good," "honorable," "strong," etc. are elaborated in a variety of combinations and contexts that become essential parts of the enduring character structures identifying the uniqueness of individuals. All these have associated concepts of self with appropriate emotional repertoires. They are rationalized with personal reality.

We have the same emotional reaction to our personal reality that we have to anything that validates and stabilizes us: We love it. Its loss fills us with the same reactions of anxiety, despair, and/or anger that we have in response to the loss of any love object. We are also as loyal to it as we are to our loved ones or groups. We champion it with even greater enthusiasm than when we root for our home teams. It is so important to us that we are even willing to kill or die for it. Testament to this are the great religious-ideological struggles of history, such as the Crusades and the "democracy versus communism" anxiety that threatened our existence for so long.

The interpersonal effects of linear personal reality have been played out on the stage of the Theater of the Absurd. The hard rules of linear personal reality's value and moral systems frequently obscure the perception and understanding of the underlying emotional relationships that are essential to loving and creative interpersonal engagements. It makes "rhinoceroses" (Ionesco, 1966) of us all. Personal reality's intimate contact with the hard objects of the external environment gives it a stability reflected in its resistance to change.

This concept of personal reality is discomforting because the individual can no longer maintain the illusion that he or she is in direct possession of a firm, objective, external guide. Indeed, we are alone, autonomous and responsible for our own constructions about who we are and how we conduct ourselves during the course of our lives. We may be trained to believe in, and thereby become "fused" with, cultural, social, religious, and parental conventions about who we are or what we should be. When this happens, we may find comfort in reassuring explanations about who we "should" be or how we "should" think and behave, but in this "comfort," we are delusional.

I have described personal reality as a massive, primarily linear, equilibratory system that cognitively organizes information about the neurological ego's relationship to everything in the external environment, including what its role in these relationships "should" be.

The equilibratory systems experienced as personal reality ordinarily function as ground processes upon which self phenomena and feelings are figurally displayed. When self phenomena and feelings are linearly formatted, they have the same experiential qualities as those that are experienced in the personal reality system. They are different only in the contents of the cognitive systems.

Personal reality is a deeply embedded part of our person. It is, for the most part, experienced as belief structures, which also requires validation to "feed" its affect hunger. With the exercise of validation, it becomes habituated. The beliefs, which are parts of personal reality, are experienced as being as "real," "natural," and as the "order of things as they should be." They become so highly automated that they operate outside the awareness of the individual. The emotional structures that emerge from the most intimate parent-child relationships endure and seek validation for as long as we live. They are active, vital, validation-seeking parts of our personalities.

Personal reality is the most stable and reliable of the personal systems. Its constant reinforcement on the stability of the external environment makes it the most believable and comforting banister upon which we can lean to stabilize our fragile emotionality. In psychotherapy, I have found that personal reality is the system most resistant to change. I have been able to help some clients escape from the delusional aspects of psychosis within relatively short periods of time, sometimes in just a year or two. However, their personal realities become almost impenetrable because the realities effectively shield them from painful emotionalities of their childhood personality formation. This is particularly true of love in its adult form.

This concludes my portrait of the person. In the next chapter, I will describe the assets and opportunities of my theory as a whole, as well as some of its limitations.

CHAPTER XI

A Glance Back
and a Look Forward

Again, I am at Ulysses' side. I have arrived at my destination, as he did. However, there is no loving Penelope waiting for me, urging me to remain home. Instead, I am presented with invitations to depart on other ventures. Looking back on where I have been, I more clearly see how much I have left undone on this journey.

In the beginning of my adventure, I wandered off my chosen path, intrigued by errant questions that caused me to lose sight of my course. As I learned more about what I wanted to say, it was easier to resist side trips into deeper explorations of theories of consciousness, the mind, the mind/body relationship, and many other ideas. However, this discipline cost me the pleasure of being able to explore the emotional parts of the person more deeply, including the exploration of love and sex, of creativity and beauty. All of these are essential dynamics in intensive psychotherapy, but they were only superficially examined. Despite the theory's limitations, it has guided me to an understanding of the nature of the therapeutic process that I would not otherwise have had.

I gradually developed a sense of the wholeness of the theory. Even though I was unable to articulate all its outlines, that wholeness enabled me to stay within the bounds of the task that I had set for myself. It helped me to roughly describe the person.

In this concluding chapter, I will discuss the strengths and limitations of the theory. In the course of writing it, I also came across four mysteries that I will share with you. I will conclude by taking a very short walk into places where "angels fear to tread." These discussions will reprise the major hypotheses of the theory.

The Theoretical Characteristics of the Theory

Its Strengths. The discussion of the strengths of the theory will be structured around Hall and Lindzey's (1957) criteria for evaluating theories of personality. These criteria are *comprehensiveness, simplicity,* and *relevance.* With respect to relevance, they focused on *research* relevance. In the following discussion, I will describe the theory's relevance to research, social process, and psychotherapy.

Comprehensiveness

This is a macrotheory of personality. There are two dimensions of comprehensiveness contained within the theory. First, it describes personality biologically, psychologically, and socially, all within an integrated and unified explanatory system.

Second, my theory describes the structure, process, and development of personality (stability and change). The theory is not confined to the psychological description of personal functioning, such as describing a self with needs influencing experience and behavior.

The idea of the core brain being both the ultimate homeostat and the individual's neurological ego sets the theory firmly within the biological domain. The bimodal equilibratory hypothesis describes the life-sustaining dynamic of the individual. Furthermore, this aspect of the theory describes emotionality in a way that is clinically relevant. It provides the therapist with information about the ongoing process of the therapeutic relationship.

The hypotheses that cognition and consciousness are internal equilibratory processes creates the psychological dimension of the theory. The concept of the person arises from the description of cognition as an automatic categorizing or classifying system. The person consists of linear and nonlinear cognitions about the neurological ego, its disturbance, and its relationship to the external environment. These cognitions emerge in experience as self phenomena, feelings, and personal reality.

The concept of consciousness as an equilibratory display function explains this ubiquitous phenomenon. It is the theoretical linchpin connecting the body with its mind. It also enables the theory to more precisely define psychological information processing functions by separating the experiential process from other psychological information-processing operations.

For example, *perception* is a term that usually describes the fusion of experiencing with the importation of sensory information. The same is true of thinking, where information classification, awareness, and self-experience are experientially fused (cf. Dennett, 1991).

The idea of action programs relates personality operations to behavior. Linear, nonlinear, and sensory, nonsensory explanatory processes become parts of behavioral programs. Cognition initiates action. Ideas about things or situations and/or feelings have behavioral instructions. The explanatory aspect of feelings also include instructions for action. For example, when one is embarrassed, one also acts to cover up the aspect of him- or herself that has been inadvertently exposed.

The theory enters the social domain of personality operations with the theory of dyadic interaction. The biological need (affect hunger) for invariant validational feedback stabilizes both the neurological ego and the psychological processes of the individual in the social engagement of the dyad. The feeding of the affect hunger of the neural structures that underlie the person in other social situations is a significant variable in all social process. These concepts provide the theory with the ability to describe social atrocities that humans can wreak upon on one another in wars, our xenophobia, our opposition to social change, and the origins of sin.

The theory not only is able to more precisely define psychological operations, but it is able, within the same explanatory frame of reference, to relate the different psychological phenomena operationally. For example, the person is a cognitive system that serves to regulate the steady-state condition of the disequilibrated neurological ego that generates emotion. Feelings are the part of the person that "explains" the bodily movement of emotion, and they are displayed in awareness because the neurological ego is unable to automatically process destabilizing information.

This theory explains a broad range of psychological phenomena within a single, simple, conceptual paradigm. The theory is truly a three-legged creature with its feet firmly planted in the biological, psychological and social domains within which the individual lives.

Simplicity

Conceptually, the theory is extraordinarily parsimonious. Occam would have chosen it over other macrotheories that presently exist. Instead of the six metatheoretical systems that psychoanalytic theory requires to explain personality (cf. Rappaport, 1960), my theory relies upon a single, bimodal, equilibratory (autopoietic) paradigm. The internal, homeostatic psychological equilibratory and the external invariant feedback processes account for the dynamics of personality operations. This bimodal paradigm can also be applied to the relationships that exist between internal and external determinants of experience and behavior.

It should be noted that this theory is not limited to describing the determinants of behavior. It also describes the internal experience of the individual. A theory of personality that does not explain experiencing cannot account for the richness of human growth and development.

Research Relevance

This theory raises many questions about its relevance to research. The most significant question that can be asked is: "Can the theory be experimentally studied and validated?" The answer is yes, and in many areas it can be easily done. In other areas, the laboratory work will be difficult and time-consuming. One such area is the mind-body relationship. Although I have presented some ideas about the general relationship of the brain to the mind, I have not been able to describe the neural dynamics that transform neurological equilibratory operations into psychological process. While work in this area is in progress (cf. Edelman, 1988, 1989), there are definitional and conceptual difficulties about the mind/body relationship that have not yet been overcome. I hope that the perspective I have presented will be helpful in clarifying definitional problems that impede neuropsychological research.

The definitions of the theory make a positive contribution to research. The clarity and the interrelatedness of the psychological terms within this theory are more readily defined than are conventional psychological definitions. These characteristics not only allow research to have greater phenomenal specificity, but they will enable the results of research in one area of investigation to be related to other areas. For example, research on emotion is rarely related to self phenomena or the person. Within the conceptual framework of this theory, the relationships among self, emotion, feelings, and personal reality are encompassed within the concept of the person. The definitions of this theory enable research to have greater specificity of topic and a wider range of relationships to other personality processes than do other theories of personality.

The theory will complicate personality research because it proposes that personality, like all psychological processes, is dichotomously formatted. This very question can be tested in the laboratory. However, if this is the case, then research must account for the differences in formatting when it elicits responses from research subjects. For example, if a hypothesis about emotionality is being tested, the scientist must ascertain whether the hypothesis refers to linear or nonlinear emotionality and then ensure that the test materials actually tap the appropriate linearity. If the research question has to do with emotional transformations, which is nonlinear processing, then conventional paper-and-pencil tests would be completely inappropriate. Paper-and-pencil tests primarily tap linear process.

While there has been no systematic research on the theory, a doctoral student tested my hypothesis about the emotionality of baseline process in the theory of the dyad (cf. Morris, 1977). The positive results of this experiment were promising not only for the validity of the theory, but also because they demonstrated that the theory was researchable.

Psychotherapeutic Relevance

The theory arose from my work as a psychotherapist, and it has enabled me and my students to work effectively in this field. Unlike any of the other dynamic theories of personality, a theory of psychotherapeutic technique can be derived from this theory of personality. The concept of the information-processing skills of the neurological ego and personal systems has enabled me to devise a psychotherapy of engagement. The theory of dyadic interaction and the person provides the conceptual foundations for a theory of psychotherapy. Ideas about interruption, rehearsal and the reinforcement characteristics of self-process are the underpinnings of the theory of change that is a necessary part of any theory of personality.

The engagement of the therapist and client provides a training ground where childhood personal formations can be transformed from anxiety-provoking structures into interesting and informative memories. The interpersonal engagement of psychotherapy enables the client to develop personal skills that are effective for the social environment within which this individual lives. This form of therapy goes beyond the pursuit of linear understanding to the creation of emotional skills. Liberating individuals from the confines of childhood formations makes them face the anxiety of adult freedom. This anxiety is readily transformed into an acceptance of one's essential aloneness and freedom.

The ideas about emotion and personal process, when tied to the theory of the dyad, expand our understanding of the therapeutic process. Transference and countertransference do not have a way of explaining the contemporary emotional dynamics of the therapeutic engagement. My theory provides us with a way of thinking about the moment-to-moment dynamics of the loving engagement of the therapeutic "dance." Therapists are increasingly leaving the confines of the blank screen model of psychotherapy. With this departure, the explanations of transference and countertransference that have depersonalized the therapeutic relationship are losing their meaningfulness.

The therapy of engagement is much more demanding on the therapist than older forms of therapy. In this engagement, therapists must not only be responsible for the nature of their participation, but they must have greater emotional skills. Without them, the therapist is unable to see the "here-and-now" process of psychotherapy.

The definitional clarity of this theory enables research to establish testable criteria to study both the effects and results of psychotherapy. Emotional skill criteria can be established and measured to evaluate the effects of psychotherapy on the creation of emotional abilities of treated clients. The cognitive structures that constitute the self and its variations with emotion can be established before and after periods of psychotherapy to evaluate psychotherapeutic effect and progress. Linear and nonlinear information-processing skills of self and personal reality can also assay the effects of psychotherapy.

Social Relevance

The social relevance of the theory is manifested in its concept of personal skills and the ways that they are developed. The concept of fixated childhood formations, an inheritance from psychoanalytic theory, and emotional skills are relevant to child-rearing practices. Fixated childhood formations and associated poor emotional skills lie at the base of all of the social pathology that I have seen.

The research literature also indicates that fixated childhood personal structures are the foundations of social pathology. The idea of emotional skills provides social process with a concrete set of operations that can be used to aid individuals to function less painfully in their lives.

The concept of personal development in the early months of the infant's life can lead to child-rearing practices that will enable the infant to maximize the creation of emotional skills. These skills will help in the prevention of the fixation of childhood personal structures that lead to violence and addiction. Clinically, I have observed that individuals who are prone to violent behavior have poor emotional skills. When confronted with emotionalities that leave them impotent, these people seek violent solutions to avoid their sense of helplessness. I have also worked with some drug abusers and have found that they too are extremely limited in both the range and intensity of emotionality with which they can cope. Should the hypotheses of this theory prove to be valid, the saving in human misery and in financial loss would be enormous. The costs of training are insignificant when contrasted with that of enforcement and incarceration.

The concept of the neurological ego adds to the social relevance of the theory through its ability to resolve the universality/individual difference paradox that has troubled both emotion theory and social/anthropological theorizing (cf. Sampson, 1991). The findings of generalized emotions by Ekman, et al. (1982) can be accounted for by the fact that all peoples have essentially the same hypothalamic-limbic systems. The cultural differences found by Lutz (1988) can possibly be explained by cognitive formatting differences. And, finally, the individual differences that exist within individuals are products of our being raised in varied cultures and families.

I hope that this theory will also be socially relevant in contributing to the demystification of both love and sex. In a sense, theories of personality have much in common with religion. They both define and explain human nature in terms of its essential characteristics and therefore draw conclusions about its social and cosmological condition. I believe that by extricating our understanding of love and sexuality from anxiety-driven explanations, we will be able to raise our children in less conflicted and confusing families.

Humiliation is a too-frequent childhood experience, and in childhood, it is a primary cause of human neurosis. In terms of numbers of people who are negatively affected during this impressionable time, I would guess that humiliation hurts more people than either sexual or physical abuse. The fragile, unskilled persons that emerge after infancy are often misunderstood or lie unseen in the turmoil of family strife. When this injury is compounded by sexual misunderstanding or abuse, its effects endure and develop into anguished adulthood. Education in parenting will reduce both the intensity and frequency of the enduring effects of childhood humiliation.

Another social implication of the theory has to do with the fact that different nationalities and cultures develop their own emotional skills. I believe that studies of these differences could enrich our understanding of cultural dissimilarities.

Limitations of the Theory

It is obvious from the global and introductory presentation of this theory that its major limitation is its lack of specificity about the nature of its own major concepts. The following list of unfinished aspects of the theory is illustrative of the theory's limitations. It is not intended to be a complete description of limitations. I hasten to say that I believe that these deficiencies can be rectified with additional study. I do not believe that any of them will invalidate the structural integrity of the theory.

The theory does not describe the regulatory dynamics that exist between the cortex and the core brain. Until we have a more complete understanding of the biochemical and neural operations of the brain's autoregulatory systems, we will not be able to describe how psychological process emerges from neural operations. The theory does make a contribution in this direction, as it does define psychological phenomena in ways that make the interface between neural and psychological process operationally closer. A psychological theory that uses ideas about the inhibition, facilitation, matching and mismatching of information is closer to neurological process than current attempts to relate ill-defined psychological concepts to specific brain areas.

As in other areas of psychological theory, this theory turns the idea of engrams on its head. An *engram* is a term that denotes the presumed existence of a stable neurological pattern underlying some psychological trait or stable process. The search for engrams has had a long and very unsuccessful history (cf. Kinsbourne's, 1988 discussion of Kissin, 1986).

The movement of personal process reflects the fluid movement of cerebral process. The stabilities of personal process also reflect the stable organization of brain systems. Our eyes consistently import visual information, which is processed by the same neural structures of the brain. The mysteries of movement are those which reside in the homeorhetic process of the brain. If it is true that psychological process emerges from internal equilibratory processes within the brain, as this theory proposes, then it would seem reasonable to understand more about the nature of equilibration within the brain. The observation of psychological process and its relationship to neural operations leads to a more dynamic picture of the mind-brain interaction than trying to find an engram that underlies a psychological trait.

Current research on memory is shifting from searching for engrams to an analysis of *processes* (cf. Report in the APA Monitor, Vol. 19, No. 11, Nov. 1988). This is a shift in research emphasis consistent with the paradigmatic structure of this theory. Here is another of the theoretical inversions that characterize this theory. This intriguing limitation calls for greater investigation and discussion.

The mind-brain relationship that I have proposed is based on a psychological theory of consciousness as a display function and does not readily interface with other information-processing models that Powers (1973) and others have used. While my suggestion, that consciousness is a display of information that cannot automatically be processed by the neurological ego, is consistent with laboratory research and everyday observation, a much more detailed understanding of its regulatory role must be achieved before the specifics of the mind-body relationship can be known.

The theory proposes that structural alterations in the personality occur when automated parts of it are interrupted, causing their display in awareness. However, the theory says little about the relationships that exist between self-process, consciousness, and cognitive autopoiesis. More needs to be known about how this interaction creates personality change.

The idea of the person as a complex set of cognitions that emerge as the self, feelings, and personal reality has a simplicity I find appealing. It relates hitherto unrelated psychological processes into a unified dynamism. The weakness of the concept lies in the fact that the theory says nothing about their underlying regulatory arrangements. The validation and invalidation of these processes has similar effects, which leads me to believe that they are parts of a unified, underlying regulatory system. My guess is that we will not know more about it until we have knowledge of the neural and biochemical regulatory operations of the brain from which the processes emerge.

These are some of the weaknesses or limitations of the theory. I will next describe four mysteries that I have confronted during the writing of this book. Then, I will finish with a very brief discussion of two implications of the theory that are most meaningful to me.

The Four Mysteries

The first two mysteries have to do with the nature of consciousness. The third mystery is about the strange hatred of sex that exists in Western civilization, and the fourth mystery raises a question about Eastern and Western ways of processing information.

During the exploration of the metaphorical planet of this theory, I pointed to the continent of consciousness and its relationship to cognition and perception. However, the equilibratory dynamics of consciousness, which we intuitively acknowledge, remained relatively untouched. I did not discuss the various states of consciousness and the roles that they play in the stabilization of the interactions of the cortex with the neurological ego. I believe that when we can solve the mystery of this equilibratory relationship, the most profound mysteries of human nature will be discovered. One of these mysteries is the nature of psychosis. It has been my observation that one of the major characteristics of psychosis is that, in a psychotic condition, persons are moved outside the normative state of consciousness.

The discovery of the equilibratory nature of consciousness will throw light on the nature of both sleep and psychosis. In both these conditions, the operations of internal equilibratory processes are displayed in dreams and delusions. These are related phenomena. In both dreams and psychosis, personal reality and emotional information are bent to fit the anguished last of tortured person/neurological ego interactions. The twisted shapes of this information are then displayed in awareness as the horror of nightmares or paranoia.

The third mystery has to do with Western hatred of sex. Ever since I was a child, I have wondered why sex was considered to be so bad. My masturbatory experiences were delightfully compulsive. Although I was troubled by my compulsivity mainly because neighborhood gossip told me that it was wrong and that bad things would happen to me if I did "it" too much, I soon found that none of the dire predictions came true. The palms of my hands remained hairless; I did not become an idiot, nor was I punished by God.

In the background of my mind, I puzzled about why sexuality was so stigmatized. In my adolescence, I studied primitive cultures and learned that some of them were less punitive and more permissive about sex than mine was. I envied them. At the same time, I saw movies where people in my culture were caught up in terrible tragedies because of the expression of their sexual desires and confusions. As I matured, I tried to explain this confusion to myself by recognizing that sex had to do with economics, love, and childbirth.

However, as I came to the conclusion of this book, I was again struck by the fact that Western civilization is strikingly different from Eastern cultures in the way that sex is used in the lives of people. For example, Eastern societies have for centuries produced many books describing and instructing in the pleasures of coitus and sex play. Until very recently in Western society, explicit, pleasure-oriented books about sexuality have either been banned and/or have been declared obscene. It has been only in the last twenty years that books on sexual pleasure, such as Alexander Comfort's (1972) *Joy of Sex,* have been popularly published in the United States. It is interesting to note that its subtitle is *A Cordon Bleu Guide to Lovemaking.* Could this be a serendipitous recognition that sex feeds affect hunger?

What in Western civilization has led to the guilt and sex-hating beliefs within it? Campbell (1988) suggests that the domination of matriarchal agriculture by nomadic patrilineal herding and hunting tribes is related to this prejudice, and Pagels's (1988) description of Augustine's anguish and its impact on church doctrine are the beginnings of a much-needed study of the tragic human misunderstanding of the nature of sexuality.

Regardless of the reasons for our destructive prejudices about sex, they contaminate our child-rearing practices and can lead to tragic adult personalities. The often-violent reaction of parents to sexuality during the early developmental years of infancy tragically extend into a person's adult life.

I know of a young woman who participated in a sex surrogate training course. At one point in the course, after intensive explanation and emotional preparation, she and the group of which she was a member were told that they could take off as much of their clothing as they wished. Except for her, all the members of her group stripped naked. At that point, she broke down. Refusing to take any of her clothing off, she announced that her body was not designed for pleasure. She further declared that her body was to be beaten and to be abused sexually. As a child, she had been repeatedly sexually abused by her father.

Sexually abused children are molested by sexually abused "children" who continue to reside in the adult bodies of the abusers. In all the cases I have seen of people who had been sexually abused or who had sexually molested their children, the abusers were persons with fixated childhood structures.

I believe that we can now develop educational programs for parents, which can reduce the anguish and distortions of our prejudiced conception of sexuality. A clearer understanding of the mystery of our sexual prejudice will not only help us in rearing children without sexual anxiety, but it will vastly improve the quality of loving that exists in our society.

The fourth mystery that intrigues me is the possibility that the peoples of Eastern and Western societies process information differently. Dorothy Lee (1950) reported that the Trobriand Islanders process information "nonlineally," as opposed to the "lineal" processing that occurs in Western logical thought. Within the terminology of my theory, "lineal and nonlineal" information processing refers to linear and nonlinear formatting of information. Should such a difference exist between Eastern and Western societies, it would greatly expand our understanding of both culture formation and the nature of thinking.

Finally, I will conclude with a brief walk into territories that have been held to fundamental human truths. During this stroll, I will challenge their verity.

Where Angels Fear to Tread

I have abandoned common sense as the conceptual tool with which I have built this theory of personality. Despite Skinner's (1978) dissatisfaction and some philosophical dissent about the use of common sense as the paradigmatic foundation of personality theory building, it remains one of the basic conceptual tools used in personality theory construction. I have found that the recognition of the doubly dichotomous nature of human nature liberated me from the confusing and misleading bonds of common sense.

This freedom permitted me to construct a theory that accounts for and describes the rich internal movement of psychological process. The equilibratory interaction of the neurological ego and the cortex is the dynamic process that underlies all of what appears in awareness to be our motivation. The dichotomy of the formatting systems of the mind allows me to describe the figural and background process that exists in all psychological operations. The idea of the brain responding both to nonsensory internal process and external sensory process enables me to describe the richness of emotionality, self process, and our unique, individuated personal realities.

However, in doing so, I have taken positions that deny the truth of a number of long-held axiomatic assumptions and ways of thinking about human nature. I will conclude this book with a brief inventory of assumptions about human nature that I believe are in error and have limited our understanding about ourselves.

First, the sense of self we have when we are intending to do something is *not* the control center of our action. The self that is experienced is simply the display of the relationship of the person to the disequilibrating situation that is triggering action. This is an expansion of William James's (1950/1890) provocative explanation of emotion. Neither the experienced "I" nor the beliefs and reasoning experienced as explanations of our motivation activate behavior. In a sense, they are simply ex post facto displays of an unexperienced equilibratory process in the brain.

These creates havoc with long-held beliefs, assumptions and ways of thinking about who we are and why we do what we do. Intentionality is an illusion; the idea of free will has to be drastically reformulated; for the same reasons, values about personal responsibility have to be recast and reassessed; the validity of the pleasure principle is denied; platonic assumptions of the rule of reason, and its corollaries "good" or "absolute beauty," have to be put aside. All these denials are blows to our narcissistic sense of self-control and the equilibratory relief we experience when we believe the "truth" of our favorite explanations.

This new way of thinking about personality may be somewhat costly in its unfamiliarity, but I think that it is a small price to pay for the expanded vision it gives us about ourselves. It can eradicate the sea monsters that inhabit the oceans of ignorance that abide in our limited, but expanding, knowledge of human nature.

APPENDIX A

The Structure of the Theory

The following table outlines the skeletal structure of the theory through and around which fluid, bimodal regulatory processes flow and emerge in experience as personality. In the left column are the major hypotheses that make up the theory. On the right are the names of those who have described the concept. I have added my name where I have modified or altered their ideas to make them compatible with the theory.

CONCEPTS OR STRUCTURES	AUTHORS
1. The *core brain,* also known as the paleo-mammalian brain and hypothalamiclimbic system, is called the *neurological ego* in this theory.	McLean, Weil, Gross
2. The cortex regulates the neurological ego.	Luria
3. Regulation is a *bimodal process,* equilibrating the neurological ego and the cortex with information from the internal and external environments of the individual.	Gross
4. Disequilibration of the neurological ego and the cortex results from mismatching information or their *affect hunger.*	Gross
5. *Affect hunger* is the biological need of neural structures for invariant stimulation.	Platt, Gross, Levy, & Ferenczi
6.. Invariant stimulation arising from stable, sensory cognitive sources feeds "affect hungry" neural systems.	Platt, Gross
7. Internal regulation occurs homeostatically and cognitively.	Cannon, Gross
8. External regulation equals "search for invariance" from physical objects in the external environment.	Platt

9.	Cognitive regulation is a form of validation. Validation is the "feeding of affect hunger" through repetitive processing of information that matches processing structures.	Gross
10.	Consciousness is a hologramic regulatory display of information.	Pribram, Gross, Orenstein
11.	The display of the neurological ego's disturbance is *emotion,* associated with an awareness of an aspect of self phenomena (see 16.)	James, Gross
12.	Cognition is a form of cortical regulation.	Luria
13.	Cognition is automatic linear/nonlinear and sensory/nonsensory classification of information in the cognitive system.	Bruner, Lakoff, Gross
14.	Cognition is organized within linear and non-linear formats and sensory and nonsensory formats.	Gross
15.	Cognitions emerge psychologically as con-structs, explanations, expectations, feelings, and attributions.	G. Kelly, Gross, Heider, H. Keeley
16.	Classifications of neurological ego are displayed as *self phenomena.*	Epstein, Gross
17.	Cognitive classifications of the disturbance of the neurological ego are displayed as *feelings.*	Gross
18.	Classifications of relationship of the neurolog-ical ego to the external environment are displayed as personal reality (see 20).	Gross, Mahoney
19.	Classifications of the neurological ego are organized in linear and nonlinear, sensory and nonsensory formats.	Gross
20.	The *person* is a holistic, doubly dichotomously formatted cognitive regulatory system that is experientially displayed as *self-phenomena, feelings,* and *personal reality.*	Gross
21.	*Action programs* are cognitive/behavioral systems developed with cognitive systems, including those of the person.	Galanter Pribram, Miller, & Gross

Glossary

Action Programs	Brain programs underlying behavior.
Affect	See *Emotion,* a synonomous term.
Affect Hunger	The need of living tissue for invariant stimulation.
Attention	Focal awareness.
Awareness	Normative state of consciousness.
Cognition	The classification of information.
Cognitive Blending	The integration of two or more different cognitions or perceptions into a unitary category.
Consciousness	The information display system activated when the person/neurological ego is unable to process information automatically.
Dyad	A two-person relationship.
Emotion	The experienced movement of the neurological ego that occurs with an experience of self.
Feelings	Cognitive classifications of emotion with an associated experience of self.
Formatting Systems	Cerebral organizations of information into linear and nonlinear formats. Linear formats are sequential, point-to-point organizations of information. Nonlinear formats organize information into systems of relationships. These relationships can be spatial, temporal, or abstract. Sensory and nonsensory information are also organized in different formats.
"I"	An aspect of the neurological ego that orients it in relationship to any source of disequilibrium.
Information	Anything within or between systems that creates change within or between systems.

Mind	All the neurological activity that emerges into experience as the psychological systems serving the equilibratory needs of the neurological ego.
Neurological Ego	Midbrain structures variously labeled the hypothalamic-limbic system, the paleo-mammalian brain, or the core brain.
Perception	The transport of information between systems.
Person	Cognition about the neurological ego, its disturbance and its relationship to the external environment. These systems of cognition are labeled self phenomena, feelings, and personal reality.
Personal Reality	Cognitions about the neurological ego's relationship to the external environment.
Psychological Systems	Cortical equilibratory structures serving the neurological ego. They transport, store, retrieve, classify, and label information into linear and nonlinear and sensory and nonsensory formats; the double dichotomy.
Self Phenomena	Cognitions about the neurological ego.
States of Consciousness	Various conditions of the display function. They are experienced as different states, such as dreams, meditation (Zazen, Samhadi), intoxication, and psychosis.
Transformations	Cognitive reclassifications that reequilibrate the neurological ego.
Validation	The variant stimulation of living tissue.

Ainsworth-Land, G.T. (1986), *Grow or die: The unifying principle of transformation*. New York: John Wiley and Sons.

Allport, G. (1937), *Personality*. New York: Henry Holt and Company

Allport, G. (1943), The ego in contemporary psychology. *Psychology Review, 50* (88), 451-478.

Bateson, G. (1972), *Steps to an ecology of mind; The new information sciences can lead to a new understanding of man*. New York: Ballantine Books.

Battegay, R. (1991), *Hunger diseases*. Lewiston, New York,: Hogrefe and Huber.

Becker, C.L. (1932), *The heavenly city of eighteenth-century philosophers*. New Haven: Yale University Press.

Berlyne, D.E. (1966), Curiosity and exploration. *Science, 153* (3731), 25-33.

Bevan, W. (1991), A tour inside the onion. *American Psychologist, 46* (5), 475-483.

Blakemore, C. (1977), *Mechanics of the mind*. Cambridge: Cambridge University Press.

Bouchard, T.J., Lykken, B.T., McGue, M., Segal, N.L., and Telegen, A. (1990), Sources of human differences: the Minnesota study of twins reared apart. *Science, 250* (4978), 223-228.

Bowlby, J. (1969), *Attachment and loss; Volume I attachment*. New York: Basic Books

Bowlby, J. (1973), *Attachment and loss; Volume II separation*. New York: Basic Books.

Breuer, J., and Freud, S. (1893-1895/1955), *Studies in hysteria, standard edition, volume II*. London: Hogarth Press.

Brody, S. (1956), *Patterns of mothering*. New York: International Universities Press.

Buber, M. (1970), *I-Thou; a new translation with a prologue "I and You" and notes*. Translated by Walter Kaufman. New York: Scribner.

Bulfinch, T. (1978), *Bulfinch's mythology*. New York: Avenal Books.

Burns, B.D. (1968), *The uncertain nervous system*. London: Edward Arnold.

Campbell, J. (1988), *The power of myth*. New York: Doubleday.

Cannon, C.B. (1939), *The wisdom of the body*. New York: W.W. Norton.

Cannon, C.B. (1957), Voodoo death. *Psychosomatic Medicine, 19* (3), 182-190.

Caplan, D. (ed.) (1982), *Biological studies of mental processes*. Cambridge: MIT Press.

Capra, F. (1975), *The tao of physics*. Boulder, Colorado: Shambala Publications, Inc.

Carroll, L. (1965), *Alice's adventures in wonderland.* New York: Avenal Books.

Comfort, A. (ed.) (1972), *The joy of sex.* New York: Crown Publishers.

Cortázar, J. (1969), *Blow-up.* New York: Collier.

Deikman, A.J. (1975), Bimodal consciousness. In R.E. Orenstein (ed.), *The nature of human consciousness; a book of readings.* New York: Viking Press.

Dennett, D.C. (1991), *Consciousness explained.* Boston: Little, Brown and Company.

Duyckaerts, F. (1970), *The sexual bond.* New York: Delacorte Press.

Eccles, J., and Robinson, D.N. (1985), *The wonder of being human; our brain and our mind.* Boston: New Science Library, Shambala Publications, Inc.

Edelman, G.M. (1988), *Neural darwinism; the theory of neuronal group selection.* New York: Basic Books.

Edelman, G.M. (1989), *The present remembered.* New York: Basic Books.

Ekman, P., Friesen, W.V., and Ellsworth, P. (1972), What emotional categories or dimensions can observers judge from facial behavior? In P. Ekman (ed.), *Emotion in the human face* (pp. 39-55). New York: Cambridge University Press.

Fierman, L.B. (ed.) (1965), *Effective psychotherapy: The contribution of Hellmuth Kaiser.* New York: The Free Press.

Fletcher, G.J.O. (1984), Psychology and commonsense. *American Psychologist, 39* (3), 203-213.

Fodor, J. (June 27, 1991), Too hard for our kind of mind? *London Review of Books,* 15-17.

Freud, S. (1915/1957), *Instincts and their vicissitudes.* London: Hogarth Press.

Fridja, N.H. (1986), *The emotions.* New York: Cambridge Press and Editions de la Maison des Sciences de l'Homme.

Friedman, R.E. (1987), *Who wrote the Bible?* New York: Summit Books.

Fromm, E. (1956), *The art of loving.* New York: Harper and Row.

Gazzaniga, M.S. (1985), *The social brain.* New York: Basic Books.

Gergen, K. (1985), The social constructionist movement in modern psychology. *American Psychologist, 40* (3), 226-275.

Goffman, E. (1959), *The presentation of self in everyday life.* New York: Anchor Books.

Granit, R. (1977), *The purposive brain.* Cambridge: MIT Press.

Greenberg, L.S., and Safran, J.D. (1987), *Emotions in psychotherapy.* New York: Guilford Press.

Gross, Z. (1954), Learning and lobotomy. *American Psychological Association Meetings.* New York.

Haggard, E. (1973). Some effects of geographic and social isolation in natural settings. In J.E. Rasmussen (ed.), *Man in isolation and confinement* (pp. 99-143). Chicago: Aldine Publishing Company.

Hall, C.S., and Lindzey, G. (1957), *Theories of personality.* New York: John Wiley and Sons.

Hampden-Turner, C. (1981), *Maps of the mind.* New York: Macmillan.

Heath, R. (1964), Pleasure response of human subjects to direct stimulations of the brain: physiologic and psychodynamic considerations. In R. Heath (ed.), *The role of pleasure in behavior.* New York: Hoeber Medical Division, Harper and Row.

Held, R. (1965), Plasticity in sensory-motor systems. *Scientific American,* 5 (213), 84-94.

Held, R. (1968), Action contingent development of vision in neonatal animals. In D.P. Kimble (ed.), *Experiences and capacity.* New York: New York Academy of Sciences.

Henley, W.E. (1980), Quotation. *Bartlett's quotations.* Boston: Little, Brown and Company.

Hinsie, L.E., and Campbell, R.J. (1960), *Psychiatric dictionary.* New York: Oxford University Press.

Hofstadter, D.R., and Dennett, D.C. (eds.) (1981), *The mind's I: fantasies and reflections on self and soul.* New York: Basic Books.

Holt, R.R. (1989), *Freud reappraised.* New York :The Guilford Press.

Inhelder, B., Bovet, M., Sinclair, H., and Smock, C.D. (1966). On cognitive development. *American Psychologist,* 21, 160-164.

International Psychoanalytic Association (April 1990), The "Round Robin" Newsletter of Section I, Psychologist-Psychoanalyst Practitioners Division of Psychoanalysis. (39), p. 1.

Ionesco, E. (1960). *Rhinoceros.* New York: Samuel French.

Ivins, W.M.J. (1953), *Prints and visual communication.* London: Routledge and Kegan Paul, Ltd.

Izard, C. (1972), *Patterns of emotion: A new analysis of anxiety and depression.* New York: Academic Books.

James, W. (1890/1950), *Principles of psychology.* New York: Dover Press.

Jaynes, J. (1976), *The origin of consciousness in the breakdown of the bicameral mind.* Boston: Houghton Mifflin Company.

Jung, C.G. (1962), *Memories, dreams, reflections.* Translated by Richard and Clara Winston. New York: Pantheon.

Kagan, J. (1989), *Unstable ideas; temperament, cognition and self.* Cambridge: Harvard University Press.

Kaplan, H.S. (1974), *The new sex therapy; active treatment of sexual dysfunctions.* New York: Bruner/Mazel.

Kinsbourne, M. (1982), Hemispheric specialization and the growth of human understanding. *American Psychologist,* 37 (4), 411-420.

Kissin, B. (1988), *Conscious and unconscious programs in the brain.* New York: Plenum Press.

Klein, M. (1975), *Envy and gratitude and other works,* 1946-1963. New York: The Free Press.

Koestler, A. (1967), *The ghost of the machine.* New York: Macmillan Co.

Kohler, W. (1959), *Gestalt psychology.* New York: Mentor Books.

Lakoff, G. (1987), *Women, fire, and dangerous things; what categories reveal about the mind.* Chicago: University of Chicago.

Lee, D. (1974), Codifications of reality: lineal and nonlineal. In R.E. Orenstein (ed.), *The nature of human consciousness: a book of readings* (pp. 128-142). New York: The Viking Press.

Levy, D.M. (1937), *Maternal overprotection.* New York: Columbia University Press.

Lewin, K. (1935), *A dynamic theory of personality.* New York: McGraw-Hill Book Company.

Lorenz, K. (1969), *Studies in animal and human behavior.* Boston: Harvard University Press.

Luria, A.R. (1973), *The working brain: An introduction to neuropsychology.* New York: Basic Books.

Lynch, J.J. (1977), *The broken heart: The medical consequences of loneliness.* New York: Basic Books.

Lynch, J.J. (1985), *The language of the heart: The body's response to human dialogue.* New York: Basic Books.

MacLean, P.D. (1973), *A triune concept of the brain and behavior.* Toronto: University of Toronto Books.

MacLuhan, M. (1965), *Understanding media.* New York :McGraw-Hill.

Mahoney, M.J. (1991), *Human change processes: The scientific foundations of psychotherapy.* New York: Basic Books.

Mandler, G. (1984), *Mind and body; Psychology of emotion and stress.* New York: W.W. Norton.

Margolis, H. (1987), *Patterns, thinking, and cognition: A theory of judgment.* Chicago: University of Chicago Press.

Marks, C.E. (1981), *Commissurotomy, consciousness, and the unity of the mind.* Cambridge: University of Chicago Press.

Masson, J.M. (1988), *Against therapy: Emotional tyranny and the myth of psychological healing.* New York: Atheneum.

Masters, W.H., and Johnson, V.E. (1974), *The pleasure bond: a new look at sexuality and commitment.* Boston: Little, Brown and Company.

Masterson, J.F. (1984), Reflections on Anna O. In M. Rosenbaum and M. Muroff (ed.), *Anna O.: Fourteen contemporary reinterpretations.* New York: The Free Press.

Menninger, K. (1958), *Theory of psychoanalytic technique.* New York: Basic Books.

Michael, M. (1991), Some postmodern reflections on social psychology. *Theory and Psychology,* 1 (2), 203-221.

Milgram, S. (1974), *Obedience to authority: an experimental view.* New York: Harper and Row.

Miller, G., Galanter, E., and Pribram, K.H. (1960), *Plans and structure of behavior.* New York: Holt.

Montagu, A. (1971), *Touching: the significance of skin.* New York: Columbia University Press.

Morris, R.S. (1977), *The disconfirmation of self presentation as a change agent in psychotherapy.* Research, California School of Professional Psychology, Los Angeles.

Morton, A. (1980), *Frames of mind: Constraints on the common-sense conception of the mental.* Oxford, England: Clarendon Press.

Natsoulas, T. (1974), Consciousness. *American Psychologist,* 33, 139-175.

Olds, J. (1977), *Drives and reinforcements: Behavioral studies of hypothalamic functions.* New York: Raven Press.

Orenstein, R.R. (ed.) (1973), *The nature of human consciousness: A book of readings.* New York: Viking Press.

Orenstein, R.R., and Sobel, D. (1987), *The healing brain.* New York: Simon and Shuster.

Pagels, E. (May 12, 1988), The origins of sin. *New York Review of Books,* pp. 28-35.

Pagels, E. (1988), *Adam, Eve, and the serpent.* New York: Random House.

Piaget, J. (1970), *Structuralism.* New York: Basic Books, Inc.

Piaget, J. (1985), *The equilibration of cognitive structures: the central problem of intellectual development.* Chicago: The University of Chicago Press.

Platt, J.R. (1970), *Perception and change: projections for survival.* Ann Arbor: University of Michigan Press.

Plutchik, R. (1962), *The emotions: Facts, theories, and a new model.* New York: Random House.

Powers, W.T. (1973), *Behavior: The control of perception.* Chicago: Aldine Publishing Company.

Pribram, K.H., and Melges, F.T. (1969), Psychophysiological basis of emotion. In Vinken, P.J., and Bruyn, G.S. (eds.) Handbook of Clinical Neurology, 3, pp. 316-342. Amsterdam: North Holland Publishing Co.; New York: John Wiley and Sons.

Pribram, K.H. (1971), *Languages of the brain.* Monterey, California: Wadsworth Publishing.

Prigogine, I. (1980), *From being to becoming.* San Francisco: W.H. Freeman and Company.

Rappaport, D. (1960), *The structure of psychoanalytic thinking: a synthesizing attempt.* New York: International Universities Press, Inc.

Reich, W. (1972), *Character analysis.* New York: Farrar, Straus, & Giroux.

Reik, T. (1948), *Listening with the third ear.* New York: Farrar, Straus.

Reiser, M.F. (1984), *Mind, brain, body: Toward a convergence of psychoanalysis and neurobiology.* New York: Basic Books.

Restak, R.M. (1979), *Brain: the last frontier.* Garden City, New York: Doubleday.

Riesen, A.H. (1975), *The developmental neuropsychology of sensory deprivation.* New York: Academic Press.

Robinson, D.N. (1980), *The enlightened machine: an analytic introduction to neuropsychology.* New York: Columbia University Press.

Rose, D. (1982), Some functional correlates of the maturation of neural systems. In D. Caplan (ed.), *Biological studies of mental processes* (pp. 27-43). Cambridge: MIT Press.

Rosen, J. (1953-68), *Direct analysis: selected papers.* New York: Grune and Stratton.

Rosenfeld, I. (1988), *The invention of memory.* New York: Basic Books.

Rosenthal, D. (1970), *Genetic studies of abnormal behavior.* New York: McGraw Hill.

Roth, G. (1982), *Feeding the hungry heart: the experience of compulsive eating.* New York: The New American Library.

Ryle, G. (1949), *The concept of mind.* London & New York: Hutchinson University Library.

Sacks, O. (1987), *The man who mistook his wife for a hat and other clinical tales.* New York: Harper Collins.

Sacks, O. (November 22, 1991), Neurology and the soul. *The New York Review of Books* (pp. 44-50).

Schacter, S. (1964), The interaction of cognitive and physiological determinants of emotional states. In L. Berkowitz (ed.), *Advances in experimental social psychology* (vol. I, pp. 49-80). New York: Academic Press.

Shah, I. (1977), *A veiled gazelle*. London: The Octagon Press.

Silverman, L.H., Lachmann, F.M., and Milich, R.H. (1982), *The search for oneness*. New York: International Universities Press.

Skinner. B.F. (October 1990), Address to American Psychological Association. *American Psychological Association Monitor* (pp. 4-6).

Sperry, R. (1985), Consciousness, personal identity, and the divided brain. In D.F. Benson and E. Zaidel (eds.), *The dual brain*. New York: The Guilford Press.

Spitz, R. (1946), Hospitalism; a follow-up report. *The psychoanalytic study of the child*. New York: International Universities Press.

Staats, A.W. (1991), Unified positivism and unification psychology; fad or new field? *American Psychologist*, 46 (9), 889-912.

Stern, D.N. (1985), *The interpersonal world of the infant: a view from psychoanalysis and developmental psychology*. New York: Basic Books, Inc.

Strunk, W.J., and White, E.B. (1972), *The elements of style*. New York: Macmillan Publishing Company.

Tomkins, S.S. (1965), *Affect, cognition and personality; empirical studies*. New York: Springer Publishing Company.

Tsu, L. (1989), *Tao te ching*. Translated by Feng, Gia-fu, and English, J. New York: Vintage Books.

Tucker, D.M. (1981), Lateral brain function, emotion, and conceptualization. *Psychological Bulletin*, 89 (1), 19-46.

Van Holtoon, F., and Oleson, D.R. (1987), *Common sense: The foundations of social science*. Lanham, Maryland: University Press of America.

Waber, D.P. (1982), Maturation: thoughts on renewing an old relationship. In D. Caplan (ed.), *Biological studies of mental processes*. Cambridge: MIT Press.

Waddington, C.H. (1974), *The strategy of the genes: a discussion of some aspects of theoretical biology*. New York: Macmillan Publishing Company.

Weil, J.L. (1974), *A neurophysiological model of emotional and intentional behavior*. Springfield, Illinois: Charles C. Thomas.

Young, P. (1973), *Emotion and man and animal* (revised edition). New York: R. Krieger.

Zubek, J.P. (ed.) (1969), *Sensory deprivation: fifteen years of research*. New York: Appelton-Century-Crofts.